'Why did some protest movements turn to force when others did not in times of austerity? How has it influenced political structures of the Eurozone states? In this empirically rich, methodologically advanced, and theoretically innovative book, Joanna Rak open-mindedly addresses important research problems of the sources and consequences of differences and similarities across cultures of political violence formed by the post-2008 anti-austerity movements in Europe. Not only does Rak's study contribute to our understanding of what happened in austerity-driven societies, but it also makes an important contribution to the Social Sciences by creating and applying a compelling non-traditional research design that allows a researcher to verify methodological correctness and analytical effectiveness of theoretical frameworks. Those who are interested in how to analyze contentious politics now have an excellent work to read!'

Roman Bäcker, *The former President of Polish Political Science Association*

'Joanna Rak has written an admirably clear, rigorously designed and conducted comparative study of European anti-austerity movements. This book does more than challenge the students of contention to think critically about conceptual and explanatory frameworks of cultures of political violence. By formulating and testing new analytical tools, the study pushes us to reconsider a traditional research process and the use of theoretical categories in comparative politics and social movement studies.'

Adam Wielomski, *The President of Political and Legal Theory Association*

'This timely and innovative research allows us to understand how broad civil historical contexts shaped placid, hector-led, and militant cultures of political violence in austerity-driven Europe. Drawing upon the pieces of data in 14 languages and a comprehensive literature review, Joanna Rak creates entirely new databases for anti-austerity movements. In skillfully combining qualitative and quantitative comparative techniques, she achieves both theory-verification and theory-generation aims. The analysis makes significant methodological and theoretical advances as Rak devises a gradable theoretical category of a culture of political violence. Her original theoretical framework introduces a refreshingly new way to bring together accomplishments in the study of contentious politics and history. Rak paves the way for further research and discussion about a nature of contemporary cultures of political violence.'

José Luis Orella Martínez, *Professor of History and Political Sciences, CEU San Pablo, Spain*

Theorizing Cultures of Political Violence in Times of Austerity

After the multidimensional financial crisis of 2008, the member states of the Eurozone imposed a set of economic policies to save their economies. Socially unpopular cuts contributed to the occurrence of violent movements that both opposed austerity policies and created animosity towards the politicians who implemented them.

Combining qualitative and quantitative comparative analyses from anti-austerity movements in 14 Eurozone states from 2007 to 2015, Joanna Rak develops an original typology of patterns of a culture of political violence to explain why some anti-austerity movements turned to violence and others did not, despite having shared goals and political values. She uncovers the very nature of the differences and similarities between cultures of political violence, identifies their sources, and determines their differing results. Simultaneously, she opens a discussion on the exploratory and explanatory utility of the category of a culture of political violence in the Social Sciences.

Theorizing Cultures of Political Violence in Times of Austerity casts new light on the scholarly debate on cultures of political violence and anti-austerity violent behavior, making it a compelling read for scholars of political sociology, political behavior, comparative politics, European politics, and sociology.

Joanna Rak is an assistant professor of Political Science and Journalism and the Chair of Political Culture at Adam Mickiewicz University, Poznań, Poland. In 2016 and 2017, she was a visiting researcher at CEU San Pablo University in Madrid. Her research interests are cultures of political violence, dynamics of radicalization, anti-austerity movements, political epistemic apparatuses, social mobilization, and cultural security. Her current research is on the culture of political violence dynamics of anti-austerity movements in Europe and contemporary Russian authoritarianism and totalitarianism.

Routledge Research in Comparative Politics

The Statecraft of Consensus Democracies in a Turbulent World
A Comparative Study of Austria, Belgium, Luxembourg, the Netherlands and Switzerland
José M. Magone

Policy Change under New Democratic Capitalism
Edited by Hideko Magara

Rampage Shootings and Gun Control
Politicization and Policy Change in Western Europe
Steffen Hurka

Growth, Crisis, Democracy
The Political Economy of Social Coalitions and Policy Regime Change
Edited by Hideko Magara and Bruno Amable

Think Tanks in the US and EU
The Role of Policy Institutes in Washington and Brussels
Christopher J. Rastrick

Institutions, Partisanship and Credibility in Global Financial Markets
Hye Jee Cho

Health and Political Engagement
Mikko Mattila, Lauri Rapeli, Hanna Wass and Peter Söderlund

Theorizing Cultures of Political Violence in Times of Austerity
Studying Social Movements in Comparative Perspective
Joanna Rak

Interest Group Organisation in the European Union
How Internal Organisational Structures Shape Interest Group Agency
Michelle Hollman

Theorizing Cultures of Political Violence in Times of Austerity

Studying Social Movements in Comparative Perspective

Joanna Rak

Routledge
Taylor & Francis Group
NEW YORK AND LONDON

First published 2018
by Routledge
52 Vanderbilt Avenue, New York, NY 10017

and by Routledge
2 Park Square, Milton Park, Abingdon, Oxon, OX14 4RN

First issued in paperback 2020

Routledge is an imprint of the Taylor & Francis Group, an informa business

Library of Congress Cataloging-in-Publication Data
Names: Rak, Joanna, author.
Title: Theorizing cultures of political violence in times of austerity : studying social movements in comparative perspective / Joanna Rak.
Description: New York, NY : Routledge, [2018] | Series: Routledge research in comparative politics ; 74 | Includes bibliographical references and index. Identifiers: LCCN 2018006553| ISBN 9780815383604 (hardback) | ISBN 9781351205740 (webpdf) | ISBN 9781351205733 (epub) | ISBN 9781351205726 (mobipocket/kindle)
Subjects: LCSH: Political violence–Social aspects–European Union countries. | Protest movements–European Union countries. | Social movements–European Union countries. | Global financial crisis, 2008–2009–Social aspects–European Union countries. | European Union countries–Economic policy–21st century.
Classification: LCC HN380.5.Z9 V573 2018 | DDC 307.1/412094–dc23
LC record available at https://lccn.loc.gov/2018006553

ISBN 13: 978-0-367-66642-2 (pbk)
ISBN 13: 978-0-8153-8360-4 (hbk)

DOI: 10.4324/9781351205757

Typeset in Times New Roman
by Wearset Ltd, Boldon, Tyne and Wear

Contents

Illustrations

Figures

Tables

Acknowledgments

A number of people have given considerable time and effort in support of my research. I would like to express my sincere thanks to Professors Tadeusz Wallas, Roman Bäcker, and José Luis Orella Martínez for their unwavering support throughout preparing this book on its every stage, from the very idea through many drafts to the complete manuscript and giving me the benefit of their critical judgment. This book is a result of the research project "The Culture of Political Violence Dynamics of Anti-austerity Movements in Europe," supported by the National Science Centre, Poland (grant number 2016/23/D/HS5/00192) and performed at the Faculty of Political Science and Journalism at Adam Mickiewicz University in Poznań. The intellectually stimulating environment of this place allowed me to develop a non-traditional research design, formulate a theoretical framework of a culture of political violence, and test their empirical effectiveness throughout a comparative study of post-2008 anti-austerity movements. I am deeply indebted to the colleagues and advisors whose critical remarks pushed me to rethink some of my views on political violence and helped me achieve research goals. I appreciate the great direction of the editors at Routledge, particularly Natalja Mortensen and María Landschoot. The book proposal was much strengthened in light of feedback from anonymous reviewers. I am also grateful to the staff of European police stations for providing me with data on protest policing over anti-austerity events.

I feel obligated to emphasize that every single work that I approached critically contributed substantially to the research. I have found a critical evaluation of current theoretical and methodological approaches the most fruitful and inspiring way to understand cultures of political violence. Hence, I would challenge students of political violence to make an effort to read the book critically so as to we can benefit further from an academic discussion on its content.

Introduction

DOI: 10.4324/9781351205757-1

Towards an Explanation for the Violent Behavior of Anti-Austerity Movements

After 2008, European governments were relentlessly undertaking austerity measures to come out of the global financial crisis and recover from its effects (Fumagalli and Lucarelli 2015; Hayes 2017; Kotz 2009). Austerity measures in the form of the deliberate deflation of domestic wages and prices through cuts to public spending were imposed to reduce the states' debts and deficits, increase their economic competitiveness and restore what is called "business confidence" (Blyth 2013a; 2013b). Inevitably, the results of their implementation were socially noticeable (della Porta 2015; Grasso and Giugni 2015; Ventriss 2013) and contributed heavily to the occurrence of new social movements (Braun 2013; McMenamin *et al.* 2015; Quaranta 2016; Seymour 2014) which swiftly became an influential player on a political scene.

Anti-austerity movements proved to be more or less violent in different European states, and it was not clear why some of them turned to force, and others did not despite the shared experience with austerity policies, political values, and goals. The existing studies on anti-austerity movements have concentrated mainly on the relations between structural changes and the transpositions of social conflict patterns (Cristancho 2015; Kriesi 2016; Perugorría *et al.* 2016; Ross 2016), the role of cultural and political representations in social conflict (Andretta *et al.* 2015; Freire *et al.* 2014; Karyotis *et al.* 2014), the mechanisms of the transpositions of interests and ideas into collective behavior (Saunders *et al.* 2015), the influence of social, political, and cultural conflict on anti-austerity movements' effectiveness (Clarke and Newman 2012, 300; della Porta, 2012, 2015; Giugni and Grasso 2015a; Guzman-Concha 2015; Hylmö and Wennerhag 2015; Ketelaars 2015; Kriesi 2015), political economy-based interpretation of social mobilization (Císař and Navrátil 2017), and the channels of diffusion of the ideas which constitute anti-austerity movements (della Porta and Mattoni 2015; Oikonomakis and Roos 2016; Smith 2016; Teixeira *et al.* 2014). Those works contributed to our knowledge of why anti-austerity movements came into being, how the idea of their continuance spread over and far beyond Europe, and why they were relatively unique while comparing it with predecessors (Cinalli and Vasilopoulos 2015; Giugni and Grasso 2015b).

No research, however, has sought to explain why the initially self-described peaceful anti-austerity movements used mental and physical political violence in a public sphere and why they did it in richly varied ways (della Porta *et al.* 2017; Wearden 2012). Although it has been on the street because of world news that the attitudes towards the usage of force differed in Europe, we have not known why Slovaks and Estonians preferred to sing their way through hardship rather than fight bitterly like Greeks, Belgians, or Spaniards (Velmet 2014). Another puzzle has been the modes of the legitimation of turning to political violence by social movements. Not only has it been unclear to what extent and how they differed in the paradigms of violent behavior but also what exactly contributed to their very nature and those differences. In general, little has been done to shed light on the use of political violence by those movements.

Current specialist literature has offered no comparative studies that identified dissimilarities and similarities between the violent behavior of particular movements. It incentivized us to formulate a research question of how and to what extent the behavior was different and similar in the particular European states. Apart from explaining some violent incidents, the literature has not proposed explanations for general patterns of violent behavior that entered Europe. It aroused a next question of why the patterns had some features in common and differed in others. Although post-2008 anti-austerity movements are a fairly new phenomenon, it was also appealing to learn if those various patterns of violent behavior resulted in either broadly based or same political consequences. On the one hand, looking for instant results seemed to be a slick way because of a limited and relatively short time perspective to assess the courses of action. It did not allow us to see the contention from a valuable historical perspective and prompted us to pose a question if it is possible at all to capture the immediate aftermaths of the activity of anti-austerity movements. On the other hand, it was tempting to resort to a rich and vast body of literature on political violence to test the explanatory power of models it offers on this particular research field involving recent events in the age of austerity. In fact, potentially useful theories have undergone testing no more than once, and thus they have not held out the promise of being something more than a description of a given political reality. Bearing in mind a threat of bias in the form of a self-fulfilling prophecy, it was of tremendous cognitive risk to choose one theory and build an explanation around it. Nonetheless, it did not counsel us against inquiring of what the repercussions of anti-austerity violent activities were and how the repercussions differed in the states.

The research questions inspired another review of the specialist literature. Whereas the first one had concentrated directly on state of the art of studies on anti-austerity movements, the second aimed to strike theories which would be forceful and comprehensive enough to identify similarities and dissimilarities between the violent behavior of social movements and explain their sources and results. Although the review found no theory of both exploratory and explanatory values, it finished with chasing down a poorly established category of a culture of political violence whose meaning and analytical value met general searching criteria. The existing literature has contained several definitions, classifications, and explanatory models that made use of the category as either an explaining factor or a factor to be explained. Admittedly, no work has formulated and implemented a holistic approach, but their elements have not been at odds, which implied that their careful elaboration might have resulted in a promising theoretical framework.

Although different in many ways, the definitions of a culture of political violence have some essential features in common (An-na'im 2006; Ayele 2011; Kling 1963; Taylor 1981; Siniawer 2008). They put emphasis on a context in which political subjects use violence to achieve their goals within social structures. The subjects are shown in relationships of power and as legitimating and delegitimating themselves and others to perform political roles and to take advantage of violence by employing diversified strategies. The commitment of political violence is introduced as the measure that may take the variety of forms ranging from physical force to mental influence. Additionally, the intensity of violence is characterized as gradable and changeable. Those defining features arm a culture of political violence with a conceptual framework applicable to identify the details of violent behavior. The lenses of the category allow us to look at the relationships between anti-austerity movements and makers of austerity measures. It involves going beyond a culture of political violence of anti-austerity movements and drifting towards observing a culture of political violence of stakeholders of anti-austerity movements. The stakeholders are political subjects in relations with movements. They are the people who participate in their structures, take part in anti-austerity protests and other forms of movements' collective activities. This approach counts representatives of the state apparatus, mainly politicians, police officers, firefighters, employees of a public sector, government officials, and public media journalists who act as loyal supporters of politicians or are perceived by movement participants as doing so. Although firefighters usually do not occupy politically relevant roles, they are figured in the category of the political subjects because movement participants linked them closely with state apparatuses and attacked over clashes in times of tensions on this account. The analytical relational perspective that embraces relations between the political subjects is indeed of higher exploratory power than a one-subject view as long as it shows the content of interactions between those who create contention (Alimi *et al.* 2015, 10). The content is the use of political violence, legitimation and delegitimation of its deployment and fulfilling political roles, and reactions to the very activities.

The literature review has also revealed the competing ways of applying the category of a culture of political violence as an explaining factor or a thing to be explained. They seemed to be more or less convincing but, thus far, none of them has analyzed social movements, which inhibited the chances to predict how they work while investigating the violent behavior of anti-austerity movements. The possible criteria for selection of the theories to be employed to drive hypotheses and a theoretical framework of the research were the extent of the plausibility of frameworks and their theoretical elaboration. However, in those cases, the research choices of likely explanatory power were limited and limited the potential of future research because the solutions breaking forth were unacceptably discretionary and blatantly subjective to approach the understudied phenomenon. There also appeared an urgent need not to follow out own research inclination, a citation index of the pieces of work, and opinions about their impact in the field. Additionally, it was not obvious how the theories compete in their methodological correctness and empirical effectiveness which is how well they perform while exploring and explaining what happens in political reality. In other words, it was much more riveting to test them all, including seemingly the least compelling theories, rather than only some favorites so as not to lose a chance for carrying out a comprehensive analysis. It resembled a quest for enjoying horse racing by watching all the runners rather than the one we gambled on. This approach, however, demanded to abstract methodically a set of theories to be tested from an existing body of specialist literature in order to avoid a selection bias.

Non-Traditional Research Design

In facing the methodological difficulties, at the research planning stage after the second literature review, a decision was made to propose and implement a non-traditional research design. Design engineering commenced with a thesis that a culture of political violence is a forceful theoretical category to explore and explain violent behavior in austerity-driven Europe. A presumption of the links between theory and reality guided the next methodological choices. The uniqueness of the approach consists in employing methodological premises to the process of reviewing the existing literature instead of discussing just the high-ranking and the newest works in the field. Strictly speaking, the research begins with the literature review that is carried out according to a scrupulously determined set of methodological assumptions. The idea is to identify all the theoretical frameworks of a culture of political violence that function in scientific circulation to discuss their methodological correctness and, most importantly, to test them empirically by working with case studies of the post-2008 anti-austerity movements. It means that the research does not advantage any theoretical approach but takes care over the verification of every relevant one. Anti-austerity movements are indeed a qualitatively new phenomenon, and as such, it is advisable to analyze them with the observance of due methodological diligence.

This approach required setting a text corpus of academic works released in specialist books and journals to show the qualitative variety of theoretical approaches towards a culture of political violence. Although there is no universally accepted system of ranking for book and journal publishers, the most influential, meaningful for the research subject, and substantial for the development of science ones from among them are indexed in major academic databases and search engines. That is why this literature review includes the works in social sciences and humanities indexed in 47 of the largest databases and search engines. It adopts two additional sources selection criteria to minimize a selection bias and the likelihood of omission of essential papers and to conduct a comprehensive review. The first one relates to books and makes use of the Socio-Economic and Natural Sciences of the Environment Research School's (SENSE 2009) broad-based list which contains book publishers frequently considered by professionals in rankings. The literature review discusses works classified as refereed book publications by the world's top of publishers. This class contains 11 publishing companies. The second criterion concerns scholarly journals and takes advantage of the International Scientific Institute's (ISP 2016) top international publisher list formulated by a number of academic journals released by a company which embraces the most influential and led by experienced editorial boards of publishing houses. The quantitative indicator allowed us to rank them, but a position on the list did not have an impact on the ranking of the papers under review. The literature review covers the first 20 publishers that put out journals devoted to social sciences and humanities. Then, the study applies a phrase searching technique to search for the studies containing the exact searching phrase "culture of political violence" in each from among the mentioned sources. It analyzes the first 50 search results, arranged in order of relevance, out of all the search results in relation to the use of the category of a culture of political violence. The works which just mention but neither define nor give it a function in the analysis are excepted from the further steps of the review because they fail to make a contribution to a theoretical framework of the category.

The next step was to collate the search results according to a criterion of the function the category has in theories. The selection of four functions was consistent with the research goals and, thereby, the review scrutinized definitions potentially useful to determine (i) the essential features of a culture of political violence, (ii) explanatory frameworks using the category as a thing to be explained to account for what contributes to cultures of political violence, (iii) explanatory frameworks employing a culture of political violence as a thing explaining other things for the purpose of accounting for the result of its emergence, and (iv) classification models to detect the criteria for the distinction of cultures of political violence.

Then, the construction of four sets of criteria for methodological correctness, applicable to critically evaluate the elements of theories under review, provided a framework for a discussion on the search results collated into four sections. The first section gathers and analyzes those works which introduce the semantic fields of a culture of political violence by stating what it is and how researchers understand it. It exclusively focuses on definitions and distinctive features of this category. The following problems explore the semantic fields: what types of meanings are attached to a culture of political violence? By what criteria are these types distinguishable? To what extent are definitions of a culture of political violence correct? What is the extent of their applicability to empirical analyses as the analytical tools? It is of vital importance to assess whether definitions have the capability to work above and beyond the scope of concrete papers and how they contribute to an operationalizable definition and a conceptual framework of the category. Every single conceptual construction of a culture of political violence undergoes a critical scrutiny according to the same set of criteria elaborated especially for this study. This part of the review seeks to inform theoretically an empirical study of the characteristics of cultures of political violence that entered Europe in the scope of the identification properties expressed by similarities and dissimilarities among their patterns.

The second section of the review takes into consideration the explanatory frameworks based on the assumption that an indicator or a set of indicators accounts for a culture of political violence. An explanatory framework is understood as a description and explanation of why a being, phenomenon, process, configuration of those, or lack thereof is the way it is or how and why it works. It stands in for the full explanation of an issue in question unless a full and effective explanation exists. The following problems structure the scrutiny of this subject field: what types of explanatory frameworks are employed to explain sources of a culture of political violence? To what extent are explanatory frameworks formulated correctly? What is the extent of their applicability to empirical analyses? Every single work identified in the process of searching literature, which offers a model for explaining how cultures of political violence come about, is critically analyzed according to the same original set of criteria formulated especially for this analysis. The goal of this section is to discover what may make for cultures of political violence in Europe, particularly what qualities they have in common and how they differ. At this stage of the research process, the study did not adopt or reject models because of their extent of methodological correctness or estimated explanatory effectiveness. Instead, the next part of the research coping with this type of explanatory frameworks tested the models empirically in their current or modified forms with respect to the correctness criteria if needed.

The third section of the literature review draws attention to the explanatory frameworks that capture unambiguously a culture of political violence presented as an explaining indicator of other things. The following problems address this subject field: what does a culture of political violence explain? To what extent are explanatory frameworks phrased correctly? What is an extent of their applicability to empirical analyses? Let us emphasize, the difference between the second and the third section consists in the role of the category in the analyses striving for providing an explanation. Whereas the second concerns possible sources of cultures of political violence, the third deals with their feasible consequences. Once again, every single theoretical contribution aspiring to build a model involving the category as an explaining factor of a being, phenomenon, process, configuration of those, or lack thereof is analyzed by the same original set of criteria elaborated especially for this analysis. This section aims to set what the outcomes of cultures of political violence may be and how those outcomes mirror the similarities and dissimilarities between the cultures. In the later part of the research which relates to this type of explanatory frameworks, the models that use a culture of political violence as an explaining factor are tested empirically in their existing or amended shapes with respect to methodological correctness if necessary. Here, just as in the second section, the models are discussed critically, but no framework is disdained or taken for granted. Instead, their explanatory effectiveness is to be verified afterward by working with case studies.

Finally, the fourth section approaches classification schemes of a culture of political violence. The following problems organize the analysis of this subject field: what types of classification schemes of a culture of political violence are in the literature? Under what rules do researchers outline them? To what extent are they correct? What is the extent of their applicability to empirical analyses? Every single classification framework identified while searching the literature is scrutinized by the same set of criteria proposed especially for this study. The purpose of this section is to recognize how and to what extent cultures of political violence may vary in what criteria. It fortifies the results of the first section's analysis with an insight into the differences between the cultures, and it has an exploratory potential to boost the analysis of distinctive features of cultures of political violence in Europe.

All the works under review are analyzed sternly and strictly in the line of the standardized sets of criteria. It shows the theoretical frameworks in the light of their methodological correctness but tells little about empirical effectiveness. An empirical analysis following the literature review evaluates their effectiveness. It does, however, double duty as it tests theories as well as explores and explains political reality. Accordingly, the further step of the research was to advance ontological, epistemological, and methodological perspectives, research problems, hypotheses, field, methods, techniques, and tools to state what and how the study addresses. Generally speaking, those methodological assumptions for empirical analysis were of vital importance to design a way for verifying an empirical effectiveness of the theories on the next step. The last step was the evaluation of research results.

Methodological Assumptions for Empirical Tests

The analysis draws upon a pragmatic rather than a paradigm-driven approach, so it states the research problems that need answers and then chooses methods for answering them (Punch 2014, 17). The structure of the problems guides the design and implementation of the methodological and theoretical premises (Evans *et al.* 2011). Ontological, epistemological, and methodological choices follow this assumption. First, ontology concerns the very nature of reality. The pragmatic ontological perspective enables us to see the political reality as incessantly negotiated and renegotiated more than constant and fixed. Second, epistemology relates to what the relationship between the researcher and the reality is and how she can generate acceptable knowledge (Punch 2014, 15). The pragmatic epistemological point of view drives the researcher into trying to achieve intersubjectively the verifiable research conclusions by proposing and following methodological assumptions. The researcher cognizes the political reality with scientific methods, techniques, and devices because the objective recognition is impossible and the subjective one does not provide her with exact results. Third, methodology concerns what methods can be employed for studying the reality. The pragmatic methodological perspective is free from the potentially biasing premise that there is a method being the only game in town applicable to approach social movements productively. Instead, the researcher eventually selects those qualitative, and quantitative in a pinch, methods which she esteems being the most appropriate and effective to solve particular research problems. In doing so, she is not confined to any paradigm-driven assumptions and gets away from a "methodolatry" trap.

The analysis is, however, theory-driven throughout each stage of the research process. The use of the term "theory" ought not to be taken to mean that it applies to denote a unified theory due to the absence of such one in the field. Instead, the term is the framework or the set of concepts that have a descriptive, organizational, and explanatory value (Cantir and Kaarbo 2016, 21). The literature review and existing substantive theoretical approaches inform and inspire the research problems, hypotheses, conceptual frameworks, and explanations.

The goals of the study are of both theory-verification and theory-generation nature. The first objective is to set down cultures of political violence of the stakeholders of the anti-austerity movements which entered Europe in the times of austerity in a way capturing similarities and differences between them. The similarities and differences that the clusters of European cases have in common are crucial for distinguishing between patterns because their particular configuration creates the types of a culture of political violence. Second, the research aims at explaining the sources of the types. Third, it aims to account for the results of the types. The point is to investigate to what extent the sources and the results of the cultures of political violence are explainable by existing explanatory frameworks. Most importantly, to inquire into the roots of differences between the cultures and the meaning of those differences for the repercussions of the cultures.

The research solves the three research problems to fulfill the aims: what patterns of a culture of political violence did stakeholders of the post-2008 anti-austerity movements have? To what extent do current explanatory frameworks explain why stakeholders of the post-2008 anti-austerity movements had particular patterns of a culture of political violence? To what extent do current explanatory frameworks account for the results of patterns of a culture of political violence had by stakeholders of the post-2008 anti-austerity movements? The research questions that motivated this study inspired the research problems.

Although one may look at the formulation of hypotheses in qualitative research as walking on thin ice (Punch 2014, 66), the research proposes hypotheses to organize a research process. Those involved are, however, general enough not to enforce an interpretation-orientation on the researcher and rigorous sufficiently to delineate an analysis direction. Predicted answers to the research problems draw upon an extensive literature review and empirical data recognition. Research hypotheses are consistent with the problems: stakeholders of the post-2008 anti-austerity movements might have had patterns of a culture of political violence diversified with respect to the values of its essential features: political subjects that deployed political violence, their mutual legitimation to the deployment, modes of the legitimation of the use, an intensity of the use of physical political violence, and forms of political violence. Current explanatory frameworks probably to a low extent explain why stakeholders of the post-2008 anti-austerity movements had particular patterns of a culture of political violence. Current explanatory frameworks probably to a low extent account for the results of patterns of a culture of political violence had by stakeholders of the post-2008 anti-austerity movements. Then, specific hypotheses deriving from given theories are introduced directly before their empirical tests. They examine a research field according to the theoretical and methodological premises.

A research field indicates what exactly a subject of research interest is. Let us begin by defining an anti-austerity movement to throw light on the subject scope of the examination. Social movements are understood as conscious, collective, and organized efforts at a social change (Edwards 2014, 4), here, at the abandonment of austerity measures, removing their results, and providing or restoring social well-being. They are not one-off events. Instead, they exist over some span of time by engaging in a conflictual issue with a particularly powerful opponent (Edwards 2014; Tilly 1999), here, the makers of austerity policies are mainly the European Union and governments. Movement participants work together to carry out, resist, or undo a social change. They share a collective identity and actively strive for an amendment of their social situation often by employing protest (Edwards 2014). Movements differ from other forms of contentious politics in their configuration of sustained campaigns of claim-making, an exceptional set of claim-making performances, and concerted displays of supporters' worthiness, unity, numbers, and commitment (Tilly 2006, 182). In many states, but not in every single case, the activity of the post-2008 anti-austerity movements indeed took the shape of political protests (Peterson *et al.* 2015; Sabucedo *et al.* 2017) organized to manifest opposition to austerity policies and solidarity with those who suffered from their establishment. The repertoire of collective action was, nonetheless, broader (McAdam *et al.* 2001; Tilly 2003). Apart from demonstrations, it embraced the creation of special-purpose associations and coalitions, public meetings, solemn processions, marches, vigils, rallies, strikes, petition drives, attacks on the public and private property as well as on representatives of the chief opponent, statements to and in public media, activities in commercial and social media, performances, *charivaris* (also "shivaree" or "rough music"), and pamphleteering (Tarrow 2013, 13). Yet, the research takes into account all the forms of political action undertaken not just exactly by anti-austerity movements (della Porta and Tarrow 2005; della Porta and Rucht 2015) but by all their stakeholders, with the object of discovering the paradigms of violent behavior which entered European states in the times of austerity in the relational perspective. It seeks to find how the behavior was produced within the relations between the political subjects engaged in the collective action due to their roles in a political structure.

Let us move on towards temporal boundaries of the research field which were of relevance while gathering empirical material. The analysis covers political behavior initiated by the stakeholders of anti-austerity movements that acted in Europe between December 1, 2007, and December 31, 2015, and came out against government and European Union austerity programs more than once. December 1, 2007, is the initial caesura of the research field because then the recession triggered by the European debt crisis began (Canterbery 2015; Thompson 2016). The crisis was an indirect underlying cause of a massive wave of public protests organized by the newly arisen anti-austerity movements in Europe. Government austerity measures imposed to battle the debt crisis threatening common currency were the direct reason for those protests and the inception of the movements (della Porta 2015; Lucarelli 2012; Zamponi and González 2017). Notably, the implementation did not take place at the exact moment in all the European states, which gave reasons to pitch on the more remote but common caesura. The research settles a broad temporal perspective just not to omit any event of consequence for the continuance of anti-austerity movements.

The closing caesura is December 31, 2015, although many of the movements faded before (Genovese *et al.* 2016) and many awakened or reawakened over time (DW 2016; Fulton 2016; Kamdar 2016). Nevertheless, it was the first year when the economic situation of European states improved after the recession, i.e., an extent of fluctuation of international financial flow declined, an extent of real GDP increased, a lending rate of bonds decreased, and government austerity programs were quenched (Copelovitch *et al.* 2016). Therefore, the direct justification for the continuance of anti-austerity movements, which opposed to the consequences of austerity policies, lapsed. Thereby, the reason for their stakeholders' existence simply vanished as well. The caesurae are the time boundaries of the research field. In turn, its territorial scope involves the epicenter of the crisis (Genovese *et al.* 2016), the European states where anti-austerity movements occurred. The subject matter research field is established by violent activities of relevant stakeholders of anti-austerity movements. The involved people form, therefore, the subject research field. Political violence ranging from a mental to physical kind is an indicator of violent behavior.

Before delving analytically into the research field, preliminary research contributed to the estimation of the availability and quality of the sources necessary and sufficient to solve the research problems, selection of research methods, techniques, and tools, and descriptive determination of case selection. The relational qualitative content analysis of specialist literature indicated that in one state, one movement existed because a collective identity was consistent within each anti-austerity movement in each state (Ancelovici 2015). Also, the analysis of all the 46 European states would be both uneconomic and ineffective. Hence, the research encompasses those observation entities which satisfy the following critical criteria: euro area states where anti-austerity movements were functioning between December 1, 2007, and December 31, 2015, and opposed to austerity measures more than once. Significantly, the analysis embraces stakeholders of anti-austerity movements which were acting in the state whose markets were directly stricken by the results of the European debt crisis. In the member states of the Eurozone, austerity measures were imposed by the European Union and governments, which created a common ground of experience for political subjects. It was of vital importance to control the analysis for confounding factors. Thus, even if anti-austerity movements acted in some other states such as England where austerity policy was not EU-imposed, they were not included in the set of cases. Fourteen cases meet the selection criteria: Austria, Belgium, Estonia, Finland, France, Greece, Spain, the Netherlands, Ireland, Germany, Portugal, Slovakia, Slovenia, and Italy. It means that the research covers all the populace of the member states of the Eurozone where the new social movements made an appearance.

The mode of the analysis is a result of research methods, techniques, and tools selection. The preliminary analysis of the sources prevented us from conducting surveys because this method would be ineffective as the past issues constitute the research field. A less expensive but also reliable method of secondary sources analysis proved to be useful to collect raw data needed to solve the research problems. Although it is time consuming because of a number, quality, and disparate locations of the pieces of secondary data, it is forceful enough to accelerate the discovery process. Thereby, the research makes use of a qualitative method of written sources analysis. The need for conceptual qualitative content analysis follows this methodological decision. The pieces of data come from various sources because there is no comprehensive and credible database which encompasses crucial information on anti-austerity movements and indicators relevant for the theoretical framework established in the literature review (della Porta 2014; Lindekilde 2014; Mosca 2014a). The research techniques of data collection are the following: an analysis of secondary data gathered in the state police databases, reports, and records, the Eurostat, the Freedom House reports, the Global Gender Gap Reports, non-government organization databases; secondary literature on the stakeholders of anti-austerity movements and indicators involved in explanatory frameworks; and articles and visual materials published in public, commercial, and social media. The sources triangulation aims to generate as reliable data as possible.

The major criterion for sources selection is their utility to verify the hypotheses effectively. Hence, the whole process of gathering the pieces of data is first and foremost purpose driven. According to the principle of theoretical sampling, the theoretical developments that occurred in an analysis of the previously gathered data lead the following stages of data collection. The cycle of alternation between data collection and analysis does not stop at two repetitions. Rather, it stands until theoretical saturation is reached. In other words, until the new pieces of data are not introducing the exemplifications of new theoretical elements but instead are confirming what has already been discovered (Punch 2014, 134). The attempts concentrate on gathering the data sets necessary and sufficient to solve the research problems (Spangler 2016, 42). This procedure aims to provide us with data for verifying all the hypotheses.

The research tools are: literature review instruction, sets of correctness criteria of definitions, explanatory frameworks, and classification frameworks, matrix of raw data, data-set observations, categorization key to content analysis, scales to interpret the research results, algebraic expressions to compute the values of time indicators, instruction to review the media of secondary data, typology of political subjects that used political violence, continuum of mutual legitimation to the use, model of the modes of the legitimation of the use, continuum of the intensity of physical political violence, and continuum of forms of political violence.

The research makes use of a statistical analysis method to verify the specific theory-driven hypotheses. The Pearson correlation technique determines the type and strength of linear correlations between the explaining indicators and the indicators to be explained. There is also conducted a two-tail test to compute the statistical significance of the correlations. In turn, when there is no need to calculate, the causal-process observations and critical discussion evaluate relations between indicators (Beck 2010; Brady and Collier 2004; Brady *et al.* 2006; Collier 2011; Collier *et al.* 2010). Choice of a set of methods, techniques, and tools heavily depends on a type of data either qualitative or quantitative as well as on a quest for research process optimization. Specific methodological assumptions are introduced in the following chapters directly before empirical tests.

Let us link the discussion on the non-traditional research design and its methodological basis. The first part of the research introduces the literature review which points out and methodologically assesses the theories of a culture of political violence. This part of the research contributes to social sciences by proposing how to create a new non-traditional research design built around a methodologically structured literature review. It allows a researcher to find the theories of potential exploratory and explanatory power while projecting a study of an understudied research field. Note should be taken, the problems that inform the literature review have a universal value and may be effectively applied to other studies as well. Although the four sets of correctness criteria for definitions, two types of explanatory frameworks, and classification schemes aim here directly to analyze theories concerning cultures of political violence, their general applicability to assess the methodological correctness of theoretical approaches is much broader. In general, they are useful to analyze theories in social sciences, but they must not take the place of an empirical test because they are invulnerable to evaluate an empirical effectiveness. The particular sets of criteria may be employed separately to analyze the respective elements of theories, but a researcher has to make a judgment what function some piece of model or model performs in a study and then to choose a set to analyze it. Accordingly, the problems and the four sets of correctness criteria make a contribution to social sciences by introducing an intersubjective, standardized, and a methodologically founded way for critical evaluation of both theories and their selected components. Finally, the literature review is the first attempt to analyze comprehensively, systematically, and critically the current body of specialist literature concerning a culture of political violence.

Critical discussion of definitions and classification frameworks paves the way for solving the three research problems. The second part of the research provides the semantic universe of a culture of political violence and its types and addresses the empirical problem. Here, by drawing on state of the art, a culture of political violence is defined as a paradigm of using political violence in a political structure, set by the temporal, subject, and subject matter indicators. This paradigm indicates who takes advantage of the use of political violence, what their mutual legitimation to the usage is, how they justify and explain the deployment, what forms of political violence they employ, and what the intensity of physical political violence is. By drawing upon empirical material, the analysis identifies the patterns of cultures of political violence of stakeholders of the post-2008 anti-austerity movements, determines similarities and dissimilarities between them, and formulates a typology. This part of the research contributes to political sociology by developing an operationalizable definition and a conceptual framework of a culture of political violence. It employs them to conduct a qualitative comparative analysis of cultures of political violence that entered European states. The analysis shows the category as a variable that takes on the values that range from placid, through hector-led to militant patterns. It is a first endeavor to create a typology of cultures of political violence in the times of austerity.

The next part of the research addresses the second problem by testing all the explanatory frameworks which recognize a culture of political violence as a thing to be explained. Those models under empirical evaluation come from the methodologically-structured literature review and show the ways for possible explanations. On the one hand, the study contributes to our knowledge of what triggered off particular patterns of a culture of political violence. On the other, it makes a contribution to studies on cultures of political violence in general by assessing an empirical effectiveness of the existing explanatory frameworks and by introducing new ways of testing theories. The added value of the study is a set of original databases presenting the theory-driven indicators for the states involved in the research.

The last part of the research deals with the third research problem and also makes use of theories discussed in the literature review but focuses on those explanatory frameworks that treat a culture of political violence as a thing explaining other things. The analysis contributes to our knowledge of results of cultures of political violence. It also introduces an empirical effectiveness of current models for the Eurozone case studies.

Indeed, this research is the first attempt to describe and systematically explain the movement stakeholders' violent behavior in various state contexts, identify similarities and differences between them, and determine the sources and results of those critical features. Let us move on towards the structure of the book that shows how the research process spreads out over the subsequent chapters.

Structure of the Book

This volume is organized into an introduction, four chapters divided into subchapters, and conclusions. The introduction presents a non-traditional research design and puts forward the methodological assumptions for the research. In particular, it reveals the research goals, temporal, territorial, subject, and subject matter field, problems, hypotheses, methods, techniques, and tools. The methodological choices that structure, organize, and fuel the discovery process are discussed and justified.

The first chapter presents a comprehensive methodologically structured literature review of theoretical approaches towards a culture of political violence. Drawing on an original extensive set of methodological assumptions, it systematically and critically analyses current specialist literature concerning this category: its semantic fields in the shape of definitions of the theoretical category, theories using a culture of political violence as a thing to be explained, theories treating a culture of political violence as a thing explaining other things, and classification schemes of the category. In other words, it sets a corpus of academic works released in specialist books and journals and then analyzes them in terms of methodological correctness. It allows us to evaluate to what extent the existing theoretical frameworks are correct and how they establish the scientific perception of the very nature of a culture of political violence. The discussion finishes with recommendations for the construction of a theoretical framework of the category.

The review of substantive literature locates the research against the background of the body of studies on a culture of political violence. It is followed by three empirical chapters which are to contribute to the field empirically. The second chapter sheds light on the post-2008 patterns of a culture of political violence in the member states of the Eurozone. It defines the core category as a paradigm of using political violence in a political structure, which is determined by the temporal, subject, and subject matter indicators. Then, it formulates a conceptual framework of a culture of political violence that encompasses five critical indicators: the political subjects that made use of political violence, mutual legitimation to the use, modes of the legitimation of the use, intensity of physical political violence, and forms of political violence. The model is designed to uphold the validity of identification and comparisons between the states. Additionally, by working with the case studies of the post-2008 violent behavior of stakeholders of 14 anti-austerity movements, the framework undergoes a test. In establishing similarities and dissimilarities between the paradigms of using political violence, it elaborates the typology introducing values taken on by cultures of political violence of stakeholders of anti-austerity movements that entered the Eurozone. As a result, it solves the first research problem of what patterns of a culture of political violence stakeholders of the post-2008 anti-austerity movements had.

The third chapter fulfills an explanatory goal. It tests current explanatory frameworks of a culture of political violence by analyzing the post-2008 incidents in which anti-austerity movements' stakeholders participated. There, the models which categorize a culture of political violence as a phenomenon to be accounted for are under scrutiny. The test is done for a theory-verification purpose to develop theories and for a theory-generation purpose to verify if and to what extent they explain why particular patterns of a culture of political violence emerged in the Eurozone of the age of austerity. Meanwhile, the analysis suggests adjustments to the existing models discussed within the literature. This chapter handles the second research problem of to what extent current explanatory frameworks explain why stakeholders of the post-2008 anti-austerity movements had particular patterns of a culture of political violence.

The last part of the empirical study checks for another aspect of a culture of political violence. The fourth chapter aims directly at verifying an empirical effectiveness of the current explanatory frameworks which put forward a culture of political violence as an explaining indicator of beings, phenomena, processes, and their configurations. It leads us to the modification and extensions of existing models identified in the literature review. The empirical study contributes to the field by mainly theory-verification attempts. This chapter addresses the last research problem of to what extent current explanatory frameworks account for the results of patterns of a culture of political violence had by stakeholders of the post-2008 anti-austerity movements.

The summary reveals the research results and introduces avenues for future studies of the research field. In particular, it weighs an extent of the hypotheses verification by discussing and summarizing arguments for and against the validity and plausibility of the final conclusions. It pays close attention to the courses and properties of modifications made within the current theoretical approaches towards the analytical category over empirical tests. Importantly, it shows the theoretical framework elaborated in the research process as a result of the theory-verification and theory-generation efforts. Last but not least, it comments on the nature of diversity and similarities between the cultures of political violence that entered the austerity-stricken member states of the Eurozone and identifies their sources and results. Simultaneously, it opens the discussion on the exploratory and explanatory utility of the category of a culture of political violence in social sciences.

Bibliography

Alimi, Eitan Y., Chares Demetriou, and Lorenzo Bosi. 2015. *The Dynamics of Radicalization. A Relational and Comparative Perspective*. New York: Oxford University Press.

Andretta, Massimiliano, Lorenzo Bosi, and Donatella della Porta. 2015. "Trust and Efficacy Taking to the Streets in Times of Crisis: Variation among Activists." In *Austerity and Protest: Popular Contention in Times of Economic Crisis*, edited by Marco Giugni and Maria Grasso, 133–154. London and New York: Routledge.

An-na'im, Abdullahi Ahmed. 2006. "Why Should Muslims Abandon Jihad? Human Rights and the Future of International Law." *Third World Quarterly* 27(5): 785–797.

Ancelovici, Marcos. 2015. "Crisis and Contention in Europe: A Political Process Account of Anti-Austerity Protests." In *Europe's Prolonged Crisis*, edited by Virginie Ruzza, Carlo Ruzza, and Hans-Jörg Trenz, 189–209. New York: Palgrave Macmillan.

Ayele, Negussay. 2011. "Legitimacy, Culture of Political Violence and Violence of Culture in Ethiopia." In *Terrorism, Identity and Legitimacy: The Four Waves Theory and Political Violence*, edited by Jean E. Rosenfeld, 212–231. Abingdon and New York: Routledge.

Beck, Nathaniel. 2010. "Causal Process 'Observation': Oxymoron or (Fine) Old Wine." *Political Analysis* 18(4): 499–505.

Blyth, Mark. 2013a. *Austerity: The History of a Dangerous Idea*. New York: Oxford University Press.

Blyth, Mark. 2013b. "The Austerity Delusion: Why a Bad Idea Won Over the West." *Foreign Affairs* 92(3): 41–56.

Brady, Henry E. and David C. Collier (eds.). 2004. *Rethinking Social Inquiry: Diverse Tools, Shared Standards*. Lanham, MD: Rowman and Littlefield.

Brady, Henry E., David Collier, and Jason Seawright. 2006. "Toward a Pluralistic Vision of Methodology." *Political Analysis* 14(3): 353–368.

Braun, Benjamin. 2013. "Preparedness, Crisis Management and Policy Change: The Euro Area at the Critical Juncture of 2008–2013." *The British Journal of Politics and International Relations* 17(3): 419–441.

Canterbery, E. Ray. 2015. *The Rise and Fall of Global Austerity*. New York: World Scientific Publishing.

Cantir, Cristian and Juliet Kaarbo. 2016. "Unpacking Ego in Role Theory: Vertical and Horizontal Role Contestation and Foreign Policy." In *Domestic Role Contestation, Foreign Policy, and International Relations*, edited by Cristian Cantir and Juliet Kaarbo, 1–22. New York and London: Routledge.

Cinalli, Manlio and Pavlos Vasilopoulos. 2015. "Feelings of Hardship and Anxiety for Contentious Politics: Economic Crisis and the Unemployed Youth in France." In *Austerity and Protest: Popular Contention in Times of Economic Crisis*, edited by Marco Giugni and Maria Grasso, 217–230. London and New York: Routledge.

Císař, Ondřej and Jiří Navrátil. 2017. "Polanyi, Political-Economic Opportunity Structure and Protest: Capitalism and Contention in the Post-Communist Czech Republic." *Social Movement Studies* 16(1): 82–100.

Clarke, John and Janet Newman. 2012. "The Alchemy of Austerity." *Critical Social Policy* 32(3): 299–319.

Collier, David. 2011. "Understanding Process Tracing." *Political Science and Politics* 44(4): 823–830.

Collier, David, Henry E. Brady, and Jason Seawright. 2010. "Outdated Views of Qualitative Methods: Time to Move On." *Political Analysis* 18(4): 506–513.

Copelovitch, Mark, Jeffry Frieden, and Stefanie Walter. 2016. "The Political Economy of the Euro Crisis." *Comparative Political Studies* 49(7): 811–840.

Cristancho, Camilo. 2015. "A Tale of Two Crises: Contentious Responses to Anti-Austerity Policy in Spain." In *Austerity and Protest: Popular Contention in Times of Economic Crisis*, edited by Marco Giugni and Maria Grasso, 193–216. London and New York: Routledge.

della Porta, Donatella. 2012. "Critical Trust: Social Movements and Democracy in Times of Crisis." *Cambio* 2: 33–43.

della Porta, Donatella. 2014. "Social Movement Studies and Methodological Pluralism: An Introduction." In *Methodological Practices in Social Movement Research*, edited by Donatella della Porta, 1–20. New York: Oxford University Press.

della Porta, Donatella. 2015. *Social Movements in Times of Austerity: Bringing Capitalism Back into Protest Analysis*. Cambridge: Polity Press.

della Porta, Donatella, Joseba Fernández, Hara Kouki, and Lorenzo Mosca. 2017. *Movement Parties Against Austerity*. Cambridge: Polity Press.

della Porta, Donatella and Alice Mattoni (eds.). 2015. *Spreading Protest: Social Movements in Times of Crisis*. Colchester: ECPR Press.

della Porta, Donatella and Dieter Rucht. 2015. "Power and Democracy in Social Movements: An Introduction." In *Meeting Democracy: Power and Deliberation in Global Justice Movements*, edited by Donatella della Porta and Dieter Rucht, 1–22. Cambridge and New York: Cambridge University Press.

della Porta, Donatella and Sidney Tarrow. 2005. "Transnational Processes and Social Activism: An Introduction." In *Transnational Protest and Global Activism*, edited by Donatella della Porta and Sidney Tarrow, 1–20. Oxford: Rowman and Littlefield.

DW. 2016. "Police in Belgium Fire Water Cannon at Anti-Austerity Protesters." *DW*, May 24. Accessed February 4, 2017. www.dw.com/en/police-in-belgium-fire-water-cannon-at-anti-austerity-protesters/a-19280167.

Edwards, Gemma. 2014. *Social Movements and Protest*. Cambridge and New York: Cambridge University Press.

Evans, Bronwynne C., David W. Coon, and Ebere Ume. 2011. "Use of Theoretical Frameworks as a Pragmatic Guide for Mixed Methods Studies: A Methodological Necessity?" *Journal of Mixed Methods Research* 5(4): 276–292.

Freire, André, Marco Lisi, Ioannis Andreadis, and José Manuel Leite Viegas. 2014. "Political Representation in Bailed-out Southern Europe: Greece and Portugal Compared." *South European Society and Politics* 19(4): 413–433.

Fulton, Deirdre. 2016. "Anti-Austerity Leftist Announces Challenge to French President Hollande." *Popular Resistance*, August 22. Accessed February 4, 2017. https://popularresistance.org/anti-austerity-leftist-announces-challenge-to-french-president-hollande/.

Fumagalli, Andrea and Stefano Lucarelli. 2015. "Finance, Austerity and Commonfare." *Theory, Culture & Society* 32(7–8): 51–65.

Genovese, Federica, Gerald Schneider, and Pia Wassmann. 2016. "The Eurotower Strikes Back." *Comparative Political Studies* 49(7): 939–967.

Giugni, Marco and Maria Grasso. 2015a. "Austerity and Protest: Debates and Challenges." In *Austerity and Protest: Popular Contention in Times of Economic Crisis*, edited by Marco Giugni and Maria Grasso, 1–15. London and New York: Routledge.

Giugni, Marco and Maria Grasso. 2015b. "Austerity and Protest: Lessons and Future Research." In *Austerity and Protest: Popular Contention in Times of Economic Crisis*, edited by Marco Giugni and Maria Grasso, 231–240. London and New York: Routledge.

Grasso, Maria and Marco Giugni. 2015. "Are Anti-Austerity Movements 'Old' or 'New'?" In *Austerity and Protest: Popular Contention in Times of Economic Crisis*, edited by Marco Giugni and Maria Grasso, 57–82. London and New York: Routledge.

Guzman-Concha, Cesar. 2015. "Understanding Conflict, Change and Power after the Financial Crisis." *Sociology* 49(4): 791–797.

Hayes, Graeme. 2017. "Regimes of Austerity." *Social Movement Studies* 16(1): 21–35.

Hylmö, Anders and Magnus Wennerhag. 2015. "Does Class Matter in Protests? Social Class, Attitudes towards Inequality, and Political Trust in European Demonstrations in a Time of Economic Crisis." In *Austerity and Protest: Popular Contention in Times of Economic Crisis*, edited by Marco Giugni and Maria Grasso, 83–110. London and New York: Routledge.

ISP. 2016. "Top International Publisher List." Accessed June 9, 2016. www.scijournal.org/top-international-journal-publisher.shtml.

Kamdar, Mira. 2016. "In Paris, a Protest Movement Awakens." *New York Times*, April 14. Accessed February 4, 2017. www.nytimes.com/2016/04/14/opinion/in-paris-a-protest-movement-awakens.html?_r=0.

Karyotis, Georgios, Wolfgang Rüdig, and David Judge. 2014. "Representation and Austerity Politics: Attitudes of Greek Voters and Elites Compared." *South European Society and Politics* 19(4): 435–456.

Ketelaars, Pauline. 2015. "Bridging the Protest Macro-Micro Gap: Investigating the Link between Motivations, Political Efficacy and Political Context." In *Austerity and Protest: Popular Contention in Times of Economic Crisis*, edited by Marco Giugni and Maria Grasso, 111–132. London and New York: Routledge.

Kling, Merle. 1963. "Violence and Politics in Latin America." *The Sociological Review* 11(S1): 119–132.

Kotz, David M. 2009. "The Financial and Economic Crisis of 2008: A Systemic Crisis of Neoliberal Capitalism." *Review of Radical Political Economics* 41(3): 305–317.

Kriesi, Hanspeter. 2015. "Political Mobilization in Times of Crises: The Relationship between Economic and Political Crises." In *Austerity and Protest: Popular Contention in Times of Economic Crisis*, edited by Marco Giugni and Maria Grasso, 19–34. London and New York: Routledge.

Kriesi, Hanspeter. 2016. "Mobilization of Protest in the Age of Austerity." In *Street Politics in the Age of Austerity: From the Indignados to Occupy*, edited by Marcos Ancelovici, Pascale Dufour, and Héloïse Nez, 67–90. Amsterdam: Amsterdam University Press.

Lindekilde, Lasse. 2014. "Discourse and Frame Analysis: In-Depth Analysis of Qualitative Data in Social Movement Research." In *Methodological Practices in Social Movement Research*, edited by Donatella della Porta, 195–227. New York: Oxford University Press.

Lucarelli, Bill. 2012. "The Break-Up of the Eurozone?" *The Economic and Labour Relations Review* 23(4): 25–38.

McAdam, Doug, Sidney Tarrow, and Charles Tilly. 2001. *Dynamics of Contention*. Cambridge and New York: Cambridge University Press.

McMenamin, Iain Michael Breen, and Juan Muñoz-Portillo. 2015. "Austerity and Credibility in the Eurozone." *European Union Politics* 16(1): 45–66.

Mosca, Lorenzo. 2014a. "Methodological Practices in Social Movement Online Research." In *Methodological Practices in Social Movement Research*, edited by Donatella della Porta, 397–417. New York: Oxford University Press.

Oikonomakis, Leonidas and Jérôme E. Roos. 2016. "A Global Movement for Real Democracy?: The Resonance of Anti-Austerity Protest from Spain and Greece to Occupy Wall Street." In *Street Politics in the Age of Austerity: From the Indignados to Occupy*, edited by Marcos Ancelovici, Pascale Dufour, and Héloïse Nez, 227–252. Amsterdam: Amsterdam University Press.

Perugorría, Ignacia, Michael Shalev, and Benjamín Tejerina. 2016. "The Spanish Indignados and Israel's Social Justice Movement: The Role of Political Cleavages in Two Large-Scale Protests." In *Street Politics in the Age of Austerity: From the Indignados to Occupy*, edited by Marcos Ancelovici, Pascale Dufour, and Héloïse Nez, 91–120. Amsterdam: Amsterdam University Press.

Peterson, Abby, Mattias Wahlström, and Magnus Wennerhag. 2015. "European Anti-Austerity Protests – Beyond 'Old' and 'New' Social Movements?" *Acta Sociologica* 58(4): 293–310.

Punch, Keith F. 2014. *Introduction to Social Research: Quantitative and Qualitative Approaches*. 3rd edition. London: Sage.

Quaranta, Mario. 2016. "Protesting in 'Hard Times': Evidence from a Comparative Analysis of Europe, 2000–2014." *Current Sociology* 64(5): 736–756.

Ross, George. 2016. "Austerity and New Spaces for Protest: The Financial Crisis and Its Victims." In *Street Politics in the Age of Austerity: From the Indignados to Occupy*, edited by Marcos Ancelovici, Pascale Dufour, and Héloïse Nez, 43–66. Amsterdam: Amsterdam University Press.

Sabucedo, José-Manuel, Cristina Gómez-Román, Mónica Alzate, Jacquelien van Stekelenburg, and Bert Klandermans. 2017. "Comparing Protests and Demonstrators in Times of Austerity: Regular and Occasional Protesters in Universalistic and Particularistic Mobilisations." *Social Movement Studies*. 16(6): 704–720.

Saunders, Clare, Silke Roth, and Cristiana Olcese. 2015. "Anti-Cuts Protests in the UK: Are We Really All in This Together?" In *Austerity and Protest: Popular Contention in Times of Economic Crisis*, edited by Marco Giugni and Maria Grasso, 171–192. London and New York: Routledge.

SENSE. 2009. "Ranking of Academic Publishers." Accessed June 9, 2016. www.sense.nl/gfx_content/documents/ABCDE-indeling%20Scientific%20Publishers%20SENSE_approved_May_2009.pdf.

Seymour, Richard. 2014. *Against Austerity: How We Can Fix the Crisis They Made*. London and New York: Pluto Press.

Siniawer, Eiko Maruko. 2008. *Ruffians, Yakuza, Nationalists: The Violent Politics of Modern Japan, 1860–1960*. Ithaca, NY and London: Cornell University Press.

Smith, Jackie. 2016. "Social Movements and Political Moments: Reflections on the Intersections of Global Justice Movements & Occupy Wall Street." In *Street Politics in the Age of Austerity: From the Indignados to Occupy*, edited by Marcos Ancelovici, Pascale Dufour, and Héloïse Nez, 205–226. Amsterdam: Amsterdam University Press.

Tarrow, Sidney. 2013. *The Language of Contention: Revolutions in Words, 1688–2012*. Cambridge and New York: Cambridge University Press.

Taylor, Stan. 1981. "Riots: Some Explanations." *Journal of Ethnic and Migration Studies* 9(2): 167–172.

Teixeira, Conceição Pequito, Emmanouil Tsatsanis, and Ana Maria Belchior. 2014. "Support for Democracy in Times of Crisis: Diffuse and Specific Regime Support in Portugal and Greece." *South European Society and Politics* 19(4): 501–518.

Thompson, Helen. 2016. "Enduring Capital Flow Constraints and the 2007–2008 Financial and Euro Zone Crises." *The British Journal of Politics and International Relations* 18(1): 216–233.

Tilly, Charles. 1999. "From Interactions to Outcomes in Social Movements." In *How Social Movements Matter*, edited by Marco Giugni, Doug Mcadam, and Charles Tilly, 253–270. Minneapolis and London: University of Minnesota Press.

Tilly, Charles. 2003. *The Politics of Collective Violence*. Cambridge and New York: Cambridge University Press.

Tilly, Charles. 2006. *Regimes and Repertoires*. Chicago, IL and London: The University of Chicago Press.

Velmet, Aro. 2014. "Estonia: Not the Neoliberal Stronghold You've Been Sold." *Left East*, May 5. Accessed February 2, 2017. www.criticatac.ro/lefteast/estonia-not-the-neoliberal-stronghold-sold/.

Ventriss, Curtis. 2013. "The Economic Crisis of 2008 and Its Substantive Implications for Public Affairs." *The American Review of Public Administration* 43(6): 627–655.

Wearden, Graeme. 2012. "Europe's Day of Anti-Austerity Strikes and Protests Turn Violent – As It Happened." *Guardian*, November 14. Accessed January 31, 2017. www.theguardian.com/business/2012/nov/14/eurozone-crisis-general-strikes-protest-day-of-action.

Zamponi, Lorenzo and Joseba Fernández González. 2017. "Dissenting Youth: How Student and Youth Struggles Helped Shape Anti-Austerity Mobilisations in Southern Europe." *Social Movement Studies* 16(1): 64–81.

1 Theoretical Approaches towards Cultures of Political Violence

DOI: 10.4324/9781351205757-2

Methodological Assumptions for a Literature Review

The goal of this chapter is to provide a comprehensive review of theoretical and methodological approaches towards a culture of political violence. It establishes a text corpus of academic works released in the specialist books and journals which apply the category to scrutinize a social reality, and then it systematically and critically analyzes their theoretical frameworks by employing methodological assumptions. In doing so, it assesses to what extent the existing approaches are formally correct and how they contribute to our understanding of the nature, sources, and consequences of cultures of political violence.

The uniqueness of the approach consists in applying methodological premises to the process of reviewing the existing literature and then making use of the results in an empirical part of the research. The idea is to identify all the theoretical frameworks of a culture of political violence that function in scientific circulation, to discuss their correctness, and to test their empirical effectiveness by working with the case studies of post-2008 anti-austerity movements. It means that the research does not advantage any theoretical approach but takes care over the verification of every one. Anti-austerity movements are a qualitatively new phenomenon and as such they have to be analyzed with the observance of due methodological diligence. A quick overview of definitions of a culture of political violence shows that although they identify a symptomatic phenomenon, they fail to provide us with a comprehensive view of relevant and operationalizable features of the movement's violent behavior. Also, it would be a tremendous research risk to apply an explanatory framework that is currently fashionable, just seems to be the most appropriate, or is the most cited. As this chapter argues, it is important to see how well the existing approaches work and compete on the field of explanation. It allows us to observe the results of an application of the variety of theoretical frameworks and assess their exploratory and explanatory potential.

First and foremost, the review establishes a text corpus to provide material for the literature review. Admittedly, there is no universally accepted system of ranking for book and journal publishers, but major academic databases and search engines contain papers that are the most influential, significant for the research subject, and contribute to the development of science (Krause 2001; McGinn *et al.*

2016). Hence, the review considers the works in social sciences and humanities indexed in the largest databases and search engines: Academic Search Complete, Anthropological Index Online, Anthropological Literature, APA PsycNET, ATLA Religion Database, AULIMP: Air University Library's Index to Military Periodicals, BASE: Bielefeld Academic Search Engine, Current Contents, EconBiz, EconLit, ERIC: Educational Resource Information Center, GENESIS, Google Scholar, IngentaConnect, International Directory of Philosophy, Isidore, JournalSeek, JSTOR: Journal Storage, Jurn, LexisNexis, Lingbuzz, Mendeley, Microsoft Academic Search, NBER: National Bureau of Economic Research, OAIster, OpenSIGLE, Philosophy Documentation Center eCollection, Philosophy Research Index, PhilPapers, POIESIS: Philosophy Online Serials, POPLINE, Project MUSE, PsycINFO, Pubget, PubPsych, Questia: Online Research Library, RePEc: Research Papers in Economics, SafetyLit, ScienceOpen, Scopus, Socol@r: Socolar, SSRN: Social Science Research Network, SpringerLink, VET-Bib, Web of Science, WorldCat, and WorldWideScience.

The review adopts two additional criteria for sources selection to minimize the likelihood of the omission of substantial works. The first one relates to books and makes use of Socio-Economic and Natural Sciences of the Environment Research School's (SENSE 2009) broad-based list which embraces book publishers frequently placed by professionals in rankings. The list is divided into (1) refereed book publications published by (A) the world top of publishers, (B) the world's semi-top of publishers, (C) other publishers and (2) non-refereed book publications published for (D) an academic public (professional publications) and (E) a non-academic general public. The studies published by the 2-category companies are of a relatively lower academic value and relevance than the 1-category because of not being refereed (Torraco 2016), so, they are beyond the text corpus. The B- and C-publishers are also excluded from the corpus on the grounds of their lower academic meaning and extent of influence on the development of disciplines. Additionally, the 1-category publishers which release studies falling outside the scope of social sciences and humanities are excluded from the corpus. Ultimately, the literature review includes studies in refereed books printed by the following A-publishers: Cambridge University Press, Columbia University Press, Harvard University Press, Johns Hopkins University Press, MIT Press, Oxford University Press, Princeton University Press, Stanford University Press, University of Chicago Press, and Yale University Press.

The second criterion concerns scholarly journals and takes advantage of International Scientific Institute's (ISP 2016) top international publisher list formulated by a number of academic journals released by the most influential companies and led by experienced editorial boards of publishing houses. The quantitative indicator allowed us to rank them, but a position in the list did not have an impact on the papers under review. The literature review covers the first 20 publishers releasing journals devoted to social sciences and humanities. They are as follows: Elsevier, Springer-Verlag, Taylor and Francis, John Wiley and Sons, Sage Publications, Walter de Gruyter, Redalyc, Inderscience Publishers, Hindawi Publishing Corporation, Project MUSE, Cambridge Journals, Oxford

Journals, Revues.org, Emerald, African Journals Online, Scientific Research Publishing, Sabinet Online Ltd, SpringerOpen, Brill Academic Publishers, and IGI Global.

Then, the review applies a phrase searching technique to search for the studies containing the searching phrase "culture of political violence" rather than any other phrases comprising a set of keywords "culture," "political," "of," and "violence" put in random order. Finally, the analysis counts the first 50 phrases out of all the search results arranged in order of relevance. For the sake of clarity, it means that 50 search results are analyzed in the case of each database, search engine, and publishing house extracted for the review. Rarely was a number of searched results higher than 50 because a culture of political violence is an understudied phenomenon.

The analysis deals with conceptual and, more broadly, theoretical dimensions of the category (Fawcett 2013, 285; Rak 2016). It collates the identified uses of the category according to a criterion of a function of a culture of political violence in a theoretical framework. Therefore, the review consists of four main parts from among each and concentrates on a different component of a theory in terms of a component's function. They are a culture of political violence as a theoretical category, the category as a thing to be explained by other things, the category as a thing explaining other things, and the types of the category.

The first part gathers and analyzes those works which present the semantic fields of a culture of political violence by describing what it is and how researchers understand it. It exclusively focuses on definitions and distinctive features of this category. The following problems explore the semantic fields: what types of meanings are attached to a culture of political violence? By what criteria are these types distinguishable? To what extent are definitions of a culture of political violence correct? What is the extent of their applicability to empirical analyses as analytical tools? The review assesses whether definitions have the capability to work above and beyond the scope of concrete papers and how they contribute to an operationalizable definition and conceptual framework of the category. Every single conceptual construction of a culture of political violence undergoes a critical scrutiny according to the same set of criteria elaborated especially for this study.

The second part of the review takes into consideration the explanatory frameworks based on the assumption that an indicator or a set of indicators accounts for a culture of political violence. An explanatory framework is a description and explanation of why a being, phenomenon, process, configuration of those, or lack thereof is the way it is or how and why it works. It stands in for the full explanation of an issue in question unless the full and effective explanation exists. The following problems structure the scrutiny of this subject field: what types of explanatory frameworks are employed to explain sources of a culture of political violence? To what extent are explanatory frameworks correct? What is an extent of their applicability to empirical analyses?

The third part of the review pays close attention to the explanatory frameworks capturing unambiguously a culture of political violence presented as an explaining indicator of other things. The following problems address this subject field: what does a culture of political violence explain? To what extent are explanatory frameworks phrased correctly? What is an extent of their applicability to empirical analyses? Let us emphasize, the difference between the second and the third part consists in the role of the category in the analyses striving for providing an explanation. Whereas the second concerns possible sources of cultures of political violence, the third is about their likely consequences.

Finally, the fourth part approaches classification schemes of a culture of political violence. The following problems organize the analysis of this subject field: what types of classification schemes of a culture of political violence are in the literature? Under what rules do researchers outline them? To what extent are they correct? What is the extent of their applicability to empirical analyses?

Those works that just mention a culture of political violence but do not offer any references to its meaning (e.g., Knight and Narozhna 2005; Ncube and Okeke-Uzodike 2015) are beyond the analysis because they fail to formulate definitions or explanatory and classification frameworks for scrutiny.

Semantic Fields of Cultures of Political Violence

The first part of the analysis deals with the semantic fields of a culture of political violence expressed by definitions and distinctive features of the category. A definition is a specification of a meaning of the term that is neither true nor false (Opp 2009, 31). The review analyzes this subject field with the five problems head-on. The first one pertains to the senses given to the category in the literature, and it investigates what types of meanings are attached to a culture of political violence. To do so, it collects the *definientia* of "culture of political violence". Each definition consists of the *definiens* (plural: *definientia*) and the *definiendum* (plural: *definienda*). The *definiens* is the word or words serving to define another word or expression. So, it is a defining part of a definition. The *definiendum* is a word or expression that is being defined. Each *definiens* constitutes a semantic field of the *definiendum* by stating the *designata* (singular: *designatum*) (Rodriguez-Priego *et al.* 2013). The *designatum* means a property contributing to the meaning of the category. The *designata* indicate the types of meanings attached to a culture of political violence.

The second problem addresses on the basis of what criteria those types are distinguishable. To solve this problem, the review puts the meanings in typological generality order and identifies the essential and distinctive features of the given meanings. If the meaning has mutated, it may be advisable to establish the chronological order of approaches towards the distinctive features of a culture of political violence to capture how they have evolved.

The third problem concentrates on the correctness of definitions and tests to what extent are definitions of a culture of political violence correct? A definition is correct if it meets the following set of criteria: (1) it determines the *designata* which are necessary and sufficient to count the thing which is characterized by these *designata* among the meaning scope of a culture of political violence

(Podsakoff *et al.* 2016, 11); (2) it is operationalizable, namely, it is feasible to translate a culture of political violence into measurable variables (Meter *et al.* 1987) because it has empirical content (Opp 2009, 13); (3) it is not contextual, i.e., the *definiens* is independent of time and space contexts; (4) the *definiens* is not replaced by examples but it has a precisely stated meaning; (5) the *designata* are not in contradiction with the reverse of a culture of political violence; (6) it is not value-laden; (7) it is not normative, i.e., it involves neither demand for making the world a better place in a particular way nor an answer to a question of how it should be (Ackermann 1964, 522); and (8) it is internally consistent. The higher the extent of the criteria fulfillment by a definition is, the higher the extent of its correctness is.

The fourth problem relates to the applicability of definitions to studies and focuses on to what extent definitions of a culture of political violence are applicable to empirical analyses as the analytical tools. Hence, on the grounds of the correctness of particular definitions, the review assesses whether and under what conditions they apply to obtain research results in an intersubjective and diligent way. When the conditions are under evaluation, a definition locates on a continuum set by the extreme points of generalness and contextuality. When a definition is contextual, the continuum serves as a scale to assess to what extent this feature is firmly attached to a semantic field of the category. The review also examines definitions in terms of properties of research fields and analytical levels they may explore. It enables us to determine a current range of exploratory of potential a culture of political violence.

Application of the methodological assumptions to a search process resulted in discovering five analytical attempts to formulate definitions of a culture of political violence and to construct its conceptual frameworks (An-na'im 2006; Ayele 2011; Kling 1963; Siniawer 2008, 2012; Taylor 1981). Each of them draws on the assumption that acceptance of the use of violence or political violence in the past, in the here and now, or acquiescence to it in the future followed by the deployment allows a researcher to verify the occurrence of a culture of political violence. It undermines, however, the validity of building the term of culture into the semantic field of the category because it rules out the possibility of the existence of the continuum of stances towards the use of violence. In the line of the authors, a culture of political violence occurs or not everywhere, and it is the same everywhere. Nevertheless, empirical research provides the evidence for the existence of the more or less violent societies representing different patterns of a culture of political violence (Karstedt 2012; Steenkamp 2014; 2009). We premise that, first, expressions of a culture of political violence differ in an extent of acceptance, and, second, non-acceptance of the employment of violence indicates a different culture of political violence than the one based on a full acceptance. The existing approaches (An-na'im 2006; Ayele 2011; Kling 1963; Siniawer 2008, 2012; Taylor 1981) miss the first part of the premise and close the door on comparing diversified phenomena. Indeed, the researchers who stand for the application of a culture of political violence to comparative studies might want to consider formulating some antinomic category, such as a culture of political non-violence. However, it is important to assume that these categories are of gradable nature when we aim at identifying similarities and dissimilarities between the expressions of the categories.

The definitions offer a relational understanding of public power. It means that political subjects of violent behavior – if introduced – are those functioning in the relation of public power: the ruling, the aiming at the ruling, and the ruled. The attitudes towards violence or political violence are the subject matter. They are, however, undefined in the existing theoretical approaches to a culture of political violence. Similarly, the subject matter of these attitudes, violence or political violence respectively, also remain puzzling. Overall, the crucial components of the definitions have unspecified semantic fields, which obscures how the category is understood. Their essential features should be determined to specify what criteria are sufficient and necessary to recognize something as an empirical expression of the category and to contribute to the operationalization of definitions. An exploratory potential of the approaches is considerably reduced because they omit a role of forms of aggressive behavior, the threat, abandonment of the use, and mental political violence. It hinders a researcher from seeing the paradigms of deploying violence comprehensively.

Let us take a closer look at the definitions by analyzing them with the already introduced problems. The first by Merle Kling describes a culture of political violence as political behavior which is manifestly violent and acceptance of violence as a legitimate means for the pursuit of power (Kling 1963, 121). Kling determines the subject matter semantic field of a culture of political violence with its three essential features. The *designatum* is in contradiction with the reverse of a culture of political violence. First, Kling identifies a culture of political violence with the political behavior which may be *ex definitione* one-time. Maintaining that the behavior is a culture is, therefore, unjustified in terms of the methodological and theoretical effectiveness of the approach. Furthermore, the location of a culture of political violence in a behavioral sphere by making it an equivalent of political behavior calls the use of the category of culture into question. Thus, the definition is not consistent internally.

Second, Kling assumes that the acceptance of violence as a legitimate tool to come to power is an essential feature of a culture of political violence (Kling 1963, 121). The mechanism of acceptance is located in an awareness sphere as a result of its very nature. The theoretical model under scrutiny does not introduce, however, whose awareness should be evaluated to reach conclusions on the key category. The definition avoids establishing unambiguously who accepts the use of violence by whom. In assuming the consistency of the subjects in the approach, one may state that a perpetrator is a person who strives for being a ruling subject and simultaneously this person accepts political violence as a device. Nevertheless, it is unjustifiable to remove from the meaning scope of the category of a political subject matter its essence – the relation between the ruling and the ruled. The relationship indicates the political dimension of violence. The role of society in creation, consolidation, and decline of a culture of political violence is neither circumscribed nor considered by Kling. This part of the definition demands to have specified the relationship between the subjects that deploy and approve political violence.

Third, in making up his model, Kling separately captures behavior and acquiescence to behavior in the category's semantic field (Kling 1963, 121). Nevertheless, a culture has a broader meaning than the behavior and encompasses it (della Porta 1995; Patterson 2014). The essential features of Kling's category are not entirely separate (Kling 1963, 121) because the acquiescence to the employment of violence precedes the act of violence and, simultaneously, it is neither the element, the indicator, nor the type of the use of political violence (Bell *et al.* 2013). Those who seek to be the ruling subjects and the setting of the relation of power have indeed separate semantic fields. The extent of the definition's precision is also reduced by the ontologization of power and not introducing a type of power. Kling avoids determining the subject field of his approach and thus undermines the extent of its applicability to empirical research. According to the criteria, the approach is of low extent of correctness and applicability in its existing form.

In the next of the approaches, Stan Taylor entirely equates a culture of political violence with a tradition of violence (Taylor 1981, 170). Just like Kling's approach, the *designatum* is in contradiction with the reverse of a culture of political violence and the definition is internally inconsistent. Taylor makes equal the two qualitatively and semantically different theoretical categories. In doing so, Taylor does not detail the essential features of the one being, the *definiens*. Besides, the limitation of a culture's semantic field to one of its elements – a tradition – is amply unjustified. This is as unjustified as the semantic reduction of a tradition's predicate, i.e., violence, consisting in putting political violence in the *definiendum* and locating violence in the defining expression. This definition is worth rethinking and reformulating because it does not meet the correctness criteria. Finally, the *definiens* is immeasurable, which imposes a considerable limitation on the approach's applicability to studies on a culture of political violence.

In turn, Abdullahi Ahmed An-na'im defines a culture of political violence as the capacity of perpetrators to use terrorist acts and the willingness of the wider population to tolerate such violent behavior. He claims that it indicates the disregard for the safety and well-being of others (An-na'im 2006, 796). There, in contrast to Kling's and Taylor's approaches, the *designatum* is not in contradiction with the reverse of a culture of political violence and the definition is internally consistent.

An-na'im's assumes that the analysis of a culture of political violence demands to delve into an awareness sphere. The first part of the *definiens* concentrates on the ability to initiate and carry out violent behavior. The ability constitutes, however, purely and simply some predisposition that is its potential hallmark. Having this competence does not mean, and does not have to lead to, the use of violence in tandem. Worth stressing is that the meaning scope of political violence is there narrowed down to terrorist acts (Armborst 2010). The other types of political violence are thereby excluded from the approach on no evidence.

The second part of the defining expression of An-na'im's definition focuses on the identifiable readiness to accept terrorist acts (An-na'im 2006, 796). In pointing out passive acceptance as an essential feature of the category, the author excludes from its semantic field the possibility and consequence of political mobilization. In fact, An-na'im's does not take into consideration the population's active political participation in initiating and carrying out a contentious collective action. In doing so, he unwarrantably rejects the assumption about the transposition potential of the tolerance of political violence as an essential feature of a culture of political violence (Kalmoe 2014). Yet, unlike Kling, An-na'-im considers a social indicator.

The last part of An-na'im's *definiens* introduces two types of the indications of the occurrence of a culture of political violence that are neglecting security and the well-being of only this part of the population which disapproves of terrorist acts (An-na'im 2006, 796). It means indeed that the results of the occurrence of a culture of political violence for commonality, including this part of the population which accepts terrorist acts, their perpetrators, and those who are able and prone to be perpetrators are disregarded. Overall, the limitations of the approach reduce its correctness and applicability to empirical research.

Then, Eiko Maruko Siniawer defines a culture of political violence as a context in which the use of physical force is viewed by political actors as a viable and acceptable strategy. It is dynamic and altering but helps perpetuate a violent brand of politics (Siniawer 2008, 2, 75, 2012, 629). There, just as in An-na'im's definition, the *designatum* is not in contradiction with the reverse of a culture of political violence and the definition is internally consistent. In line with this approach, a context in which political actors consider the use of physical violence to be an acceptable game plan is a culture of political violence. The nature of the strategy, the game plan, determines the analytical level of the political process which is the content of the category of a culture of political violence (Wood 2016). The absence of any predicate of the strategy contributes to the extension of the category's semantic field to a vague content and size. It is a result of not circumscribing its boundaries. Siniawer clarifies neither what strategy has a high extent of relevance for the *definiendum* nor what the essential features of the context are. Instead, he sets the context forth as dynamic and changing but helping maintain politics which is marked by the use of violence (Siniawer 2008, 2, 75, 2012, 629). Nevertheless, in focusing entirely on the productive violence, Siniawer does not take into account the destructive violence, a result of relations between political violence and politics in general (Ayyash 2013), which reduces the scope of the category's applicability to studies. Siniawer also avoids offering the model of context dynamics and the trajectory of changes.

In keeping with Siniawer, the context is the condition of politics, in which violence is employed to achieve political goals. The relations of power between the ruling subjects, between the ruled subjects, and between the ruling and the ruled subjects draw upon violent behavior. Violence is the instrument for determining the scope of liberties and duties of political subjects and for creating, protecting, and distributing public goods, including public security. As Siniawer shows, the identification of the use of physical violence as the object of perception of political subjects allows a researcher to verify the occurrence of a culture of political violence. The very use of violence does not determine, therefore, the trajectory of a continuance of a culture of political violence. It points out that the possibility of the use of Siniawer's category in its current form to conduct empirical research is considerably limited by its relatively low extent of formal correctness.

The last of the identified definitions, as the only one, is contextual in terms of a territorial criterion (Ayele 2011, 226) because its *definiens* is not independent of a space context. Hence, it is marked by a lower extent of abstraction and theoretical generalization than the other approaches, which reduces its applicability to empirical research (Floyd 2016). Negussay Ayele introduces a culture of political violence as an intrinsic and inevitable reality in Ethiopia. As Ayele reckons, it is the normative mode of exercising political power in the country's history. In this case, the *designatum* is in contradiction with the reverse of a culture of political violence and the definition is inconsistent internally. The socially accepted employment of political violence to attain, use, and perpetuate power in the state is the distinctive feature of this mode. Moreover, the power seekers or power brokers avoid raising and discussing the question of the legitimacy of authority in this political context. According to Ayele's approach, claimants to power are aware that they have to wrest power by force of arms and no one stints them or acknowledges the exercise of political violence as illegitimate or immoral.

After removing all the direct references to Ethiopia from Ayele's approach, it becomes possible to isolate an array of essential features of a culture of political violence. Ayele identifies the category with, first, a reality. This feature is, however, neither necessary nor sufficient to verify the existence of a culture of political violence. It only points out that the author strives to underline the commonness of political violence in the Ethiopian context. Second, a culture of political violence is a specific normative mode of ruling in the history of the state. Nevertheless, Ayele avoids discussing the implications of normativity in relation to a culture of political violence and thus the types of relationships between the category's parts remain undetailed. One may merely suppose that the very nature of this mode of the ruling is establishing compulsory standards, falling within the standards, and being determined by them.

Ayele, just like Kling (1963, 121), ontologizes power and totally abandons defining its type (Ayele 2011, 226–227). Power is situated in relation to power in the state. Indeed, this relation consists in generating the socially accepted use of political violence for the purpose of rising to power, wielding authority, and maintaining power in the state. Ayele, not unlike Siniawer (2008, 2; 75, 2012, 629), builds the notion of context into the definition of a culture of political violence. In contrast to Siniawer, however, he does not identify it with a culture of political violence, and he limits the scope of its meaning strictly to its political dimension. According to Ayele, a political context is composed with the agency of this relation which grows out of the social acceptance of violent behavior undertaken to achieve political goals. Noteworthy, in the context, the political subjects taking part in the processes of political decision making exclude from public discourse the questions of legitimation, relegitimation, delegitimation, and redelegitimation of power. The questions are beyond a political agenda setting.

The next implications of the context are the established rules of political elites' turnover. As Ayele emphasizes, those who make efforts to become the ruling subjects are aware of the necessity to employ physical violence to change their role in a political structure. The use of armed forces is unrestrained for those who deprive the ruling subjects of their role and take it over. Nevertheless, the reduction of the model in the scope of the means of violent behavior to armed forces is not theoretically informed because an array of means other than armed forces that may be applied to achieve this goal is broad (Hanneman 1985). The freedom of the use of armed forces consists in the lack of restrictions in the use of violence in the simultaneous widespread social acceptance and legitimizing the deployment of violence in a public sphere. Logically inconsistent is to bring the ruling subject to her role and to ontologize power in the definition because the first option means assuming taking part for the consequence of the existence of the relation of power, concretely for this facet of the relation of power which encompasses relationships between the ruling and the ruled. Ontologization, on the other hand, follows the assumption that power is a subject. The colloquial use of the notion of power is incompatible with a research need for considering its structural relational nature. Taking into account the arguments, one may state that Ayele's analytical approach is of a relatively low extent of correctness and applicability to empirical research in its current form.

The analysis of the literature has shown that the category of a culture of political violence is determined by remarkably diverse semantic fields. Each attempt to construct the category consists in generating a completely different *designatum*. They are the configuration of the use of political violence and the acceptance of violence as a legitimated means to take on the role of the ruling subject (Kling 1963), the tradition of violence (Taylor 1981), the configuration of perpetrators' abilities to organize terrorist acts, the readiness of the majority of a given population to accept those acts, and the disregard for security and wealth of those people who form the remaining part of the population (An-na'im 2006), the context in which the use of political violence is acceptable (Siniawer 2008; 2012), and the involved and inevitable reality in Ethiopia and a normative mode of ruling in the history of the state (Ayele 2011).

None of them defines closely a comprehensive set of *designata* which is necessary and sufficient to count what is characterized by these *designata* among the meaning scope of a culture of political violence. In addition, they are not operationalizable and it is feasible to translate a culture of political violence into measurable variables to a highly limited extent. Fortunately, however, examples restricting an exploratory value of definitions replace no *definiens*. It means that they may explore more and different examples than the ones investigated by the authors. They are also neither normative nor value-laden. Although an extent of applicability of the five variants of the theoretical category in their current forms is low, they introduce an array of essential features relevant to identify a culture of political violence in a political reality. These are the types of relationships between political violence and the elements of a political structure and public goods as a subject matter of violent behavior. They also suggest linking the category with the deployment of excessive political violence.

Worth bearing in mind is that the number of definitions of a culture of political violence which function in the specialist literature is extremely low. The semantic fields are authorial and usually intuitively outlined. The particular authors do not cite each other, and they develop their approaches independently. Putting the definitions in chronological order (Rocco and Plakhotnik 2009) would be then cognitively ineffective. Although the conceptual frameworks show some directions of thinking about the distinctive features of the category, they also indicate to what extent, and in what terms the research area is understudied.

Explaining Indicators of Cultures of Political Violence

This part of the analysis discusses the explanatory frameworks which aim directly to explain the sources of cultures of political violence. The four problems are utilized to study this subject field. The first one seeks to present what, according to the existing literature, explains the occurrence of a phenomenon. Thereby, it pays close attention to what types of explanatory frameworks are employed to explain the sources of a culture of political violence. A culture of political violence is the *explanandum* (plural: *explananda*) which is explicated through its *explanans* (plural: *explanantia*). Whereas the *explanandum* is a thing to be explained, and the *explanans* is an explaining thing. In other words, each *explanans* is a set of statements clarifying a property or an occurrence of a being, phenomenon, process, their configuration, or lack thereof in the *explanandum* (Nowak 2007, 352). The review sets down the sources of a culture of political violence stated in the literature, organizes them in subject order to determine the spectrum of a culture of political violence explanations, and recognizes the types of explanatory frameworks proposed by the authors.

The second problem sheds considerable light on the structures of the *explanantia*, and it asks about to what extent are explanatory frameworks correct? An explanatory framework of a culture of political violence is entirely correct if it meets the following set of criteria: (1) it determines a cause and effect relationship between the *explanandum* and the *explanans*, i.e., it consists of general sentences expressible in the form of the zero or the first conditional sentences and its apodosis (the consequence) comprises a sentence declaring the occurrence of an event or phenomenon to be explained or describing a property being explained, (2) it contains the individual sentences which declare that the events designated by a protasis or protases (the condition) of general sentences happened (Nowak 2007, 352), (3) it is operationalizable and thus verifiable, (4) it is not value-laden, (5) it is not normative, (6) it does not offer the statements in the form of the second, the third, and the mixed conditional (a mixture of the second and the third conditionals) sentences, and (7) it is internally consistent. The greater the extent of the criteria fulfillment by an explanatory framework is, the higher the extent of its correctness is.

The third problem concerns the employment of explanatory frameworks to studies and asks about the extent of their applicability to empirical analyses. The review examines the essential features of the research fields and analytical levels they may explore, and it evaluates whether and under what conditions they may achieve research results intersubjectively and thoroughly. The highly applicable explanatory framework ought to, first, be capable of accounting for a relatively broad range of beings, phenomena, and processes. Second, it should explain which phenomenon from a given class of phenomena occurs as a result of the occurrence of particular factors (Opp 2009, 24). The more specific and detailed the description of causal relations between an explaining indicator or a set of explaining indicators and an issue to be explained is, leading to a high accuracy and precision of the explanation, the bigger the extent of applicability of the framework is (Risjord 2005). Also, the broader the range of the model application is, the more informative the model is (Opp 2009, 25). When theories address specific groups or types of individuals, we lose the opportunity to learn anything about other groups or individuals (Opp 2009, 25). Therefore, the review scrutinizes explanatory frameworks employable to studies in terms of the possibility of driving their reach up.

The literature offers 11 explanatory frameworks of a culture of political violence (Ayele 2011; Dexter and Guittet 2014; Eubank and Weinberg 2000; Gerwarth 2011; Kling 1963; LaPorte and Worley 2008; Okwong 2012; Onslow 2011; Pensado 2013; Theobald 1999; Waldman 2007). They compete for the ways of a culture of political violence explanation, but they do not claim to be full explanations (Daigneault and Béland 2015). Each of them starts with the premises that a culture of political violence is non-gradable and the acceptance of the use of violence points out its emergence. Moreover, they all draw on an unwritten assumption that unless an explaining indicator or a set of explaining indicators occurs, a culture of non-violence exists. They significantly differ, however, in their views on the indicators or the sets of indicators contributing to a culture of political violence.

Negussay Ayele avoids formulating a universal theoretical framework of a culture of political violence (Ayele 2011, 216–217). Instead, he limits his approach to the Ethiopian political context by claiming that the basic defining dimensions of the persistent culture of political violence in Ethiopia (1769–2009) are intrastate, regional, and colonial indicators. Intrastate elements of political violence involve vicious struggles for the pinnacle of political power by aspirants of collective political subjects such as ethnic groups or inhabitants of geographical entities. A rivalry between regions and colonization of the land determine the second and the third indicators respectively. All the indicators are operationalizable, and thus their existence is verifiable. The relations between the explaining indicators and a culture of political violence are operationalizable and thereby verifiable as well. They constitute an internally consistent model. According to Ayele, if the configuration of the three indicators occurs, a culture of political violence emerges. Thus, the framework determines a cause and effect relationship between the *explanandum* and the *explanans*. It consists of the general sentences expressible in the form of the zero conditional sentences, and its apodosis comprises the sentences declaring the occurrence of the explaining phenomena. The in-depth outlined relation between the explaining indicators and a culture of political violence arms the framework with applicability to empirical research.

On the grounds of the detailed analysis of rising to power, mode of rule, transfer of rule in Ethiopia in 1769–2009, Ayele stakes out the interplay of forces and indicators in the creation and consolidation of Ethiopia's culture of political violence. The explanatory framework contains the individual sentences which declare that the events designated by the protasis of the general sentences happened. They are, however, the model's limitation. According to Ayele, the sources of colonial violence which emerged on the subsequent analytical levels are the following: (1) rise to power: Tigre rebel became Emperor Yohannes IV with British support; Menyelek II of Shewa became Emperor Italians in Asmera; Benito Mussolini invaded and occupied Addis Abeba; the British escorted Emperor to Addis Ababa; Cold War drew USA/USSR to Ethiopia; the Eritrean People's Liberation Front (EPLF) and the Tigrayan People's Liberation Movement (TPLF) occupied Addis Ababa and Asmera, supported by Sudan and the United States; (2) mode of rule: Somalia invaded Ethiopia; Meles Z. carried on ethnic-based reign of terror in Ethiopia TPLF invaded Somalia; and (3) transfer of rule: Sudanese dervishes behead Emperor Yohannes IV in Metemma; Ethiopian patriots defeated and ousted Italians with some British support; USSR and USA carried on proxy Cold War in Somalia/Ethiopia; Eritrea seceded EPLF vs. TPLF border war. Intrastate and regional political violence are treated altogether and thereby their joint sources are as follows: (1) rise to power: Mussolini invaded and occupied Addis Abeba; Military group (Derg) under Major Mengistu H.M. took over; and EPLF and TPLF occupied Addis Ababa and Asmera, supported by Sudan, the United States; (2) mode of rule: Ras Teferi and supporters launched *coup d'etat*; semi-feudal, more centralized rule; brutal Italian fascist violence and protracted resistance by Ethiopians; H.S.I. restored centralized rule; centralized military rule, continuous internal wars; Somalia invaded Ethiopia; and Meles Z. carried on ethnic-based reign of terror in Ethiopia TPLF invaded Somalia; and (3) transfer of rule: Gonder rebel Kassa subdued warlords; British invasion of Ethiopia; suicide of Emperor Tewodros; violent overthrow of ruler by Kassa M; Sudanese dervishes behead Emperor Yohannes IV in Metemma; Lij Iyassu ousted, jailed; Ethiopian patriots defeated and ousted Italians with some British support; people's revolution cum military mutiny toppled Emperor HIS; and Eritrea seceded EPLF vs. TPLF border war (Ayele 2011, 221–222).

Division of political violence into types is moderately useful for the study and empirical research in general. Admittedly, it allows us to identify the expressions of diverse types of violence, but it fails to distinguish the interstate violence from the regional one. It is methodologically ineffective to differentiate them in the explanatory framework. Also, some expressions meet all the criteria of all of the types. It means that some pieces of data may be overrepresented in the research. This facet of the model is worth reformulating to improve a moderately high extent of the correctness of the framework. Although Ayele's model applies to empirical research, a researcher should take into account the reservations about its structure before employing it to any methodological assumptions of empirical research so as to evade the already discussed difficulties.

Robert Gerwarth indicates that a culture of political violence is a result of the noisy and turbulent politics of the street, the town square, and the factory, in which socioeconomic grievances, hostility to the state authority, and the new and recycled dreams of a purified community are expressed (Gerwarth 2011, 518). The author determines a cause-and-effect relationship between the *explanandum* and the *explanans*. The apodosis of the zero conditional sentences comprises the sentence declaring the occurrence of the explaining event. According to this model, a culture of political violence emerges if the three explaining indicators occur. Gerwarth plausibly presents the individual sentences which prove that the events introduced by the protasis of the general sentences took place. The relation between the apodosis and the protasis is verifiable, which makes the relation between the components of the set of explaining indicators and a culture of political violence possible to verify. In short, the explanatory framework is correct because it fully meets the evaluation criteria. No essential feature limits its high extent of applicability to empirical research. Gerwarth indeed introduces the detailed description of the causal relations between the set of explaining indicators and the issue to be explained. It generates a high accuracy and precision of the explanation.

Also, three, but qualitatively different, indicators account for a culture of political violence, according to the next model. Norman LaPorte and Matthew Worley state that German party militants' seminal experiences of war, revolution, and civil war explain the emergence and the continued maintenance of a culture of political violence (2008, 246). This explanatory framework is encumbered with the reference to German history, which makes it highly contextual in terms of temporal and territorial dimensions. It considerably confines an extent of the model's applicability to empirical research to the one state. After removing the reference from the semantic scope of the *explanandum*, the experiences of war, revolution, and civil war remain as the explaining indicators. The model is formally correct because it satisfies the correctness criteria handsomely. These features contribute to the applicability of LaPorte and Worley's model to empirical studies. The description of the causal relations between the explaining indicators and a culture of political violence is rather general. The hallmarks of the major category are unspecified. Thus, it may not lead a researcher to the highly accurate, insightful, and in-depth explanation. It does not mean, however, that the model is rigid. Rather, the critical futures of LaPorte and Worley's approach are vulnerable, and thus a researcher may easily shape the model so as to perform research goals effectively.

Robin Theobald strives to account for what contributes to the occurrence and perpetuation of an undefined culture of political violence. He emphasizes that the highly mobilized and urbanized civil societies in the developed Latin American states with strong democratic traditions, e.g., Argentina and Chile, were for many years threatened by the ruthless and determined military governments. According to Theobald's framework, these states did not confine their militaries to the narrowly constitutional role this agency supposedly performs in the developed states (Theobald 1999, 153). Thereby, Theobald introduces the two explaining indicators and includes them in the two separate causal relations between an explaining indicator and an issue to be explained.

Let us delve analytically deeper into Theobald's model. First, if the highly mobilized and urbanized civil society, in the developed Latin American states with strong democratic traditions, identified with the state does not confine its militaries to the narrowly constitutional role, a culture of political violence occurs (Theobald 1999, 153). Second, if the ruthless and determined military governments threaten at length the civil society, a culture of political violence emerges. This framework is of contextual nature because of the references to the Latin American states in the *explanandum*, which narrows the scope of its applicability to this area. Additionally, it is employable to verify the occurrence of a culture of political violence in a particular type of society: civil, highly mobilized, and urbanized. Although the framework meets the correctness criteria, the causal relations between the explaining indicators and the issue to be explained are biased. Theobald just names a culture of political violence, but he introduces its two explaining indicators in detail. The specificity of the depiction of the indicators does not redound to the presentation effectiveness of the relations. They are just two, and their nature is simplified by not delving conceptually into their essence, which largely confines Theobald's model explanatory properties. They may not lead a researcher to a high accuracy and precision of the explanation.

In contrast to Theobald, the next model is not context-laden. Thomas Waldman claims that the tribal and religious loyalties create a culture of political violence (2007, 70). So, if the tribal and religious loyalties exist, a culture of political violence occurs. This internally consistent model consists of two explaining indicators and determines two relations between the *explanandum* and the *explanans*. The framework is correct, and thus applicable to empirical research. Nevertheless, Waldman fails to provide an in-depth description of the causal relations between the explaining indicators and a culture of violence. The accuracy and precision of the explanation provided by the model are, therefore, to some extent limited. A researcher may develop them effectively by setting down the essential features of the explaining indicators and clarifying what exactly tribal and religious loyalties create a culture of political violence.

Merle Kling provides an internally consistent explanatory framework of a culture of political violence. He assumes that the psychological capability for violence is used: directly to conduct acts of homicide and fights between individuals, indirectly by exhibitions of verbal aggression, or vicariously through attendance at bullfights. Moreover, according to Kling, early socialization creates the tensions that look for resolution in violence, accepted social styles for males support combative behavior, participation in political violence may provide reassurance for those who glory in masculinity that is suspect, and prevailing values condone acts of violence, including political violence. Therefore, as Kling notices, an active minority involved in acts of political violence is not restrained by a political system that brands such acts as illegitimate or by the internalized values that censure the resort to violence to perform any tasks. Individuals may encourage their intellectual resources of aggression to participate in student riots, demonstrations, political terrorism, and revolution when the standards of society and conscience are influenced by outbreaks of political violence (Kling 1963, 129–130).

Kling refers to Gabriel A. Almond and Sidney Verba's theory of political culture (1972) to show that the individuals' induction into politics happens through the experience with violent revolution. Hence, as Kling sums up, the congruence between early socialization and the later modes of political action exists when the non-political agencies of socialization produce a culture of political violence (Kling 1963, 129–130). In spite of being elaborated, the framework comprises one explaining indicator. Kling determines a cause-and-effect relationship between the *explanandum* and the *explanans* by formulating the zero conditional sentences: if particular non-political agencies of socialization take place, a culture of political violence exists. The particular agencies are the family, the Church [*sic*], and less formally organized institutions (Kling 1963, 129) which engrain violent role models into people. The model is of utmost applicability to empirical research because it fulfills all the correctness requirements. The detailed presentation of the relation between the *explanandum* and the *explanans* contributes to the framework's usefulness.

Atte Enyenihi Okwong proposes a relatively narrow explanatory framework of a culture of political violence determined by one explaining indicator. He premises that youths' engagement in electoral violence contributes to a substantial level of the existing culture of political violence in Nigeria, the country which is currently undermining people's confidence in the electoral system, ascent democracy, and the rule of law (Okwong 2012, 129). This model determines a cause and effect relationship between the *explanandum* and the *explanans* by assuming that if the young engage in electoral violence, a culture of political violence occurs. Okwong's model meets most of the correctness criteria, and thus it applies to empirical research. Although the model is of a contextual nature because of the reference to Nigeria in the *explanandum*, it may be deprived of this feature by removing the reference. The model's applicability is not high due to the lack of a detailed description of causal relations between the explaining indicator and a culture of political violence. Taking into consideration the features of just one relation may not guarantee a researcher a high accuracy and precision of the explanation.

William Eubank and Leonard Weinberg reckon that the repeated expressions of political violence may lead to a culture of political violence and to the breakdown of the democratic rule itself (2000, 294). According to this model, if the repeated expressions of political violence take place, a culture of political violence occurs. The zero conditional sentences set a cause and effect relationship between the *explanandum* and the *explanans*. Although the model is correct and thus applicable to empirical research, its extent of applicability is not very high due to the merely sketchily introduced causal relation. Providing that Eubank and Weinberg had offered a more detailed description of causal relations between the explaining indicator and a culture of political violence, the explanatory framework would have been of higher accuracy and precision. This aspect of the model still requires rethinking. First and foremost, a researcher should define a culture of political violence to foreclose the possibility that the explaining phenomenon squares with the phenomenon to be explained and settle if the category is gradable or there are some antinomic cultures of political peace or non-violence. Second, one ought to elaborate the mechanism of "leading towards," in particular in the scope of conditions under which it works, to determine the essential features of the relationships between the *explanans* and the *explanandum*.

Helen Dexter and Emmanuel-Pierre Guittet assume that the fictions of political violence may explain the occurrence of a culture of political violence. The fictions are the novels, short stories, plays, movies, or parts thereof, where political processes and political views are reasonably close to the surface (2014, 380). The authors structure this internally consistent model by indicating that if the particular fictions of political violence make an appearance, an undefined culture of political violence emerges. The model is correct and highly applicable to empirical research, but its usefulness is relatively low because of the simple relation between the explaining indicator and a culture of political violence. Although Dexter and Guittet define and elaborate the category of the fictions of political violence, they just intimate the relationships between the indicators. Thus, the approach covers the limited part of a political reality which may contribute to a culture of political violence. The accuracy and precision of the explanatory framework are not as high as they might have been if the authors had framed a more detailed set of relationships.

Sue Onslow asserts that some structural indicators explain the enduring culture of political violence within the Zimbabwe African National Union – Patriotic Front, in the alliance between the army and the party that emerged in the 1970s. As Onslow indicates, the Zimbabwe African National Liberation Army cadres were brutalized in the liberation war to implement solidarity and discipline. Furthermore, during the liberation war, the use and range of violence to browbeat Shona-speaking ethnic groups inside Rhodesia were deliberately systematic and extreme, to the extent that it produced a political language. The post-independence state-directed violence in the continuing Zimbabwean civil war in Matabeleland against the Ndebele and Kalanga people did not spark any reaction from the international community, because Zimbabwe was needed as an international success story in the larger struggle against apartheid South Africa (Onslow 2011, 8). A high extent of generalness of the internally consistent explanatory framework shows that an extent of the model's applicability to empirical research is equally high. It relates directly to the macro-level analysis (Opp 2009, xv). Nevertheless, Onslow reduces the intrinsically broad category of structural indicators to the description of Zimbabwe's politics in the particular period in its history. Territorial and time aspects make the framework contextual.

As Onslow claims, if some structural indicators occur, a culture of political violence emerges. Although the model creates a cause-and-effect relationship between the *explanandum* and the *explanans*, it is rather obscure. The presentation of the model contains the individual sentences which declare that the events designated by the protases of the general sentences happened in Zimbabwean context. In its current form, the model is hardly applicable to empirical research. First, a researcher should deprive it of the contextual aspects to boost its utility in research. Second, one ought to conceptualize which structural indicators contribute to a culture of political violence and how they do this because the phrase "some structural indicators" insufficiently determines the scope of the model. Third, before the application of the category of structural indicators to an explanatory framework, a researcher should build the operational definitions of a culture of political violence and its explaining indicators into the model. These changes would significantly improve the level of the verifiability of the framework. Fortunately, the model is neither value-laden nor expressed in the form of the second, the third, and the mixed conditional sentences. The framework is correct, and its explanatory potential is relatively high, but it requires changes to become a powerful analytical tool, especially, it has to have the relationship between the explaining category and a culture of political violence established.

The explanatory frameworks drawing on the vague beings, phenomena, and processes which cannot be captured by any social science category are to a low extent applicable to empirical studies. The analysis of the last *explanantia* provides us with a range of arguments to come out in favor of this statement. Jaime M. Pensado reckons that the internationalist spirit of the 1960s gave rise to a new culture of political violence (2013, 14). Although the framework determines a cause-and-effect relationship between the *explanandum* and the *explanans*, it does not contain the individual sentences which would declare that the events designated by the protasis of the general sentences happened. It fails to offer the detailed description of causal relations between the explaining indicator and a culture of political violence which would provide a high accuracy and precision of the explanation. Hence, the explanatory potential of the framework is scant. The explaining concept has no precise semantic field. Furthermore, the time reference to the 1960s limits its extent of applicability to a historical context. It is also far from clear what new culture of political violence is and how it differs from the old one. Thus, the relation between the *explanandum* and the *explanans* is unverifiable. Admittedly, the approach is internally consistent, not value-laden, and not normative but in the light of the previously discussed flaws, these features do not contribute to its usefulness. Overall, this framework is of low applicability to empirical research because of its methodological incorrectness.

Let us sum up the arguments concerning the model correctness and research utility. In constructing the explanatory frameworks of a culture of political violence, the authors look for different sources of its occurrence. They consider the following indicators or sets of indicators as the sources of a culture of political violence: intrastate elements of political violence involving vicious struggles for the pinnacle of political power by aspirants of collective political subjects such as ethnic groups or inhabitants of geographical entities, rivalry between regions, and colonization of the land (Ayele 2011), noisy and turbulent politics of the street, the town square, and the factory, in which socioeconomic grievances, hostility to the state authority, and the new and recycled dreams of a purified community are expressed (Gerwarth 2011), German party militants' seminal experiences of war, revolution, and civil war (LaPorte and Worley 2008), highly mobilized and urbanized civil society, in the developed Latin American states with strong democratic traditions, identified with the state, does not confine its militaries to the narrowly constitutional role and the ruthless and determined military governments threatens at length the civil society (Theobald 1999), tribal and religious loyalties (Waldman 2007), non-political agencies of socialization (Kling 1963), youths' engagement in electoral violence (Okwong 2012), repeated expressions of political violence (Eubank and Weinberg 2000), fictions of political violence defined as the novels, short stories, plays, movies, or parts thereof, where political processes and political views are reasonably close to the surface (Dexter and Guittet 2014), internationalist spirit of the 1960s (Pensado 2013), and some structural indicators (Onslow 2011).

The authors assume that if the explaining indicator or indicators make an appearance, a culture of political violence occurs. It spawns the assumption that some societies are cursed with the acceptance of the widespread use of political violence. However, we are far from claiming that either a culture of political violence or non-violence enters societies. Instead, we presume the category is gradable and useful to examine a social reality providing that a researcher makes use of a criterion of the extent of the acceptance of the use of political violence which varies. We are certain it is not the only underlying criterion to determine the differences and similarities between the patterns of a culture of political violence.

We argue that time can remove the curse. Removing the curse is the process which has its dynamics stipulated by a range of indicators. Here, we would pose the questions of how much time has to intervene to say the curse was removed? And what periods do the stages of a culture of political violence determine? We assume that these periods are different for the specific indicators. But another puzzle is what are the dissimilarities and what contributes to them? Finally, do the explaining indicators truly matter in every single or most of cases? Does a national context matter (Dufour *et al.* 2016; Zamponi and Bosi 2016)? Do the explanatory frameworks work when different examples than the already tested ones are the research fields to be explored with them? Or, on the contrary, shall we look for an entirely new explanatory framework of a culture of political violence?

Cultures of Political Violence as an Explaining Indicator of Other Things

In this part of the analysis, the explanatory frameworks treating a culture of political violence as an explaining indicator take center stage. Four problems investigate the subject field of the results of the phenomenon. The first one regards possible consequences of a culture of political violence and frames the question of what does a culture of political violence explain? Political beings, phenomena, processes, their configuration, or lack thereof are the *explananda* which are explicated through their *explanans*, a culture of political violence. Arguably, the review sets down the results of a culture of political violence stated in the literature, and it organizes models in subject order to determine the spectrum of a culture of political violence usage to explain events or properties. Then, it recognizes the types of the explanatory frameworks proposed by the authors.

The second research question throws light on the structures of the *explananda*, and it handles to what extent are explanatory frameworks phrased correctly? An explanatory framework is correct if it meets the following set of criteria: (1) it conceptualizes a cause-and-effect relationship between the *explanandum* and the *explanans*, i.e., it consists of the general sentences which may be conveyed in the shape of the zero or the first conditional sentences and its apodosis (the consequence) consists of the sentence declaring the occurrence of an explained event or phenomenon or describing a property being explained; (2) it contains the individual sentences which declare that the events designated by a protasis or protases (the condition) of general sentences took place; (3) it is operationalizable and thus verifiable; (4) it is not value-laden; (5) it is not normative; (6) it does not offer the statements put forward in the form of the second, the third, and the mixed conditional (a mixture of the second and the third conditionals) sentences; and (7) it is internally consistent. The higher the extent of the criteria fulfillment by an explanatory framework is, the higher the extent of its correctness is.

The third problem deals with the applicability of explanatory frameworks to studies, and it asks about what is an extent of their applicability to empirical analyses? Overall, on the grounds of the correctness of the particular approaches, the review evaluates whether and under what conditions they apply to achieve research results in an intersubjective and diligent way. Additionally, it assesses properties of research fields and analytical levels explorable with models. The more specific and detailed the description of the causal relations between an explaining indicator or set thereof and an issue to be explained is, giving access to a high accuracy and precision of explanation, the bigger the extent of the applicability of the framework is. Also, the broader the range of the application of a model is, the more informative the model is. The review scrutinizes explanatory frameworks employable to studies in terms of their analytical reach.

The literature offers the 19 broadly based models treating a culture of political violence as an explaining indicator of beings, phenomena, processes, their configuration, and lack thereof (Ayele 2011; Coleman 1998; Kling 1963; Forti and Maina 2012; Gohel 2014; Le Vine 2000; Moniruzzaman 2009; Njoku 2010; Obi 2011; Omotola 2010; Siniawer 2008, 2012; Taylor 1981; Theobald 1999; Waldman 2007). Most of them just mention a culture of political violence without specifying its essential features, but they give it an explaining function. The category often serves as an umbrella term to name the unidentified explaining things. We are not against the explanatory frameworks which introduce a semantically unspecified explaining category as long as we see the chance to define and operationalize both it and the relations between it and a thing or things to be explained. The review discusses the ways of thinking about relations between the *explananda* and the *explanans* and the scope of the possible *explananda.* It scrutinizes definitions and their operationalization potential because they are of practical relevance for evaluating the exploratory and explanatory power of a theoretical framework.

Negussay Ayele presents Ethiopian culture of political violence as the explaining indicator of its political culture (2011, 219) in Gabriel A. Almond, Sidney Verba and Lucian W. Pye's meaning (Almond and Verba 1972; Pye and Verba 1972). On the one side, the model is marked by considerable usefulness for research because of the determined, specified, and well-justified relations between the explaining category and the category to be explained. On the other side, Ayele introduces a simplified and contextual framework to assess Ethiopian political culture. It consists of three levels of political orientations by people about government. They are traditional or parochial levels of minimal awareness of political phenomena and virtually no role in governmental activities, some basically suppressed awareness of political matters and rights, and remaining subject to authoritarian centers of power, and the highest form of citizenship and participation in governmental activities, as in modern democratic governments (Ayele 2011, 219).

Ayele applies this framework to set out the results of a culture of political violence. He reveals that for the most part, Ethiopia has had the monarchic authority systems reinforced by feudal, aristocratic coteries, which usually have exercised tyrannical or absolute rule over the masses to this day. Furthermore, for centuries the Ethiopians have been subordinated subjects, rather than citizens, and they have had little or no say, role or share in governing or political participation. As such, the political subjectivity of the ruled was greatly reduced and relatively close to the political objectiveness. Their attitudes towards politics have been parochial to a high extent and to some extent subdued obeisance. Sometimes the ambitious person who covets high office gathers supporters and unleashes armed rebellion. If such an armed rebel succeeds, the person defeats the incumbent and seizes the state. A new ruler's rule fails to differ markedly from the reign of a predecessor. Kings and emperors asserted that "God" chose them to rule. The analysis also shows that nearly all the rulers in Ethiopia assumed power by removing incumbents with political violence. Arms and political violence are the integral parts of political superiority achievement and maintenance of power. In other words, according to Ayele's approach, Ethiopian political culture emanates from the long-time history of its culture of political violence. As the researcher emphasizes, this particular culture of political violence has unfolded over the centuries of simultaneous and constant internal, regional, and colonial armed conflicts, battles, and wars (Ayele 2011, 219).

Ayele's internally consistent model precisely conceptualizes a cause-and-effect relationship between the *explanandum* and the *explanans*. As Ayele assumes, if a culture of political violence exists, a specific pattern of political culture appears. This pattern locates between the ideal types of the parochial and the subject political culture, close to the former. The framework satisfies the criteria of correctness, which makes it applicable to empirical research. Nevertheless, the semantic field of the category of political culture reduces the applicability because it is modified to fit merely the Ethiopian context. Ayele presents convincing arguments that his explanatory framework has a use for accounting for the pattern of political culture occurring in Ethiopia. We are unsure if it is equally useful to explain other patterns of political culture. Questionable as well is whether the essential features derived from Almond, Verba, and Pye's model may serve to modify Ayele's framework to endow it with a wider scope of applicability and a universal character.

Ayele proposes one more approach towards a culture of political violence as an explaining category. Just like the first framework, the second one has a considerable explanatory power because of the way and results of setting the relations between the *explanandum* and the *explanans*. In the second, Ayele argues that the analysis of the history of the use of political violence to accomplish political goals in Ethiopia intimates that the "violence of culture" is an outcome of a long-standing culture of political violence (Ayele 2011, 226). As the researcher maintains, in Ethiopia, political violence has become the preoccupation of a "culture of masculinity." Moreover, according to Ayele's research results, for the majority of the population, the culture of masculinity is fixed as a "default" norm of male behavior. It is the long-lasting expression of the long history of Ethiopia's culture of political violence maintained in the ruthless "violence of political culture" (Ayele 2011, 226). The internal consistency of the model is eroded by naming the *explanandum* "violence of culture" either "violence of political culture" or "culture of masculinity" without any justification. Ayele uses them interchangeably to characterize the same phenomenon. Thus, despite different meanings, the names cover the same semantic field in the framework (Edwards 2006). The categories are not well established in the specialist literature, which makes their semantic establishment challenging. Before applying the model to research, a researcher should adopt one name to avoid confusing a reader or to reserve they have equivalent meanings. Although the model meets most of the correctness criteria, it is anchored in the Ethiopian context. A researcher may, however, remove the references to the context to improve the model's level of applicability.

Just like Ayele, Merle Kling provides a highly developed elaboration of a culture of political violence as an explaining indicator. Kling's framework meets the correctness criteria and is of high applicability to empirical research, but it focuses on essentially different research field than Ayele. According to Kling, in Latin American societies, a culture of political violence produces conditions in which the provocation and organization of violence are not the sole domain of professional soldiers. Although Kling refers to the territory, the model is not contextual in general. The author reckons that political subjects other than professional soldiers compete for power by using violence to achieve their public goals. Kling emphasizes that students become involved in riots, store and fire weapons from in the legal sanctuary of universities, and express a high extent of militancy and belligerency in advocating public policies. Moreover, their engagement in public affairs and experience in combatting the organized police and military forces make them professional revolutionists (Kling 1963, 126).

Kling defines the professional revolutionists as those who sustain interest in the pursuit of governmental authority by using violence. Thus, as the researcher indicates, a culture of political violence accommodates the expert, counter-expert, and amateur in violence. The differences between the three individuals become fluid when some of the amateurs secure training in guerrilla tactics and terrorism. Kling points out that when the expectations of peaceful governmental transition are low, the individuals and groups not integrated into regular military formations strive to gain expertise in the techniques of violence. The revolutionist serves to differentiate a culture of political violence and to highlight the role of experts in violence or in such a culture (Kling 1963, 126). The differences between political subjects who chose to use violence in a public sphere to achieve goals are slightly obscure but, fortunately, they do not contribute to the very nature of the model. Kling bases the framework on the zero conditional sentences: if a culture of political violence exists, the society uses physical violence to accomplish political goals regardless of their social roles. In doing so, he makes a welcome contribution to the understanding of the essence of a culture of political violence production.

So, Kling puts a strong emphasis on perpetrators of political violence rather than the results of their activities. Stephen Coleman, on the other hand, forsakes incorporating political subjects to his explanatory framework and focuses predominantly on the outcomes of the unidentified people's activities. In drawing on the case of Northern Ireland, Coleman states that if a culture of political violence appears, people are killed, maimed, disfigured, beaten, tortured, incarcerated, and exiled because of political goals (1998, 6). One may assume that, according to Coleman, aiming at the achievement of political goals with the use of political violence against people is a consequence of a culture of political violence. The author does not specify the essential features of the explaining indicator, but he outlines the relationship between its nature and the vicious political actions taken against people because of the objectives of political nature and relevance. Although the model meets the correctness criteria and applies to empirical research, it does not allow us to obtain a nuanced explanation and reliable conclusions due to its apparent and excessive theoretical simplicity.

Notably, Kling offers one more explanatory model which is formally correct and applicable to empirical research. He assumes that a culture of political violence creates the context in which an array of likely results accompanying a revolution is vast. As Kling highlights, the higher the extent of the compatibility between the acceptance of violence and the prevailing norms of a political system is, the more extensive the range of the policy results that may attend the use of violence is. According to Kling, if a culture of political violence emerges, a revolution may carry out the function of an election because violence does not need justification in this context. The similarity of a revolution to an election consists in leading to a personnel rotation and serving as a prelude to the introduction of the relatively limited changes in public policies. However, as Kling notices, in contrast to an election, a revolution may indeed shift personnel, erase certain social classes, substantially modify the capabilities of diverse interest to exert influence and power and transform the system for absorbing and resolving public conflicts. Kling adds that revolutionary means are compatible with diverse ends (1963, 130–131). In a culture of political violence, a revolution per se may or may not be a portent of radical alteration.

The two next models introduce the relation between a culture of political violence and violence during and after elections. Admittedly, Shola Omotola avoids defining a culture of political violence, but the researcher assumes that it is one of the indicators which explain electoral violence (2010, 70). According to Omotola, favorable for electoral violence are the contexts where issues of military co-exist with authoritarian remnants of previous regimes and a prevailing culture of political violence feature prominently, the nature of the African state and its politics, weak economic foundations of the democratization process, including pervasive poverty, and the weak institutionalization of democratic architectures, particularly political parties, electoral management bodies and the judiciary (Omotola 2010, 70–71). Here, a culture of political violence is just a part of the unfinished explanatory model. It contributes to electoral violence, but it has to occur along with the range of other indicators in a comprehensive explanatory framework.

In turn, according to Daniel Forti and Grace Maina, a culture of political violence explains the 2007–2008 post-election violence, a substantial proportion of the population that participated in protests, and the reality that may be attributed to the snowball effect of grassroots mobilization (2012, 74). Although both Omotola's and Forti and Maina's model meets the correctness criteria, the latter is contextual due to the time reference. Admittedly, they apply to empirical research but in the limited scope because a culture of political violence is undefined and its link with the various phenomena to be explained is obscure. It is a result of the use of the underdeveloped conceptual frameworks proposed to produce the theoretical models.

Robin Theobald argues that an undetermined culture of political violence creates the conditions under which Latin American militaries and paramilitaries are routinely deployed against dissidents. As Theobald strongly emphasizes, although Mexico has not abided military government since the reign of the Partido Revolucionario Institucional, its political system has always been based on the army to cope with the opposition as an after effect of a culture of political violence. In the line of the approach, a culture of political violence also explains that after several years, in formally democratic Argentina, critics of the regime of Carlos Menem are harassed and killed (Theobald 1999, 153). Theobald assumes that a culture of political violence is of a long-standing nature.

While mindful of the context, Theobald introduces three results of a culture of political violence and tests the model empirically. First, if a culture of political violence appears, it creates the conditions under which Latin American militaries and paramilitaries are routinely deployed against dissidents. Second, if a culture of political violence originates, a political regime uses the army to cope with the opposition. Third, if a culture of political violence comes into sight, the critics of the regime of Carlos Menem are harassed and killed in formally democratic Argentina. The model satisfies the correctness criteria, but it is slightly limited by the lack of semantic boundaries of the explaining category. Correctness of the model implies that it is of high applicability to empirical research. Nonetheless, its contextual nature determined by the references to the territory and time reduces the extent of its analytical utility. A researcher should remove the contextual components and underpin the conceptual framework to increase an explanatory potential of Theobald's model.

The literature also offers no-frills models organized into one-sentence assumptions. Their authors premise that a culture of political violence triggers off some beings, phenomena, processes, and lack thereof. The frameworks share an extent of correctness, and they are of a similar applicability to empirical studies.

Cyril Obi claims that a semantically undetermined culture of political violence causes problems to Nigeria's electoral democracy (2011, 373). This model is largely contextual in the scope of the reference to the state rather than universal. Although the category of problems is vague, the model implies that as long as a culture of political violence exists, Nigeria's electoral democracy does not work according to its fundamental rules. A researcher may deprive the approach of the contextual feature by removing the reference to Nigeria. Then, a culture of political violence would explain the transposition of democracy into or towards a non-democratic regime.

Thomas Waldman's view on the meaning of a culture of political violence for the state is close to Obi's. As the author asserts, in Iraq, a culture of political violence minimizes the chances of the establishment of peaceful democratic rules (Waldman 2007, 70). As Obi does, Waldman avoids defining the explaining category. This framework is also of the contextual nature as it makes reference to Iraq. Nevertheless, according to Waldman, if a culture of political violence occurs, peaceful democratic rules are less probable in Iraq. Whereas in Obi's account, a culture of political violence undermines a democratic system (2011, 373), in Waldman's perspective it precludes its establishment (2007, 70).

More similar to Obi's model is Victor T. Le Vine's model. The researcher maintains that a culture of political violence contributes to the collapse of democracy. As Le Vine premises, a culture of political violence resulted in the death of Lebanese democracy (2000, 276). His approach is contextual because of the direct reference to the state. Nevertheless, Le Vine offers also a more general framework by pointing out that a culture of political violence explains a democratic breakdown (2000, 277–278). None of them sets a semantic field of a culture of political violence.

Le Vine's second model is supported by Eiko Maruko Siniawer who claims that a culture of political violence explains the breakdown of democracy in Japan in 1930 (Siniawer 2008, 73, 179). Siniawer defines the explaining indicator as the context in which the use of political violence is acceptable. This approach is also sharply contextual as it refers to the time and state.

In his different work, Siniawer does not define a culture of political violence as the context. Instead, he assumes that a culture of political violence produces the context in which ruffianism, understood as vandalism, hooliganism or, simply, brutal, violent, and lawless behavior, is tacitly accepted as a routinely used tool of political life (Siniawer 2012, 629). This model satisfies the correctness criteria and is employable in empirical research, even if one should determine semantic fields of the categories involved to make it complete. Siniawer's previous definition of a culture of political violence has no use for this framework because it would generate tautology: the context accounts for the context.

Alphonsus O. Njoku claims that a political situation in Nigeria is a result of a pervasive culture of political violence in the body politic of the country. Njoku notices that Nigeria has presently sustained an uninterrupted democratic government for the last 10 years. In spite of this seemingly enduring democratic system, the country is harassed with troubled polity (Njoku 2010, 16). Since a political situation is always dynamic, its particular representation captured in the space and the time cannot be used as a theoretical category. It is just an exemplification. As Njoku implies, a culture of political violence undermines democratic consolidation. The framework is, however, strictly located in and produced by the context defined by the references to the state and time.

The other no-frills frameworks seek to use a culture of political violence to account for a political change. M. Moniruzzaman indicates that a culture of political violence creates the enormous public distrust in the capacity of major parties to come out of the destructive political legacy and initiate a new political alternative (Moniruzzaman 2009, 96). A culture of political violence contributes to the particular political attitudes towards political change.

Then, Stan Taylor assumes that a culture of political violence, defined as a tradition of violence, performs a pivotal role in promoting riots (1981, 170). The explaining indicator is, therefore, even if high-ranking, one of many undefined phenomena contributing to the promotion of riots. Far from clear is what the non-pivotal and concurrent factors are and how to identify them. Another puzzle is the criterion of the distinction of the promotion of riots and bringing the pivotal role under this political activity.

Siniawer, in his highly contextual explanatory framework, reckons that a culture of political violence explains the institutionalization of *sōshi*, the young activists of the Freedom and People's Right Movement, into party politics (Siniawer 2008, 73, 179). He sees the explaining category as the context in which the use of political violence is acceptable and firmly attaches to it a crucial role in the process of the institutional transposition of the political movement into party politics.

Finally, Sajjan M. Gohel does not define a culture of political violence, but he indicates that it undermines the secular and nationalist foundations of moderate Bangladesh (2014, 88–89). This model is also contextual because of the reference to the state. Gohel focuses mainly on a destructive influence of a culture of political violence but avoids specifying how it undermines the foundations of Bangladesh. Despite satisfying the correctness criteria, the no-frill models require elaboration before using them in empirical research because of their contextual character as well as the partial and biased conceptual frameworks.

In the existing models, a culture of political violence explains the remarkably diversified beings, phenomena, processes, their configuration, and lack thereof – the pattern of political culture: between the parochial and the subject, close to the former (Ayele 2011); the violence of culture identified with the culture of masculinity and the political violence of culture (Ayele 2011); the conditions in which the provocation and organization of violence are not the sole domain of professional soldiers (Kling 1963); bringing about revolution to being able to carry out the function of an election (Kling 1963); electoral violence (Omotola 2010); the 2007–2008 post-election violence; a substantial proportion of the population participating in protests; and the reality that may be attributed to the snowball effect of grassroots mobilization (Forti and Maina 2012); problems with Nigeria's electoral democracy (Obi 2011); minimization of the chances of the peaceful democratic rules establishment in Iraq (Waldman 2007); death of Lebanese democracy (Le Vine 2000); democratic breakdown (Le Vine 2000); breakdown of democracy in Japan in 1930 (Siniawer 2008); creation of the conditions under which Latin American militaries and paramilitaries are routinely deployed against dissidents; basing a political regime on the army to cope with the opposition, and harassing and killing critics of the regime of Carlos Menem in formally democratic Argentina (Theobald 1999); the political situation which undermines democracy (Njoku 2010); promoting riots (Taylor 1981); the production of the context in which ruffianism is tacitly accepted as a routinely used tool of political life (Siniawer 2012); the political situation in which people are killed, maimed, disfigured, beaten, tortured, incarcerated, and exiled because of political goals (Coleman 1998); enormous public distrust in the capacity of the major parties to come out of the destructive political legacy and usher in a new political alternative (Moniruzzaman 2009); undermining the secular and nationalist foundations of moderate Bangladesh (Gohel 2014); the institutionalization of *sōshi* into party politics (Siniawer 2008). The researchers verified or just discussed the frameworks but most of the relations between the indicators are of contextual quiddity, which makes us pose the challenging questions, if they work when applied to some other empirical research and to what extent they keep their explanatory values while exploring different research fields.

Classification Frameworks of Cultures of Political Violence

This part of the analysis involves classification schemes of a culture of political violence. Whereas the first part of the analysis presents the one-type approaches, this fourth section deals with two-class and more extended frameworks. The review scrutinizes them to solve four problems. The first one enables us to determine classification approaches towards a culture of political violence and it closely inquires into what types of classification schemes of a culture of political violence are in the literature. The review pays attention to an object of their semantic fields and a number of criteria applied to set classes. It recognizes a type of a classification framework by evaluating what and how many criteria organize a model and what classes it encompasses.

The second problem connects directly with the first one, and it delves into the structure of classification schemes by asking about under what rules do researchers outline classification schemes. Frameworks differ in the content and configuration of classes. Researchers establish them under the rules of (1) antinomy, or (2) gradation, (3) property, state or occurrence they are subjected to, and (4) relations between a culture of political violence and an object. The classification schemes based on the rule of antinomy are worked out according to the contradictory features, and they take on the form of dichotomy divisions. A scheme may consist of any number of dichotomies. The others draw upon a modification of gradable features and translate the sets of features into the multi-classes divisions. Each classification framework discloses the values of a culture of political violence which are the classes of a category, stages, or ranges.

The third problem leads directly up to the evaluation of the correctness of classification approaches, and it poses the question of to what extent are classification schemes correct? A classification scheme is correct if it meets the following set of criteria: (1) a division of a culture of political violence into classes is according to one homogenous criterion or one homogenous and invariable configuration of criteria; (2) it is exhaustive, i.e., each exemplification of the category belongs to one of the classes; (3) it is disjunctive, i.e., none of the exemplifications of the category belongs to more than one class; (4) it is complete, i.e., the sum of all classes is a semantic equivalent for the entirety of the divided category; and (5) it fulfills the saturation condition, i.e., each class includes some component (Tarchi 2017). The higher the extent of the criteria fulfillment by a classification scheme is, the higher the extent of its correctness is.

Finally, the last problem strives for the adjudication of the classification approaches' applicability to studies and it inquires into the extent of applicability of classification schemes to empirical analyses. Therefore, on the grounds of the correctness of classification frameworks, the review weighs up whether and under what conditions they have a use for achieving research results systematically, intersubjectively, and diligently. It assesses the applicability in terms of the properties of the research field and analytical levels they may examine to stake out a current range of a culture of political violence exploratory potential.

The literature presents merely three attempts to conceptualize any kinds of the category (Gerwarth 2011; Miller 1998; Waldman 2007). The classification fields of their frameworks differ in subject matter and are the same in avoiding making reference to a subject aspect of a culture of political violence. Each model applicable to classify cultures of political violence draws on a different division criterion and explores a variant classification field.

Thomas Waldman distinguishes an entrenched and a pure culture of political violence (2007, 70). The critical criterion of their distinction is an extent of the rooting in the shape of the perpetuation of a culture of political violence in a population's social awareness. It seems to be the division based on two antinomic classes, but the rule of antinomy is not stated directly. The classification framework is simple, consistent, and constructed on the basis of one and homogenous criterion. On the one hand, it establishes the one-dimension classification field which is simply divided into two classes. On the other, it does not allow a researcher to see the semantic differences between the classes because they are undefined. One may merely assume what hallmarks of the classes are.

The underlying limitation of the classification framework is its undetermined content and boundaries of the classification field of a culture of political violence. Additionally, Waldman avoids presenting features which would allow a researcher to identify and diversify the examples of a culture of political violence. As a result, it is unverifiable whether the framework is exhaustive, disjunctive, and fulfills the saturation condition. In its current form, the extent of correctness and applicability of the model (Waldman 2007, 70) to empirical studies is very low because it does not define what an entrenched culture of political violence is and how to distinguish it among other political beings, phenomena, processes, their configurations, or lack thereof in a political reality. Nevertheless, it considerably contributes to our understanding of the phenomenon by presenting the criteria of continuance and perpetuation as the potentially useful indicators of its variety.

The second classification framework is also marked by the absence of essential features the category superordinate to its distinct classes (Gerwarth 2011, 518). Not unlike Waldman, Robert Gerwarth distinguishes the two classes: a localized and an informal culture of political violence. Gerwarth avoids, however, pointing out a homogenous criterion or a configuration of criteria used to determine the classes. In determining the localized pattern, the researcher might have employed a territorial criterion, but it is not stated explicitly. In turn, in the informal pattern, Gerwarth might have used an extent of formality, but it is not introduced as well. Nevertheless, the criteria that we suggest are not applicable to describe all the elements of the classification framework. Formality does not characterize the localized class and the localization fails to depict the informal class. Just as in Waldman's model, the boundaries of the classification field are undetermined. The reconstruction of the essential features of the classes is hardly possible. It is also far from clear how to determine antinomic classes, e.g., a formal and an unfocused culture of political violence on the grounds of the absence of their features and criteria for distinction. The model is not exhaustive, disjunctive, and complete, and it does not fulfill the saturation condition. The arguments uncover a low extent of correctness and applicability of Gerwarth's classification framework to empirical research.

Then, Daniel Miller singles out a material culture of political violence but avoids indicating the relation between the category and a pure pattern. The material class is constituted by the material images, forms of banners, and space of parading which produced violence and political conflict when other channels were generating compromise and peace (Miller 1998, 382). The author anthropomorphizes the material pattern by bringing the power to produce violence and political conflict intrinsically under the culture, so, the category embraces not only violent behavior but also discrepancies of political interests, without any human indicator. The model omits an intangible culture of political violence. The examples which do not meet the essential features of the material class are beyond the classification framework. It shows that the framework is incomplete and does not allow us to capture in-depth the differences between phenomena.

Miller's approach lacks the category of a political subject mainly as a result of the anthropomorphism of the subject matter (1998, 382). Thereby, a human role is played by a thing. Arguably, an inanimate subject is not able to commit violence or cause political conflict. Such a being may become the component of the concept of a material culture of political violence only when we premise that a political subject's awareness adopts the meaning of material incentives and this person starts to act because of it (Sjørslev 2012). Hence, only if there is an element of individual awareness, an incentive may be the indicator contributing to a culture of political violence (Szewczak 2005). Miller calls a culture of political violence a material stimulus which may encourage somebody to behave aggressively. The category may be, however, of a higher exploratory potential when we assume that it determines if and to what extent a political subject uses a material resource to deploy violence.

Admittedly, Miller does not offer a superordinate category to a material culture of political violence, but the material culture class's *definiens* implies its essential features (1998, 382) which are material and immaterial beings and phenomena marked by the potential and predisposition to trigger off political violence. One and homogenous criterion of the division of this classification field is a type of beings and phenomena. It divides its scope consistently into the material and immaterial patterns but defines just the former.

Miller's approach indeed goes far beyond the scope of the classification field of a culture of political violence with respect to the political reality that can be explored with this model. It introduces a possibility to determine the antinomic classes of – *explicite* – a material and – *implicite* – an immaterial culture of political violence (Miller 1998, 382), namely, material and immaterial cultures of compromise and peace. As the analysis of the *definiens* discloses, they are marked by essential features antinomic to their antinomic classes.

Formal correctness of Miller's classification framework shows that it applies to empirical research to a low extent. It is not exhaustive or disjunctive and does not fulfill the saturation criterion but a researcher may improve it according to the already introduced remarks. One should rethink the relation between behavioral and awareness spheres and extend the model to obtain a tool to identify and compare the examples of cultures of political violence. It would demand to implement additional criteria for sub-classes of material and immaterial cultures of political violence. Reformulating the *definientia* and creating a conceptual framework would be of great relevance to the model's applicability as well.

The analysis points out that the classification frameworks of a culture of political violence are widely diversified. Each model is entirely original because they divide the classification fields by using the different criteria which are an extent of rooting a culture of political violence in the social awareness of populations (Waldman 2007), the territory where a culture of political violence emerges and concentrates on as well as an extent of a culture of political violence formality (Gerwarth 2011), and the type of beings and phenomena constituting a culture of political violence (Miller 1998). Identification of their empirical validity makes an important contribution to the field because it reveals what features of cultures of political violence are worth evaluating in comparative studies.

The literature offers the three classification schemes that consist of: an entrenched and a pure (Waldman 2007), a localized and an informal (Gerwarth 2011), and a material and a pure culture of political violence (Miller 1998). No model makes use of either antinomy or graduation rule to determine the classes of the category. Hence, the classes cannot be put in any order. Moreover, neither the property, state, and occurrence classes are subjected to, nor the relations between a culture of political violence and an object are common to all the classes within any of the frameworks. The review reveals that they are of low formal correctness and applicability to empirical research.

Recommendations on the Construction of a Theoretical Framework of Cultures of Political Violence

Undoubtedly, a culture of political violence is an understudied topic in the scholarly literature. The analysis of its definitions, classification schemes, and explanatory frameworks considering a culture of political violence to be an explaining indicator or an indicator to be explained reveals a range of challenges for those researchers who might want to use them effectively in their studies.

A theoretical category of a culture of political violence has to consist of its essential features. The set of features has to satisfy the correctness criteria and contribute to an operationalizable definition. A researcher should carefully establish the *explananda* and the *explanantia* of explanatory frameworks so they introduce the causal relations and do not overlap semantically to avoid tautology, understood as the needless repetition of the same sense in different words and redundancy. Most of the explanatory frameworks under review fail to present any semantic field of a culture of political violence, thus making the models flexible.

This flexibility is not always an asset since the explanatory frameworks are not the parts of any broader theoretical approaches. The causal relations between phenomena are often discretionary. Questionable is what really and exactly triggers off cultures of political violence, what their results are, and how to determine them. Regardless of methods, techniques, and tools employed to deal with the relations, a researcher is often able to observe merely the fact of correlation but not its direction. The proven ways of coping with this problem may be undependable as long as a culture of political violence is understudied. An extent of the correctness and applicability of the models is worth improving through methodological, theoretical, and empirical contributions. Hence, some thought should be given to a culture of political violence as an explaining indicator and a thing to be explained to develop an explanatory potential of the category.

The classification schemes are the underbelly of the literature on a culture of political violence. No approach towards the classification of its patterns meets all the correctness criteria. They do not define a culture of political violence, which generates the question of how to identify its expressions when one does not know how to understand this poorly established category. The authors fail to set the criteria of the classes' distinction, and thereby it is also impossible to compare any would-be manifestations of the category. Therefore, the classification framework which would allow a researcher to identify and compare cultures of political violence is still a challenging task to be undertaken.

The critical discussion on the methodological and theoretical correctness of the frameworks is not able to take the place of solid empirical research. In spite of the determined limitations, the models should not be decisively rejected because there is no perfect theoretical approach in social science. Similarly, the frameworks assessed as correct and applicable to empirical analysis ought not to be taken for granted due to the complexity of the social reality that is often difficult to predict on the stage of research preparation.

The research to follow neither adopts some theoretical approaches nor dismisses others without an empirical test. Therefore, Chapter 2 draws upon the existing insights into the necessary and sufficient essential features to identify and compare cultures of political violence. It makes use of the discussion on the semantic fields and the classification frameworks of the category. Chapters 3 and 4 take advantage of the literature review in the different ways. The former evokes all the explanatory frameworks reviewed in terms of the explaining indicators of a culture of political violence and tests those theoretical approaches one by one. They are examined to observe their empirical effectiveness to explain what contributes to cultures of political violence. Chapter 4, on the other hand, concentrates on the explanatory frameworks discussed with respect to a culture of political violence as an explaining indicator of other things. All those frameworks undergo tests to see how forceful they are to account for the results of cultures of political violence.

Bibliography

Ackermann, Robert. 1964. "Normative Explanation." *Philosophy and Phenomenological Research* 24(4): 522–529.

Almond, Gabriel A. and Sidney Verba. 1972. *The Civic Culture: Political Attitudes and Democracy in Five Nations*. Princeton, NJ: Princeton University Press.

An-na'im, Abdullahi Ahmed. 2006. "Why Should Muslims Abandon Jihad? Human Rights and the Future of International Law." *Third World Quarterly* 27(5): 785–797.

Armborst, Andreas. 2010. "Modelling Terrorism and Political Violence." *International Relations* 24(4): 414–432.

Ayele, Negussay. 2011. "Legitimacy, Culture of Political Violence and Violence of Culture in Ethiopia." In *Terrorism, Identity and Legitimacy: The Four Waves Theory and Political Violence*, edited by Jean E. Rosenfeld, 212–231. Abingdon and New York: Routledge.

Ayyash, Mark Muhannad. 2013. "The Paradox of Political Violence." *European Journal of Social Theory* 16(3): 342–356.

Bell, Sam R., David Cingranelli, Amanda Murdie, and Alper Caglayan. 2013. "Coercion, Capacity, and Coordination: Predictors of Political Violence." *Conflict Management and Peace Science* 30(3): 240–262.

Coleman, Stephen. 1998. "BBC Radio Ulster's Talkback Phone-In: Public Feedback in a Divided Public Space." *Javnost – The Public* 5(2): 7–19.

Daigneault, Pierre-Marc and Daniel Béland. 2015. "Taking Explanation Seriously in Political Science." *Political Studies Review* 13(3): 384–392.

Dexter, Helen and Emmanuel-Pierre Guittet. 2014. "Teaching (Something About) Terrorism: Ethical and Methodological Problems, Pedagogical Suggestions." *International Studies Perspectives* 15: 374–393.

Dufour, Pascale, Héloïse Nez, and Marcos Ancelovi. 2016. "Place-Based Movements and Macro Transformations." In *Street Politics in the Age of Austerity: From the Indignados to Occupy*, edited by Marcos Ancelovici, Pascale Dufour, and Héloïse Nez, 295–304. Amsterdam: Amsterdam University Press.

Edwards, Tim. 2006. *Cultures of Masculinity*. London and New York: Routledge.

Eubank, William and Leonard Weinberg. 2000. "The Italian Regions and the Prospects for Democracy." *Terrorism and Political Violence* 12(3/4): 293–307.

Fawcett, Jacqueline. 2013. "Thoughts about Conceptual Models, Theories, and Literature Reviews." *Nursing Science Quarterly* 26(3): 285–288.

Floyd, Jonathan. 2016. "Normative Behaviourism and Global Political Principles." *Journal of International Political Theory* 12(2): 152–168.

Forti, Daniel and Grace Maina. 2012. "The Danger of Marginalisation: An Analysis of Kenyan Youth and their Integration into Political, Socio-Economic Life." In *Opportunity or Threat: The Engagement of Youth in African Societies*, edited by Grace Maina, 55–86. Umhlanga Rocks and Durban: African Centre for the Constructive Resolution of Disputes.

Gerwarth, Robert. 2011. "Control and Chaos: Paramilitary Violence and the Dissolution of the Habsburg Empire." In *Control of Violence Historical and International Perspectives on Violence in Modern Societies*, edited by Wilhelm Heitmeyer, Heinz-Gerhard Haupt, Stefan Malthaner, and Andrea Kirschner, 517–534. London: Springer.

Gohel, Sajjan M. 2014. "Bangladesh: An Emerging Centre for Terrorism in Asia." *Perspectives on Terrorism* 8(3): 84–91.

Hanneman, Robert A. 1985. "The Military's Role in Political Regimes." *Armed Forces & Society* 12(1): 29–51.

ISP. 2016. "Top International Publisher List." Accessed June 9, 2016. www.scijournal.org/top-international-journal-publisher.shtml.

Kalmoe, Nathan P. 2014. "Fueling the Fire: Violent Metaphors, Trait Aggression, and Support for Political Violence." *Political Communication* 31(4): 545–563.

Karstedt, Susanne. 2012. "Contextualizing Mass Atrocity Crimes: The Dynamics of 'Extremely Violent Societies.'" *European Journal of Criminology* 9(5): 499–513.

Kling, Merle. 1963. "Violence and Politics in Latin America." *The Sociological Review* 11(S1): 119–132.

Knight, Andy W. and Tanya Narozhna. 2005. "Social Contagion and the Female Face of Terror: New Trends in the Culture of Political Violence." *Canadian Foreign Policy Journal* 12(1): 141–166.

Krause, Jürgen. 2001. "Www – Search Engines, an Alternative to the Social Science Databases?" *Bulletin de Méthodologie Sociologique* 72(1): 37–46.

LaPorte, Norman and Matthew Worley. 2008. "Towards a Comparative History of Communism: The British and German Communist Parties." *Contemporary British History* 22(2): 227–255.

Le Vine, Victor T. 2000. "Violence and the Paradox of Democratic Renewal: A Preliminary Assessment." *Terrorism and Political Violence* 12(3/4): 261–292.

McGinn, Tony, Brian Taylor, Mary McColgan, and Janice McQuilkan. 2016. "Social Work Literature Searching: Current Issues with Databases and Online Search Engines." *Research on Social Work Practice* 26(3): 266–277.

Meter, Karl M. van, Marten W. de Vries, Charles D. Kaplan, and Chantal I. M. Dijkman. 1987. "States, Syndromes, and Polythetic Classes: The Operationalization of Cross-Classification Analysis in Behavioral Science Research." *Bulletin de Méthodologie Sociologique* 15(1): 22–38.

Miller, Daniel. 1998. "Groans from a Bookshelf: New Books in Material Culture and Consumption." *Journal of Material Culture* 3(3): 379–388.

Moniruzzaman, M. 2009. "Party Politics and Political Violence in Bangladesh: Issues, Manifestation and Consequences." *South Asian Survey* 16(1): 81–99.

Ncube, Cornelias and Ufo Okeke-Uzodike. 2015. "Constituting Power and Democracy: Zimbabwe's 2013 Constitution Making and Prospects for Democracy." *African Renaissance* 12(3/4): 129–157.

Njoku, Alphonsus O. 2010. "Political Violence and Its Implications to Democratic Consolidation in Niger." *Knowledge Review* 21(4): 16–22.

Nowak, Stefan. 2006. *Metodologia badań społecznych*. Warszawa: Wydawnictwo Naukowe PWN SA.

Obi, Cyril. 2011. "Taking Back Our Democracy? The Trials and Travails of Nigerian Elections since 1999." *Democratization* 18(2): 366–387.

Okwong, Atte Enyenihi. 2012. "IT-Based Solutions to the Electoral System in Nigeria." *West African Journal of Industrial and Academic Research* 5(1): 127–139.

Omotola, Shola. 2010. "Explaining Electoral Violence in Africa's 'New' Democracies." *African Journal on Conflict Resolution* 10(3): 51–73.

Onslow, Sue. 2011. *Zimbabwe and Political Transition*. London: The London School of Economics and Political Science.

Opp, Karl-Dieter. 2009. *Theories of Political Protest and Social Movements: A Multidisciplinary Introduction, Critique, and Synthesis*. London and New York: Routledge.

Pensado, Jaime M. 2013. *Rebel Mexico: Student Unrest and Authoritarian Political Culture during the Long Sixties*. Stanford, CA: Stanford University Press.

Podsakoff, Philip M., Scott B. MacKenzie, and Nathan P. Podsakoff. 2016. "Recommendations for Creating Better Concept Definitions in the Organizational, Behavioral, and Social Sciences." *Organizational Research Methods* 19(2): 159–203.

Pye, Lucian W., and Sidney Verba (eds.). 1972. *Political Culture and Political Development*. Princeton, NJ: Princeton University Press.

Rak, Joanna. 2016. "Kultura przemocy politycznej w regionie Azji Centralnej jako wyzwanie badawcze." In *Unia Europejska wobec Azji Centralnej. Uwarunkowania regionalne i międzynarodowe*, edited by Radosław Fiedler and Tadeusz Wallas, 309–331. Poznań: Fundacja na rzecz Czystej Energii.

Risjord, Mark. 2005. "Reasons, Causes, and Action Explanation." *Philosophy of the Social Sciences* 35(3): 294–306.

Rocco, Tonette S. and Maria S. Plakhotnik. 2009. "Literature Reviews, Conceptual Frameworks, and Theoretical Frameworks: Terms, Functions, and Distinctions." *Human Resource Development Review* 8(1): 120–130.

Rodriguez-Priego, Emilio, Francisco J. García-Izquierdo, and Ángel Luis Rubio. 2013. "References-Enriched Concept Map: A Tool for Collecting and Comparing Disparate Definitions Appearing in Multiple References." *Journal of Information Science* 39(6): 789–804.

SENSE. 2009. "Ranking of Academic Publishers." Accessed June 9, 2016. www.sense.nl/gfx_content/documents/ABCDE-indeling%20Scientific%20Publishers%20SENSE_approved_May_2009.pdf.

Siniawer, Eiko Maruko. 2008. *Ruffians, Yakuza, Nationalists: The Violent Politics of Modern Japan, 1860–1960*. Ithaca and London: Cornell University Press.

Siniawer, Eiko Maruko. 2012. "Befitting Bedfellows: Yakuza and the State in Modern Japan." *Journal of Social History* 45(3): 623–641.

Sjørslev, Inger. 2012. "The Material Subject as Political: Style and Pointing in Public Performance." *Anthropological Theory* 12(2): 209–228.

Steenkamp, Christina. 2009. *Violence and Post-war Reconstruction: Managing Insecurity in the Aftermath of Peace Accords*. London: Palgrave Macmillan.

Steenkamp, Christina. 2014. *Violent Societies: Networks of Violence in Civil War and Peace*. New York: Palgrave Macmillan.

Szewczak, Wiktor. 2005. "Funkcjonalne ujęcie kultury politycznej i jego konsekwencje teoretyczno-metodologiczne." In *Teoretyczne i metodologiczne problemy badań nad kulturą polityczną*, edited by Zbigniew Blok, 69–84. Poznań: WNINPiD.

Tarchi, Marco. 2016. "Populism: Ideology, Political Style, Mentality?" *Politologický časopis – Czech Journal of Political Science* 23(2): 95–109.

Taylor, Stan. 1981. "Riots: Some Explanations." *Journal of Ethnic and Migration Studies* 9(2): 167–172.

Theobald, Robin. 1999. "Conclusion: Prospects for Reform in a Globalised Economy." *Commonwealth & Comparative Politics* 37(3): 149–159.

Torraco, Richard J. 2016. "Writing Integrative Literature Reviews: Using the Past and Present to Explore the Future." *Human Resource Development Review* 15(4): 404–428.

Waldman, Thomas. 2007. "British 'Post-Conflict' Operations in Iraq: Into the Heart of Strategic Darkness." *Civil Wars* 9(1): 61–86.

Wood, Matthew. 2016. "Politicisation, Depoliticisation and Anti-Politics: Towards a Multilevel Research Agenda." *Political Studies Review* 14(4): 521–533.

Zamponi, Lorenzo and Lorenzo Bosi. 2016. "Which Crisis? European Crisis and National Contexts in Public Discourse." *Politics & Policy* 44(3): 400–426.

2 Post-2008 Cultures of Political Violence in the Eurozone

DOI: 10.4324/9781351205757-3

Methodology for Examining Cultures of Political Violence

Dealing with cultures of political violence demands to face a challenge of measuring the immeasurable because those phenomena are unavailable for direct observation (Bruter 2013, 34; Lane 2016, 1141; Moustaki 2000, 211). As the literature review has shown, there is no available analytical tool to identify, describe, and compare cultures of political violence. But it has also revealed the array of concepts employable to characterize the things in the real world which are of relevance to devise such a model. Hence, the aims of this chapter are: to propose a precise and operationalizable definition of a culture of political violence, to construct a conceptual framework of that category, to test its empirical efficiency by analyzing the cases of post-2008 incidents in which anti-austerity movements' stakeholders took part, and to determine cultures of political violence which emerged in the crisis-ridden Eurozone of the times of austerity. Whereas the goals of this chapter are of an exploratory nature, the next chapters move on into an explanation.

This chapter solves the first research problem of what patterns of a culture of political violence did stakeholders of post-2008 anti-austerity movements have? By doing so, it strives to verify the first hypothesis organizing an analysis: stakeholders of post-2008 anti-austerity movements might have had patterns of a culture of political violence diversified with respect to the values of its essential features: (i) political subjects that made use of political violence; (ii) their mutual legitimation to the use; (iii) modes of the legitimation of the use; (iv) the intensity of physical political violence; and (v) forms of political violence. The five essential features covered by the hypothesis are the criteria for characterizing and distinguishing the patterns of cultures of political violence that constitute a typology. It sheds new light on the diversity of the cultures that are symptomatic of the European context.

Let us move on towards the process of collecting and elaborating data. The study employs a qualitative method of written sources analysis to gather the data sufficient and necessary to identify the values of the essential features for 14 European states. A particular configuration of the values is a value of a culture of political violence. The research technique of data collection is a relational qualitative content analysis of secondary data: reports, records, and databases of the states' police and 305 articles and visual materials published in public, commercial, and social media in 2007–2015, and secondary literature on the stakeholders of anti-austerity movements. The role of sources triangulation is to empower the basis of arguments and to minimize a selection bias. The research tools are: categorization key to content analysis, instruction to review the media of secondary data, typology of political subjects that deployed violence, continuum of mutual legitimation to use political violence, model of the modes of the legitimation of the use, continuum of the intensity of physical political violence, and continuum of forms of political violence.

The main criterion for sources selection is their utility to verify the hypothesis effectively. Therefore, the whole process of gathering the pieces of data is first and foremost purpose-driven. According to the principle of theoretical sampling, the theoretical developments that occurred in an analysis of the previously gathered data lead the following stages of data collection. This cycle of alternation between data collection and analysis does not stop at two repetitions but it stands up to the achievement of theoretical saturation. In other words, until the new pieces of data are not introducing the exemplifications of new theoretical elements but instead are confirming what has already been discovered (Punch 2014, 134). The attempts concentrate on gathering the data sets necessary and sufficient to solve the research problem (Spangler 2016, 42).

The research offers a new definition of a culture of political violence to project what it covers by its conceptual framework. A meaning of the category is not semantically determined by the modes of understanding of particular words constituting its *definiendum* (what is to be defined). Therefore, the semantic establishment of the *definientia* (the words or phrases that define) of culture, violence, political violence, and the predicate of political is not necessary to set down what the very nature of a culture of political violence is. The meaning of the category is not the sum of the meanings of the words which occur in its name. It is, however, crucial to define political violence as long as it remains a part of the *definiens* (the word or phrase that defines) of a culture of political violence. In other words, if political violence contributes to our conception of a culture of political violence, it has to have an operationalizable definition to serve as an indicator of the culture.

A culture of political violence is a paradigm of using political violence in a political structure, which is determined by the temporal, subject, and subject matter indicators. This paradigm indicates who takes advantage of the use of political violence, what their mutual legitimation to the use is, how they justify and account for the use, what forms of political violence they employ, and what the intensity of political violence is. This definition is the basis for an original conceptual framework applicable to describe and analyze cultures of political violence.

Let us specify the meanings of the components of the definition. A political structure is constituted by its internal political subjects and relationships between them. The subjects may be either individual or collective, and their violent behavior is under scrutiny when describing a culture of political violence. The political subjects extrinsic to a particular political structure are irrelevant when a culture of political violence is evaluated as long as they are not in relationships with domestic actors. Whereas political subjects are the subject indicator of the category, the use of political violence is the subject matter. Political violence is intentional influencing by a political subject(s) the thinking process, behavior, or physical state of other political subject(s), despite the lack of authority of the political subject under the influence, to achieve political goals. These goals are the creation, destruction, protection, deprivation of protection, distribution, and abandonment of distribution of public goods. Political violence may be an overt action or a non-action on the level of motivation.

The analysis offers a conceptual framework to identify and compare cultures of political of violence in the member states of the Eurozone. It embraces the major things to be examined and the presumed relationships between them (Miles *et al.* 2013, 37; Spanakos 2016, 2). For the sake of clarity, the conceptual framework should not be mistaken for an explanation because it avoids settling causal relations. It does not perform explanatory goals, but it precedes the creation of an explanatory framework. It serves to determine the reference categories for the empirical study. The conceptual and explanatory frameworks are the parts of the theoretical model which is to offer lenses to study the nature, sources, and results of the phenomena (Anfara and Mertz 2015). The conceptual framework is the product of a qualitative process of theorization made to help a researcher construct an interpretative approach towards social reality. It is the network of the interlinked concepts that together generate a comprehensive understanding of a phenomenon (Jabareen 2009, 50; Punch 2014, 116). In this research, the conceptual framework consists of the interlinked theoretical categories in the form of concepts taking on particular values (Rosenberg 2016, 85; Weber 2012).

Conceptualizing Cultures of Political Violence

The definition-driven conceptual framework applies to evaluate the qualitative features of cultures of political violence. It is necessary to determine the temporal dimension of the phenomena under evaluation because a researcher may employ the category to generate both static and dynamic views on the cases. This analysis adopts a static perspective and focuses on the cultures of 2007–2015, the time of the first great wave of anti-austerity events. It may, however, contribute to some broader research by establishing the dynamics of the cultures over time or become a field for a detailed study on the phenomenon dynamics within the period.

If we understand the category of a culture of political violence as a paradigm of using political violence in a political structure, which is set by the temporal, subject, and subject matter indicators, five concepts constitute the very nature of the paradigm. They allow us to operationalize the essential features of the category. It means that we have to answer the five questions to see what culture of political violence emerged in each case: who uses political violence? If and to what extent do political subjects in their political roles accept and find justified the way in which others perform their political roles in the scope of using political violence? How do political subjects justify and explain the use of political violence? What is the intensity of physical political violence? And what forms of political violence are in use? Five concepts drive the data collection questions to create a structured model for describing and comparing empirical cases (Punch 2014, 62). Those concepts do double duty as research tools to answer the questions systematically and intersubjectively. The analysis applies the same set of questions and concept-based scales to examine each culture of political violence.

The first concept allowing us to assess a culture of political violence derives from an array of answers to the question of who uses political violence. The literature review has shown that individual and collective political subjects deploy it. This study, however, demands to adopt a more specific approach to characterize the nature of the relationships between the stakeholders of anti-austerity movements. The perpetrators are, therefore, the political subjects that range from representatives of a state apparatus to anti-austerity movement participants. The representatives of a state apparatus are politicians, police officers, firefighters, employees of a public sector, government officials, and the public media journalists who act as loyal supporters of politicians or are perceived by movement participants as doing so. Although firefighters usually do not perform political roles, they are involved because movement participants considered them to be linked with the state apparatuses and on this account attacked them over clashes in times of tensions (BBC 2015a; Onyanga-Omara 2015; Spiegel 2015b; Wessel and Ewing 2015; Yan 2015). In turn, movement participants are those engaged in its structure and supporting it over protests and other activities (Tarrow 2011, 6; VanDusky-Allen 2017).

The next question deals with the mutual legitimation of representatives of a state apparatus and movement participants to use political violence. It asks if and to what extent political subjects in their political roles accept and find justified the way in which others occupy their political roles in the scope of using political violence. The literature review has revealed that cultures of political violence differ in how perpetrators perceive themselves and others in a political structure in terms of the violent means they provide for the use. Additionally, a political role itself predestines legitimation to the use or lack thereof because it forms a political subject's scope of rights and duties concerning the usage. When she misuses violence or her right to control its commitment, she loses her previous political role. If a political subject legitimated to use political violence exceeds her authority, she inevitably becomes a political subject non-legitimated to the use. Mutual legitimation is gradable with respect to the extent of cohesion between political subjects' actual usage of political violence and agreement on the use.

Accordingly, the scale necessary to measure the cohesion and interpret the data referring to mutual legitimation is the continuum established by two extreme values, the maximum and the absence (Figure 2.1). Real values locate between the extreme points in various distances to them and vary in the extent of cohesion. The largest value (A), the highest extent occurs when there is no

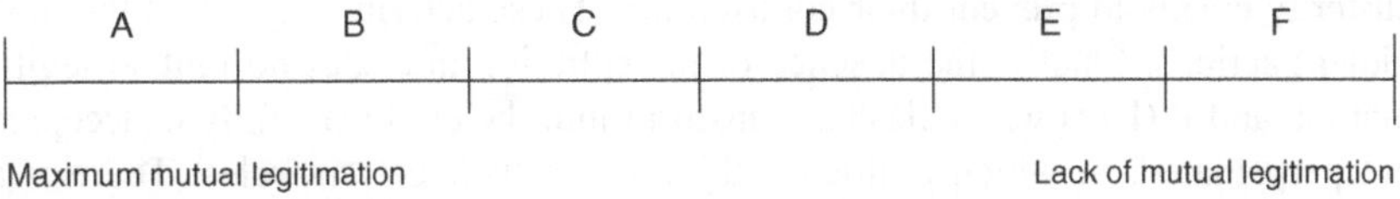

Extents of mutual legitimation:

A – maximum
B – very high
C – high
D – low
E – very low
F – absence

Figure 2.1 Continuum of mutual legitimation to use political violence.

Source: Author's own study.

strength confrontation between the political subjects. Movement participants avoid organizing protests and engaging in their activities representatives of a state apparatus. The action and non-action of political subjects achieve complete mutual legitimation. A very high extent (B) is when movement participants stage events in a public sphere and employ mental political violence to express their opinion in a widely accepted manner. They neither deploy nor provoke the use of physical political violence. In turn, representatives of a state apparatus take part in the proceedings, but the protest policing makes use of the threat in the way approved by a movement. The actions of a movement are recognized as a potentially and presumptively dangerous threat against public order, safety, and security and not fully approved. Therefore, this mode does not take on the greatest value of the cohesion. A high extent (C) is when the incidents of the use of physical political violence take place, and they are not legitimated. Political subjects approve others in a political structure and the mode and purpose of applying political violence. A disagreement appears over the incidents that are not very frequent. Moderate is, therefore, a discrepancy between political subjects' actual usage of political violence and agreement on the use. A low extent (D) is marked with the use of excessive physical political violence unaccepted by those who attended clashes. Political subjects recognize others as non-legitimated to act in the way and for the purpose they do. High is a discrepancy between political subjects' actual usage of political violence and agreement on the use. A very low extent (E) makes an appearance when active physical political violence is misused by movement participants and representatives of a state apparatus, and both oppose to the misuse. A discrepancy between political subjects' actual usage of political violence and agreement on the use achieves a very high level. Political subjects do not accept how others exercise their rights and perform duties within political roles. Representatives of a state apparatus are often publicly and widely accused in social media of initiating violent clashes in plain-clothes. Movement participants may be detained before taking part in anti-austerity events to prevent their contribution. Those activities may fuel the next violent actions. Finally, the absence of the cohesion indicates no mutual legitimation, and it (F) is when clashes transform into the civil war, fully unaccepted but perpetuated, in which political subjects lose their current roles. There is a full discrepancy between political subjects' actual usage of political violence and agreement on the use.

The two essential features relate strictly to the political subjects empowered to use political violence. They are indeed legitimated or non-legitimated to carry out violent behavior by their roles in a political structure. Mutual legitimation is produced within political relations between the subjects (Alimi *et al.* 2015, 7; Bosi *et al.* 2014, 2). Not only does an issue of political subject legitimation matter but also the legitimation of political violence contributes to our understanding of the paradigm (Huff and Kruszewska 2016, 1774; Virta and Branders 2016, 1150).

As the literature review has underlined, the ways of how perpetrators justify turning to force influence the diversity of cultures of political violence. The modes of the legitimation of the use of political violence range from the law to the will when we address the question of what justifies and accounts for the use of political violence. Nonetheless, this dual model, which is based on one essential feature (the indicator of the mode of the use of political violence legitimation) taking on the two extreme values (the law and the will), fails to cover in full swing all the possibilities and nuances of the processes of legitimation, relegitimation, delegitimation, and redelegitimation (Vaara 2014, 501). Therefore, it is of particular relevance to determine an exact meaning and primary types of the legitimation of the use of political violence.

The analysis adopts a broad meaning of legitimation to describe and evaluate this aspect of a culture of political violence. Legitimation is the discourse that accounts for and justifies the deployment of political violence. It involves providing reasons, grounds, and motivations for past, present, and future violent behavior. It generates answers to the questions of "why should we use political violence?" and "why should we use it in this way?" (Oddo 2011, 289). Therefore, it is relevant to the content of the conceptual framework to ask about how political subjects justify and explain the use of political violence. In order to offer a simple but not excessively simplifying approach towards the modes of the legitimation of the use of political violence, a four-category model is adopted. It draws on Theo van Leeuwen's typology of legitimation (2007, 92) that consists of authorization, moralization, rationalization, and mythopoesis.

In the line of this model, authorization is the legitimation by reference to the personal or impersonal authority, custom authority of tradition or conformity, and commendation authority of an expert or role model (van Leeuwen 2007, 97). It is of constitutive, regulative, and evaluative nature (Wiener 2014, 18). When undiluted personal authority is discussed, legitimate authority is vested in a person because of her status or role in a particular institution (van Leeuwen 2007, 94). Expert authority draws on an expertise providing legitimation (van

Leeuwen 2007, 94). In the case of the role model authority, role models or opinion leaders are followed (van Leeuwen 2007, 95). Not all of the types of authority legitimation are personal. Impersonal authority is based on laws, rules, and regulations (van Leeuwen 2007, 96). Authorization by tradition still may be invoked, particularly through keywords like "tradition," "practice," "custom," and "habit" (van Leeuwen 2007, 96). Conformity legitimation takes the form of a direct comparison or is realized through high-frequency modality (van Leeuwen 2007, 97).

Moral legitimation, also called moralization, makes use of evaluation, abstraction, and positive or negative comparison (van Leeuwen 2007, 100). According to van Leeuwen, this mode of legitimation is built on moral values, rather than imposed by some genre of authority without further justification. Moral values may be simply asserted by troublesome words such as "good" and "bad" which unrestrainedly travel between moral, aesthetic, and hedonistic spheres and often occur in configuration with authority legitimation (van Leeuwen 2007, 97). Most frequently, evaluation connects with specific discourses of moral value, which often are neither made explicit nor debatable. They are merely alluded to, by using predicates such as "healthy," "normal," and "useful." Admittedly, they trigger a moral concept but are out of the system of interpretation they come from, at least on an awareness level (van Leeuwen 2007, 97). They reshape moral discourses into generalized motives (van Leeuwen 2007, 98). Moral evaluation legitimation employs evaluative adjectives to show what something is like or should be just due to some moral value or values and avoids setting out any arguments. A popular form of moral evaluation legitimation is naturalization legitimation constructed with references to time or the concept of profound change. In this case, a moral order takes the shape of a natural order (van Leeuwen 2007, 98). Then, moral legitimation based on abstraction consists in referring to practices or one or more their component actions or reactions in the abstract modes that moralize them (van Leeuwen 2007, 99). Analogies as the way of moral legitimation benefit from implicit or explicit comparisons. An activity that belongs to one social practice is presented by using the term which, literally, refers to an activity belonging to another social practice, and the positive or negative values which, in a given sociocultural context, are attached to that other activity, are then transferred to the original activity (van den Broek 2017; van Leeuwen 2007, 99).

Rationalization is the argument-driven legitimation by reference to the goals and uses of institutionalized social action and to the knowledge produced by society to arm itself with cognitive validity. Van Leeuwen distinguishes two major types of rationality. First, instrumental rationality legitimates practices by making reference to their goals, tools, and effects. Purposes serve to account for why social practices exist and why they take their current forms (van Leeuwen 2007, 99). Accordingly, it may be goal-, means-, or effect-oriented. Second, theoretical rationality legitimates practices by reference to a natural order of things but in contrast to moral evaluation, it is followed by argumentation. It takes experimental, scientific, definition, explanation, or prediction forms (van Leeuwen 2007, 105).

Finally, mythopoesis is the legitimation through story-telling. It constructs the narratives whose results reward legitimate and punish non-legitimate actions (van Leeuwen 2007, 92). They take the shape of moral or cautionary tales (van Leeuwen 2007, 107). In the former, protagonists are rewarded for taking part in legitimate social practices or restoring the legitimate order (van Leeuwen 2007, 105). The latter communicate what will happen if somebody does not conform to the norms of social practices. Their protagonists engage in deviant activities that guide to undesired endings (van Leeuwen 2007, 106). Single-determination and over-determination (inversion or symbolization) mythopoetize social actions (van Leeuwen 2007, 92, 2008, 120).

Authorization, moralization, rationalization, and mythopoesis in van Leeuwen's meaning are the modes of the legitimation of the use of political violence. All the discussed forms of legitimation serve to both legitimize and delegitimize the deployment of political violence (van Leeuwen 2007, 92; 2008, 120). They show how political subjects justify and account for resorting to political violence to perform their goals. Thereby, they contribute to the very nature of a culture of political violence.

The literature review has shown that the intensity of physical political violence leaves its mark on a society lastingly. Hence, the fourth essential feature of a culture of political violence is conceptualized by answering the question of the extent of the intensity of physical political violence. In order to circumscribe the values of the feature, one may check for how long political violence was and was not used in a given period on a given territory, or how much of this territory was and was not a scene of the use of violence over time. Notwithstanding, here, the intensity of physical political violence ranges from the maximally intense active to the abandonment of the use (Figure 2.2). The extreme theoretical categories establish a continuum. Making the threat is passive physical violence and locates halfway across the continuum. Then, the use of force localizable between the maximally intense physical political violence and the threat, excluding the latter, is active physical political violence.

The scale applicable to evaluate empirical cases systematically is the continuum presenting the values of the feature. It is divided according to the extent of the intensity of physical political violence. The largest extent appears (A′) when movement participants and representatives of a state apparatus make use of maximally intense physical force. Not only are the participants detained or arrested but they are being also wounded and killed. A high extent (B′) is when a case is between the maximally intense active physical political violence and the threat. The use is just slightly more often than the threat or the threat transforms frequently into the use. A moderate extent (C′) occurs when political subjects utilize the threat regularly but do not cross its qualitative line. It means that they avoid turning to active physical political violence. The intensity is low (D′) if the deployment of physical violence is between making the threat and the abandonment. There, passive physical political violence is deployed but not on a regular daily basis. Its complete absence indicates the abandonment of the commitment of physical political violence (E′).

As the literature review has emphasized, the configuration of forms of political violence allows us to see how cultures of political violence differ. The tool

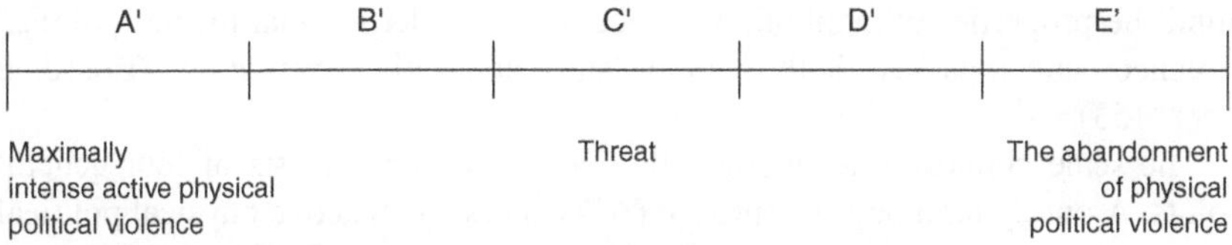

Extents of intensity of physical political violence:

A' – maximum
B' – high
C' – moderate
D' – low
E' – absence

Figure 2.2 Continuum of the intensity of physical political violence.
Source: Author's own study.

under construction is far from turning to the traditional definition of political violence which equates it solely with war or active physical violence (Bernal 2017, 32; Finlay 2017, 72). Instead, it approaches a culture of political violence from the perspective of answers to the question of what measures do political subjects adopt to commit political violence? An analytical approach towards the variety of means clinches the comprehension of political violence. All the answers fit in the continuum that ranges from a hard to soft power approach (Ad'ha Aljunied 2011, 656; Nye 2004). The discernment is not a simple reference to the demarcation between coercive power or payments on the one hand and attraction on the other (Nye 2004) but mirrors its very core (Figure 2.3). The hard power approach is based on the use of active physical political violence and bribery. In turn, the soft power approach is founded on the commitment of mental political violence and passive physical political violence. The mental

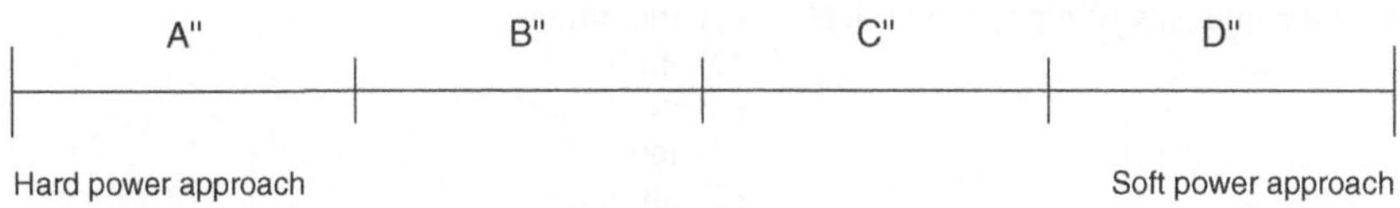

Configurations of forms of political violence:

A'' – the extreme predominance of active physical political violence
B'' – the combination of mental, and active and passive physical political violence
C'' – the combination of mental and passive physical political violence
D'' – the predominance of mental political violence and the absence of physical political violence

Figure 2.3 Continuum of forms of political violence.
Source: Author's own study.

type aims directly at gaining influence through multifarious appeal. Keeping in mind the properties of symbolic violence, let us underline that mental political violence encompasses both verbal and non-verbal activities (Bourdieu 1991, 153).

The scale applicable to interpret the pieces of data consists of four general points. A purely hard power approach (A″) occurs when active physical political violence is overwhelmingly predominant. A combination of soft and hard power approaches with the latter predominant (B″) appears when mental, and active and passive physical types of political violence are combined. A blend of soft and hard power approaches with the former dominant (C″) emerges when a blend of mental and passive physical political violence is in use. A purely soft power approach (D″) exists when just mental political violence originates.

The conceptual framework of a culture of political violence consists of the set of the five concept-based observable indicators which take on values (Table 2.1). The comparative qualitative analysis employs it to examine paradigms of violent behavior of stakeholders of the post-2008 anti-austerity movements in Austria,

Table 2.1 Essential features of cultures of political violence and their extreme values

No	*Essential features of cultures of political violence*	*Values of essential features of cultures of political violence*
i	political subjects that made use of political violence	(1) representatives of a state apparatus (2) anti-austerity movement participants
ii	mutual legitimation of political subjects to use political violence	(1) maximum (2) very high (3) high (4) low (5) very low (6) absence
iii	modes of the legitimation of the use of political violence by political subjects	(1) authorization (2) moralization (3) rationalization (4) mythopoesis
iv	the intensity of physical political violence	(1) maximum (2) high (3) moderate (4) low (5) absence
v	forms of political violence	(1) the extreme predominance of active physical political violence (2) the blend of mental, and active and passive physical political violence (3) the combination of mental and passive physical political violence (4) the predominance of mental political violence and the absence of physical political violence

Source: Author's study

Belgium, Estonia, Finland, France, Greece, Spain, the Netherlands, Ireland, Germany, Portugal, Slovakia, Slovenia, and Italy. Each type of a culture of political violence is a particular configuration of the values of the essential features under scrutiny. To put it more concretely, the research examines what values were taken on by the concept-based indicators that create the hard core of a culture of political violence – its paradigm – in each case.

The following parts of the chapter concentrate directly on those patterns. The analysis does not reproduce the broad-based activities of movements and of the police described in detail in current academic works (e.g., Andretta 2017; Craddock 2017; Davies *et al.* 2016; della Porta 2017; Fernandes 2017; Flesher Fominaya 2017; Katsambekis 2016; Konak and Dönmez 2017; Lombardo 2017; O'Connor 2017; Pickerill *et al.* 2015; Romanos 2017; Vogiatzoglou 2017). It also omits the causes and results of pursuing austerity policies because they are not its subject and have been broadly discussed in the substantive literature as well (e.g., Amenta 2016; Betz 2016; Borooah 2014; Cooper 2016; Dunn 2015; Jordà and Taylor 2016; Keller 2014; Klandermans and van Stekelenburg 2016; Mailand 2014; Major 2014; Pelagidis and Mitsopoulos 2016). It avoids describing all the activities of the stakeholders engaged in the activities initiated by the movements. As the matter of fact, it does not count exactly what objects were thrown by protest participants at police officers, what forms political mobilization took, or how many times protesters deployed physical and mental political violence. Rather, it is of the essence to investigate what values the indicators took on in European states. The next sections of the chapter analyze cultures of political violence and present their values graphically by using the continua to illustrate the similarities and differences between patterns in a comparable and vivid way.

Empirical Study of Placid, Hector-Led, and Militant Cultures of Political Violence

A qualitative comparative analysis allows us to observe the three major patterns of a culture of political violence that entered post-2008 Europe. They range from the most peaceful, through the moderately aggressive to the fiercely blazing types. The patterns are diversified intrinsically within their clusters, but they also differ widely from each other in terms of the criterion of forms of political violence. In fact, a type of a configuration of hard and soft power approaches is the critical feature that shapes the structures of the types. The form of violence entails what the intensity of political violence is and how stakeholders shape their political relationships. The conceptual representations of the components of cultures of political violence have individual semantic fields and empirical expressions, and as such, they are forceful to cluster the patterns.

Placid Cultures of Political Violence

The most peaceful type, placid cultures of political violence, entered Estonia and Slovakia. Their purely soft approach built upon mental political violence. The mildly aggressive hector-led type emerged in Austria, France, and the Netherlands. Political subjects reached out for the soft power approach by combining mental and passive physical political violence. Dominant was, however, the former. In contrast to the placid, the cases of the hector-led pattern took advantage of the implicit threat. Political subjects employed active physical violence neither in the placid nor the hector-led cases. The last type, militant cultures of political violence were the least peaceful and occurred in Belgium, Finland, Greece, Spain, Ireland, Germany, Portugal, Slovenia, and Italy. Just like the hector-led, this pattern drew on the blend of soft and hard power approaches. They differed, nevertheless, in the qualities of this configuration. The most aggressive type combined mental, and active and passive physical political violence. It means that the deployment of active violence characterized only the militant pattern.

The further parts of the chapter present an account of empirical research structured into the state sections. The theory-driven case studies introduce the character of placid, hector-led, and militant cultures of political violence systematically by discussing similarities and differences between their expressions. The first part of the analysis focuses on the most peaceful types, Estonian and Slovak.

Estonia: "Welcome to the Titanic"

Let us start from the first peaceful case and the political subjects within that contributed to the quality of its culture. In Estonia, representatives of the state apparatus and movement participants used political violence to express necessity and fear of the consequences of the financial crisis for the member states of the Eurozone respectively. The former, mainly political elites adopted the strategies of persuasion and information to influence the social reception of austerity measures by using mass media. Their action took the form of mental political violence, and they avoided deploying physical force (AFP 2013a; Ames 2012; Amundsen 2013; Bandow 2013; Guralnik 2017; Konwicki 2013; Mitchell 2012; Sahu and Jordaan 2013; Wagstyl 2012). In turn, among Estonian movement participants, in contrast to Germany, Austria, Belgium, Finland, France, the Netherlands, and Ireland, attitudes towards the member states of the Eurozone which suffered from austerities were far from supporting or manifesting solidarity with others (Alter Summit 2015; Repečkaitė 2015). Although they were not manifestly hostile, they admonished the society against the following austerity policies. Estonian opposition to austerity measures, however, did not transform into mass political protests. According to the official information from Police and Border Guard Board, no event was organized in a public sphere to manifest a revolt over anti-austerity measures (Guralnik 2017). Instead, in a public sphere, movement participants located the banners expressing their clear opinion about the crisis and the austerity as the way of coming out of it. The banners showed a sinking ship named the Titanic. Smoke rose from its four chimneys marked with the sign of euro. The smoke was labelled with four names of the states: Greece, Ireland, Portugal, and Spain. The comment on the situation was the greeting:

"Estonia! Welcome to the Titanic" (in Estonian: *Eesti! tere tulemast titanicule*) (Moulds 2012). It was the indicator of mental political violence focused on making a pitch for a particular interpretation of the topical political situation.

The modes of the legitimation of the use of political violence were: authorization, mythopoesis, and rationalization. This set was unique in its lack of moralization, and it entered merely Estonia. The activists introduced the authorization as the result of the freedom of speech and the manifestation of opinion within the legal boundaries. The mythopoesis drew upon the storytelling to account for and justify the use of political violence. It was the cautionary tale (van Leeuwen 2007, 106) about the Titanic concentrated on conveying what would have happened if Estonia had not banned austerity measures. Mythopoesis should not be confused with the one-time internet memes common for the whole Eurozone which presented ironic messages but avoided telling stories, e.g., "If smoking doesn't kill you, austerity certainly will" or " 'Never forget that everything Hitler did in Germany was legal.' Martin Luther King Jr" (Anti-Austerity Anti-Corruption Ireland 2017). Finally, just as in the other European cases, the goal-, effect-, and means-oriented rationalization dominated in social media. It focused mainly on putting forward arguments against austerity policies and their makers, mainly particular politicians and the European Union.

Worth stressing is, however, that in Estonia, as in Slovakia, representatives of the state apparatus and movement participants abandoned both using active physical political violence and making the threat (Figure 2.2: E′).

The location of the case on the continuum was a result of the absence of physical political violence. Political subjects applied only a mental form to perform their goals. The arguments indicate that the soft power approach occurred in a pure form (Figure 2.3: D″). The Estonian culture of political violence had this essential quality of placid patterns in common with the Slovak type.

In Estonia, just as in Slovakia, an extent of cohesion between political subjects' actual usage of political violence and agreement on the use took on the largest value because movement participants manifested their opposition to austerity measures within the law and in the way fully accepted by representatives of the state apparatus. Similarly, Estonian politicians engaged in public relations concerning austerity measures made their point within the commonly accepted boundaries of public discourse (Figure 2.1: A). Moreover, opponents of the movement did not go beyond their rights to express opinion freely. The commitment of mental violence fitted the rights and duties of political subjects considered by them to be fully appropriate.

The values of the essential features of the conceptual framework point out that a placidly-observing culture of political violence emerged in Estonia. This pattern is the configuration of the following properties: (1) both representatives of a state apparatus and movement participants use political violence; (2) a maximum extent of mutual legitimation to the use; (3) the modes of the legitimation of the use are authorization, rationalization, and mythopoesis; (4) an abandonment of physical political violence; and (5) a mental form of political violence constitutes a purely soft power approach.

Slovakia: "No"

As in the case above, in Slovakia, representatives of the state apparatus and movement participants took advantage of political violence. A maximum extent of cohesion between political subjects' actual usage of political violence and agreement on the use occurred there (Figure 2.1: A). Just as in Estonia, there was no strength confrontation between political subjects. Movement participants avoided engaging representatives of the state apparatus in their activities. Not unlike Estonia, in Slovakia, the action and non-action of political subjects achieved complete mutual legitimation.

Furthermore, in Slovakia, as in Estonia, political subjects abandoned using active physical force and making the threat, and they used only mental political violence (Figure 2.2: E′).

The political subjects involved in the movement's public activities employed authorization by law as the mode of the legitimation of the use of mental political violence. Movement participants organized peaceful strikes bound by local works. They carried banners and flags with the symbols of the Slovak trade unions. According to the available information, police did not secure the events (Balogová 2010; Cutler 2010). On the internet, mainly social media and discussion platforms, the activists argued against anti-austerity measures (Císař and Navrátil 2015, 51, 53; Kubišová 2011; Malová and Dolný 2016; SITA 2013; SITA, Plus JEDEN DEŇ/vip, ds, md 2013; Sulík 2013). They made use of the effect-, means-, and goal-oriented instrumental rationalization. Similarly, representatives of the state apparatus made use of these types of rationalization by applying the information and persuasion strategy (Kubišová 2011; Sulík 2013). In contrast to Germans, Austrians, Belgians, Finns, Frenches, Dutchmen, and Irishmen, Slovaks did not manifest support and solidarity with Southern Europe, which was typical for placid cultures of political violence but not only for them. Moralization and mythopoesis did not originate in the Slovak context, which was a unique property of this pattern.

The purely soft power approach in the form of mental political violence emerged in Slovakia (Figure 2.3: D″). This feature occurred in Estonia as well.

The Slovak case is the exemplification of a placidly rationalizing culture of political violence. The configuration of its properties encompasses: (1) both representatives of a state apparatus and movement participants use political violence; (2) a maximum extent of mutual legitimation to the use; (3) the modes of the legitimation of the use are authorization and rationalization; (4) an abandonment of physical political violence; and (5) a mental form of political violence is a purely soft power approach. This pattern differs from the Estonian placidly observing pattern solely in terms of how political subjects legitimated resorting to violence. Whereas Estonians employed authorization, rationalization, and mythopoesis to justify and account for the use of violence that was to admonish people against austerity, Slovaks made attempts to authorize and rationalize the use perceived as a tool to improve their social well-being. In contrast to Estonians, Slovaks did not warn about the results of austerity measures but crossed them.

Hector-Led Cultures of Political Violence

While the placid cultures of political violence were the peaceful paths towards goals, the hector-led ones manifested or implied a promise of a resort to active physical violence conditional on non-acceptance of certain expectations and demands of stakeholders of the anti-austerity movements. In Estonia and Slovakia, movement participants decided not to hold protests, which limited the scope of circumstances favorable to the use of physical violence. They avoided creating such an environment and settled for mental violence. As a result, representatives of the state apparatus were not obligated to confrontation, but they took part in the public discourse about austerity by employing mental violence. Police officers did not engage in events organized by movement participants. In contrast to the placid patterns, in the states of the hector-led pattern, the activists of anti-austerity movements staged protests. They created and perpetuated the opportunities to use active physical political violence to perform their aims. Vivid manifestations of readiness to deploy active physical force caused the engagement of representatives of the state apparatuses in the tense relationships between political subjects. The anxiety about crossing a qualitative line between passive and active physical violence fueled violent behavior of stakeholders of the anti-austerity movements and tensions between them. Dread was the emotion that marked the ways they perceived their use of political violence and themselves in political structures. This part of the chapter analyzes the hector-led Austrian, French, and Dutch cultures of political violence which were more violent than the placid but less aggressive than the militant patterns.

Austria: "Too Much EU Is Not Good for You"

In Austria, both representatives of the state apparatus and movement participants committed political violence when they were approaching austerity measures in a public sphere. The former used rationalization and authorization by law as the means to legitimate the use of political violence. They made attempts to show how Austria may have benefited from the EU-imposed policies (Bloomberg/Hahn 2012; Neugera 2012). In turn, activists employed authorization by law, rationalization, and moralization (Klandermans *et al.* 2015, 155) during objecting austerity. They functioned within the boundaries of their political roles and authorized the use of violence by their rights. They also made use of moral evaluation. The primary value underscored on banners was solidarity with Southern Europe, most notably Greece (Wearden 2012). The public discourse concentrated on expressing a tremendous support for all those Europeans who suffered from austerity measures. References to abstraction, such as the future, well-being, and mothers' love for the young affected by growing up in the times of austerity, and the future of cuts-stricken education of Austrian children, were also in use as the modes of legitimation. They occurred in banners with slogans, e.g., "With a whole heart for our children" (in German: *Mit ganzem Herzen für unsere Kinder*) (Press TV Videos 2013). Social well-being did double duty as a vehicle to moralize and rationalize violent behavior. Whereas moralization avoided providing justifications but was the justification itself, rationalization drew upon the value's nature to introduce arguments.

Movement participants employed the instrumental goal-, means-, and effect-oriented rationalization to justify the use of threat and mental political violence against austerity. They based argumentation on the social well-being-driven justification (van Leeuwen 2007, 101). The protesters manifested a vehement opposition to the austerity measures implemented not only in Austria but also in the European Union as a whole. They justified the stance they pleaded by claiming that the government programs are ruinous (in German: *ruinös*) (Wearden 2012). The role of the internet – in particular, social media – to rationalize the use of political violence was a standard feature of the European anti-austerity movements (Anti Austerity Alliance 2017a; Anti Austerity Alliance Galway 2017; Europe says OXI 2015; TVXS 2015a). The set of authorization, rationalization, and moralization typified all the hector-led and militant patterns that entered: Austria, Belgium, Finland, France, Greece, Spain, the Netherlands, Ireland, Germany, Portugal, Slovenia, and Italy.

Representatives of the state apparatus used regularly mental political violence through the mass media content. Passive physical political violence emerged as well when they attended the places where protests occurred to maintain and ensure public order, safety, and security. It took the form of protest policing, the control of protest (della Porta *et al.* 2006, 3). They were ready to employ coercive and preventive measures and thus made the threat. The protesters did not use active physical political violence but concentrated their concerted efforts on mental measures that co-occurred with the threat. The verbal expressions used by Austrians allow us to see the features of their soft power approach. They were grounded in "saying no to austerity measures" (Wearden 2012). In a public sphere, activists displayed banners with anti-austerity slogans, e.g., "Too much EU is not good for you" and "Our Europe, your choice" (in German: *Unsere Europa ihre Wahl*) (Waites 2014).

Not unlike in the Netherlands, in Austria, an extent of cohesion between political subjects' actual usage of political violence and agreement on the use was very close to the largest value (Figure 2.1: B). As the analysis has shown, movement participants staged events in a public sphere and made use of mental political violence to express their opinion in a commonly accepted way. They neither deployed nor provoked the use of physical force. Representatives of the state apparatus, on the other hand, took part in the events and used the threat over demonstrations. Movement participants accepted both the fact that and how the representatives used the threat. Police officers participated in anti-austerity events because viewed the activity of protest attendees as potentially and presumptively dangerous. They did not entirely approve activists' behavior perceived as the threat to public order, safety, and security. In protest policing, officers used passive physical political violence. Hence, this mode did not take on the maximum value of the cohesion.

The forms of political violence contributed to the soft power approach (Figure 2.3: C″) in the shape of the blend of mental and passive physical political violence. On the continuum, the Austrian case was at some distance from the purely soft power approach because the employment of the threat was not in the minority. The mental mode did not function as predominant. However, no political subject chose to make use of active physical force. Therefore, the forms of political violence were at a greater distance from the hard power approach than from the soft one. This quality also typified the Netherlands and France, which means that it was a common feature for the hector-led patterns.

After the juxtaposition of empirical evidence, the analysis of the Austrian case identifies a low extent of the intensity of physical political violence. On the continuum of the intensity, just like the Netherlands and France, Austria was between making the threat and the abandonment of the use of physical political violence (Figure 2.2: D′). Although the threat was common, political subjects avoided bringing about its dangerous escalation not to transform it into active physical force. Passive physical violence was not dominant, and stakeholders were far from making it the major mode of operation.

The pattern of a culture of political violence that entered Austria is a hector-consenting culture of political violence. Its properties are: (1) both representatives of a state apparatus and movement participants use political violence; (2) a very high extent of mutual legitimation to the use; (3) the modes of the legitimation of the use are authorization, rationalization, and moralization; (4) the intensity of physical political violence is on the continuum between the threat and the abandonment; and (5) the mental and passive physical forms of political violence compose a soft power approach.

The Netherlands: "No Euro, No Cry"

In the Netherlands, the spirit of solidarity with Southern Europe was similar to that observed in Germany, Austria, Belgium, Finland, France, and Ireland. The Dutch anti-austerity movement acted in fellowship with Spain and Greece by displaying the states' flags and banners with slogans "No euro, no cry" (Euronews 2015c), and it turned against the EU-imposed austerity measures in the Eurozone (Connolly and Chrisafis 2012; The Economist 2013; Worldcrunch/Expatica 2012). Representatives of the state apparatus and movement participants resorted to political violence while they were establishing their relationships over austerity. In the Netherlands, like Austria, an extent of cohesion between political subjects' actual usage of political violence and agreement on the use was very high, very close to the largest value on the continuum (Figure 2.1: B).

In the Netherlands, as in Austria, Belgium, Finland, France, Greece, Spain, Ireland, Germany, Portugal, Slovenia, and Italy, political subjects employed authorization, rationalization, and moralization to legitimate the use of political violence. Movement participants staged events in a public sphere and made use of mental political violence to manifest their opinion in a commonly accepted manner. They neither deployed nor provoked the deployment of active physical force. In turn, representatives of the state apparatus participated in the proceedings, but they policed protests by using the threat, which was accepted by the movement. Police officers recognized the actions of activists as potentially and presumptively dangerous and impending public order, safety, and security. Therefore, just like Austria, in the Netherlands, the extent of the cohesion did not take on a maximum value.

Representatives of the state apparatus employed mental political violence by adopting the information and persuasion strategies and made the threat by taking part in protests as the guards of public order, safety, and security. They revealed the readiness to deploy coercive measures if needed. Then, movement participants used mental political violence by marching against austerity policy and carrying flags and banners. They abandoned, however, employing active physical political violence and making the threat. Hence, in the Netherlands, the extent of the intensity of physical political violence was on the continuum between the threat and the abandonment (Figure 2.2: D′). Just as in Austria and France, it took on a low value.

Anti-austerity event participants used the authorization by law as the mode of legitimation of the commitment of political violence. They also applied the instrumental goal-, effect-, and means-oriented rationalization. There was no difference between their performance in the Netherlands and the already discussed countries. Furthermore, the protesters who manifested solidarity with Southern Europe employed moralization by moral evaluation. As in the Netherlands, Austria, Belgium, Finland, and France, it consisted in evoking the value of fellowship in a public sphere. They also had a deep mistrust of representatives of the state apparatus in common (Smith-Spark 2012). The current decision-making processes that brought about the implementation of austerity measures were shown as the incentive to use political violence.

In the Netherlands, as in Austria and France, the forms of political violence were on the continuum between hard and soft power approaches, close to the latter (Figure 2.3: C″). The identification of the Dutch case as the soft power approach was a result of the occurrence of the configuration of passive physical and mental political violence. Importantly to the nature of the pattern, no political subject used active physical force.

The same pattern of a culture of political violence that entered Austria also occurred in the Netherlands. The features defining a hector-consenting culture of political violence are: (1) both representatives of a state apparatus and movement participants use political violence; (2) a very high extent of mutual legitimation to use political violence; (3) the modes of the legitimation of the use are authorization, rationalization, and moralization; (4) the intensity of physical political violence is on the continuum between the threat and the abandonment; and (5) the mental and passive physical forms of political violence compose a soft power approach.

France: "Enough Is Enough"

Across France, activists staged angry protests against austerity measures and in the name of social services protection, public transport, and equality in employment (Le Monde 2014; McPartland 2015; The World Post 2013). Just as in

Austria and the Netherlands, they used authorization, rationalization, and moralization to legitimate the use of political violence. According to movement participants, they tried to explain to the government the necessity to change its economic policy because the effect of austerity was impacting on employment, public investments, and wages in an unacceptable and ravaging way (AFP 2015; Chabanet and Lacher 2016; McPartland 2015). They made use of banners with slogans to express their opinion and rationalize the commitment of political violence. Amidst them, the following were dominant: "Hollande, that's enough," "When you are leftist you support employees" (Wire services 2014); "Enough is enough!" (in French: *Maintenant ça suffit!*); "Against finance and austerity" (in French: *Contre la finance et l'austérité*) (McPartland 2015); "No to austerity!" (in French: *Non à l'austérité*) (Euronews 2015a); "Give Greece a chance," "We support Greece #StopAusterity" (TVXS 2015b); "For a solidarity-based Europe, not for the austerity treaty" (in French: *Pour une Europe solidaire, non au traité de l'austérité*), "Resistance!" (in French: *Résistance!*) (Le Roux 2012); and "Labor, social equality, solidarity" (in French: *Du travail, de l'égalité sociale, de la solidarité*) (Julian 2012). French movement participants openly expressed their determined opposition to anti-austerity measures and gave voice to solidarity with Greece and the whole of Europe, just like the activists from Germany, Austria, Belgium, Finland, the Netherlands, and Ireland (News247 2015; Zougla 2015b). The expressions of support and solidarity with Southern Europe were typical for the hector-led cultures of political violence.

Apart from banners, protesters carried flags, badges, flares, colorful balloons, and caricatures of Nicolas Sarkozy (The Globe and Mail 2010). They seldom burnt pallets and other flammable things to make the threat (The Globe and Mail 2010). More often, however, they blocked access to public buildings and blockaded oil depots and airports (Wolf 2010). The Eiffel Tower was unavailable to tourists because its staff decided to take part in protests (McPartland 2015; The Local staff 2015). Public and private sector workers stopped working and joined anti-austerity events. Also, senior citizens and students took to the streets (BBC 2012b; Gleize 2015; John, Ireland, and Heinrich 2015; The Globe and Mail 2010). Movement participants used mainly mental political violence and rarely the threat. They abandoned employing active physical political violence.

Activists authorized the deployment of violence by a right to express their opinion in a public sphere. They rationalized violent behavior by the references to the goals, effects, and uses of the institutionalized social action and common knowledge (van Leeuwen 2007, 92). Apart from those dominant modes of legitimation, they made use of moralization by moral evaluation. The values of social solidarity, equality, and justice as the means of moralization were in the minority. This set of modes was the feature of the hector-led and militant cultures of political violence.

In France, just as in Austria and the Netherlands, representatives of the state apparatus were ready to deploy the coercion means, but active physical political violence did not occur. They controlled the use of political violence and made the threat. Summing up the arguments, not unlike the other hector-led patterns, the extent of the intensity of physical political violence was low. The case was on the continuum between the threat and the abandonment (Figure 2.2: D′).

As in Austria and the Netherlands, in France, politicians and police officers legitimated the use of political violence by the instrumental rationalization and the authorization by law. The extent of cohesion between political subjects' actual usage of political violence and agreement on the use was close to a maximum level (Figure 2.1: C). Both representatives of the state apparatus and movement participants used their duties and rights within the boundaries of their political roles in a manner accepted by the political subjects. They did not approve of incidents of the use of physical political violence. Anti-austerity event participants accepted each other in the political structure as well as the modes and purposes of applying political violence. A disagreement made an appearance just exactly over the incidents that were uncommon eventually. Hence, just as in Finland, the mutual legitimation took on a high level in France. This value was unique for those two cultures that were of different patterns. Whereas the French pattern was the most aggressive from among the hector-led examples, the Finnish militant pattern was the least violent within the militant cluster.

The forms of political violence were between soft and hard power approaches, close to the former (Figure 2.3: C″). Just as in Austria and the Netherlands, in France, the configuration of mental and passive physical political violence emerged. Political subjects kept themselves from the use of the active type.

An original pattern of a culture of political violence made an appearance in France. A hector-acknowledgment culture of political violence is featured with: (1) both representatives of a state apparatus and movement participants use political violence; (2) a high extent of mutual legitimation to use political violence; (3) the modes of the legitimation of the use are authorization, rationalization, and moralization; (4) the intensity of physical political violence is on the continuum between the threat and the abandonment; and (5) the mental and passive forms of physical political violence set a soft power approach.

This pattern differed from the hector-consenting culture of political violence that entered Austria and the Netherlands in terms of mutual legitimation to commit political violence. The value of this feature took on a slightly lower level in France than in Austria and the Netherlands. Whereas the acknowledgment symptomatic of the French pattern consisted in passive countenancing how other political subjects use violence, the Austrian and Dutch consent based on general approval. The hector-led types had the remaining properties in common.

Militant Cultures of Political Violence

The most aggressive type of a culture of political violence that occurred in the times of austerity was also the most frequent. Whereas the placid patterns made an appearance in two cases and the hector-led pattern in three, the militant type entered nine states. The unique feature of the latter was the deployment of active physical political violence by stakeholders of anti-austerity movements to gain their goals. They passed the qualitative line between passive and active force impassable for the placid and hector-led patterns. The evidence of the activity of political subjects shows that within the militant cultures of political violence the threat often transformed into active physical force. Furthermore, just as in the case of the moderately belligerent patterns, movement participants organized protests and thus generated numerous occasions to clash with representatives of state apparatuses. This part of the chapter scrutinizes the militant cultures of political violence that entered Finland, Belgium, Germany, Portugal, Slovenia, Italy, Greece, Spain, and Ireland after 2008.

The militant cultures of political violence differed in the mutual legitimation of political subjects to deploy political violence. Whereas in the aggressively militant pattern this feature took on a very low extent, in the obstreperously militant pattern just a low extent, and in an indulgingly militant a high extent. The aggressively militant and obstreperously militant types differed from the indulgingly militant one in terms of the intensity of physical political violence. While the former located on the continuum very close to the maximally intense active physical political violence, the latter was just close. It indicates that the aggressively militant pattern was the most violent from among the militant cultures of political violence. The use of physical force was fully accepted by stakeholders of the anti-austerity movements, which is mirrored by the highest level of the intensity in Greece, Spain, and Ireland. Nevertheless, simultaneously, those political subjects legitimated others to commit political violence to the lowest degree. Overwhelming brutality contributed to an extremely aggressive nature of that pattern. The obstreperously militant type was marked by a slightly higher extent of mutual legitimation to commit political violence than the most aggressive cultures. Despite the impetuousness of the former, it had a lower transformation potential than the latter to change into warfare. The narrowly represented indulgingly militant pattern was driven by general mutual legitimation to permit physical political violence. Although within the indulgingly militant type the extent of the intensity was higher than in the other cases, it was still the acquiescence to crossing a qualitative line between the threat and the use of active physical force. In fact, stakeholders of the Finnish anti-austerity movement were indulgent while they were shaping relationships and discourse about austerity measures.

Finland: "People's Power"

Austerity measures caused one of the largest protests in Finland's history, which resulted in closing down ports, canceling or delaying flights, and general disruption of other means of transport (Whitman 2015; YLE 2015b). Protesters staged anti-austerity events in many cities in the whole state. Publicly funded institutions stopped working for one day in 2015 (BBC 2015b; S2W 2015). In Finland, both movement participants and representatives of the state apparatus employed political violence. The former who took part in protests made claims that they called three theses: against austerity politics in Finland, Europe, and the rest of the world; an adequate livelihood for everyone; and human and basic rights for everyone (Väisänen 2015). Moral evaluation built on the references to human rights justified and accounted for violent behavior. Just as in Austria and Belgium, the activists made references to the value of solidarity with the countries suffering from austerity.

Over protests, movement participants carried colorful balloons, flags, electronic devices playing pop music, and placards with writings: "People's Power – Fuerza collective" (in Finnish: *Joukkovoima*) (Väisänen 2015); "#STOP," "NO WAY" (in Finnish: *EI ONNISTU*) (The Malaymail Online 2015; TRT World 2015; Press TV 2015); "No to cuts" (in Finnish: *Ei leikkauksia*; *ei leikata!*), "Cooperation not competition!" (in Finnish: *Yhteistyötä ei kilpailua!*) (Ei leikata 2015; RT 2015a); "That's Enough Now!" (in Finnish: *Riittää Now!*) (Finland Times 2014); and the scissors crossed out (Banjo 2015). Worth noticing is that the slogan "People's power" directly mirrored the core of the new protest wave, the discourse of citizenship (Bosi *et al.* 2016, 7; Gerbaudo 2017). It was keenly and across the board employed to legitimate the use of political violence.

Just as in all the hector-led and militant patterns, in Finland, movement participants took advantage of authorization, moralization, and rationalization to legitimate the deployment of political violence. The claims and banners showed that the rationalization was instrumentally means-, effect-, and goal-oriented. Activists authorized the use of violence by evoking a right to express their opinion.

Representatives of the state apparatus legitimated the use of political violence by the authorization of law too. During all the protests, officers made the threat by exposing direct coercive and preventive measures (Banjo 2015). Nevertheless, they did not settle for the use of passive psychical violence but made use of tear gas and pepper spray to disperse the agitators when the latter made attempts to break through a police barrier and approach the parliament building (Finland Times 2014). Active physical political violence was often in use because anti-austerity event participants fought with riot police. On the continuum, an extent of the intensity of physical political violence was moderately high. It placed the case between the maximally intense active physical political violence and the threat, close to the former. To be more specific, a value of the feature located between a high extent of the intensity and a moderate extent, close to the former, and thus the case took on a moderately high value (Figure 2.2: B′~). A tilde sign (~) in the figure indicates a close similarity of the case to the point of high extent, but simultaneously it means that the intensity did not crest and the property was of somewhat lower or higher intensity than the high and the moderate extents respectively. Although physical political violence was not incessant, the threat more than often transformed into the use. This property made the Finnish pattern, which was the least violent from among the militant cultures of political violence, unique in the Eurozone.

In Finland, the configuration of soft and hard power approaches emerged (Figure 2.3: B″). The case was on the continuum in a larger distance from the former. It was a consequence of the configuration of the means employed by representatives of the state apparatus and movement participants. In Finland, as in Belgium, Germany, Portugal, Slovenia, Italy, Greece, Spain, and Ireland, political subjects made use of the blend of mental, and active and passive physical political violence. It was a standard property of militant patterns.

In Finland, not unlike in France, the extent of cohesion between political subjects' actual usage of political violence and agreement on its use was close to the greatest point (Figure 2.1: C). The feature took on a high value. Anti-austerity event participants condemned incidents of the employment of physical political violence. Political subjects approved each other in a political structure and the mode and purpose of applying political violence. A disagreement occurred over the incidents that, however, were not very often. Therefore, the discrepancy between political subjects' actual usage of political violence and agreement on its use was moderate. Notably, the Helsinki Police detained the movement participants that were blocking roads after the anti-austerity protests and refused to make way for traffic on Siltasaarenkatu (YLE 2015a). Activists informed officers about the other activists who did not want to leave the road (YLE 2015a). Representatives of the state apparatus co-operated with movement participants in the field of controlling the use of political violence.

An indulgingly militant culture of political violence is the original pattern that entered Finland. The following properties are of its nature: (1) both representatives of a state apparatus and movement participants use political violence; (2) a high extent of mutual legitimation to use political violence; (3) the modes of the legitimation of the use are authorization, rationalization, and moralization; (4) the intensity of physical political violence is on the continuum between the maximally intense active and passive physical political violence, close to the former; and (5) the mental, and active and passive physical forms of political violence constitute the blend of soft and hard power approaches.

Belgium: "Nothing but Crumbs for Us"

Just as in Finland, representatives of the state apparatus and movement participants used physical political violence in Belgium. They did not accept each other's violent behavior. Although police officers deployed coercive measures within the boundaries of their political roles, movement participants went beyond the scope of their rights. Politicians and police officers did not leave it without comment and fierce reaction respectively. Therefore, the extent of cohesion between political subjects' actual usage of political violence and agreement on its use was low (Figure 2.1: D). The Belgian pattern had this property in common with the German, Portuguese, Slovene, and Italian cultures of political violence.

In Belgium, the modes of the legitimation of the use of political violence were diversified in the way common for the hector-led and militant patterns. Political subjects used authorization, rationalization, and moralization to legitimate resorting to political violence. Representatives of the state apparatus took advantage of the authorization by law and the goal-, means-, and effect-oriented instrumental rationalization. In turn, movement participants utilized the authorization by law, the moralization by moral evaluation, and the same types of rationalization. Not unlike in Finland, in Belgium, the stakeholders made references to their political roles in the state. Thus, they justified and explained their brutal acts by an array of rights and duties in the political structure.

Just like Austrian, Dutch, French, Finnish, German, Italian, and Irish activists, Belgians expressed the solidarity with those who suffered badly from austerity policies (Protothema.gr 2015) to moralize the employment of force. The fellowship among Europeans was instrumentally employed in justifying the use of political violence. Activists carried Greek flags, banners with the manifestation of solidarity with Greece and Spain, and chanted anti-austerity slogans (Ls/sms, AP, dpa 2015; Protothema.gr 2015). Furthermore, they directly opposed the austerity measures implemented by Charles Michel's government. The intensity of the verbal political violence expressed via banners took on a relatively low value. The slogans used by activists in the widespread protests shed considerable light on the ways of accounting for and justifying the use of physical political violence. The dominant cries rationalizing the modes of operating were the following: "Nothing but crumbs for us" (in French: *Rien que des miettes pour nous*), "Austerity does not work" (in French: *L'austérité ne fonctionne pas*), "No to austerity, priority to jobs and growth" (BBC 2010a), "Austerity = sustainable poverty," "Austerity measures = sustainable poverty" (in French: *Austérité = pauvreté durable*; *Mesures d'austérité = pauvreté durable*), "No to the impoverishment of the weakest" (in French: *Non a l'appauvrissement des plus faibles*), "Don't touch the index!!!" (in French: *Touchez pas a l'index!!!*), and "People, not profit" (AFP 2014; France TV Info 2014; Le Monde 2015; Ouest France Justice et Liberté 2015; La Tribune 2014). They expressed the instrumental rationalization. In turn, representatives of the state apparatus rationalized their violent behavior by showing it as a response to savage activists. They underscored the importance of performing duties.

Then, as in Greece, Spain, Ireland, Germany, Portugal, Slovenia, and Italy, in Belgium, the extent of the intensity of physical political violence was very high. It located the case between the maximally intense active physical political violence and the threat (Figure 2.2: A′~), considerably closer to the former extreme stage (Le Monde 2015). It has been marked with A′~ because it is the closest point on the continuum to the Belgian case. A tilde sign (~) in the figure means a close similarity between A′ and A′~, but simultaneously it indicates that the exact value of A′ did not crest.

Movement participants threw things at police officers. The things utilized as weapons were stones, paving stones, firecrackers, flares, smoke flares, bottles, parts of fences, barriers, sticks, whistles, horns, and garbage mustered in the time of incidents (BBC 2010a, Le Monde 2015; L'obs 2014; La Tribune 2014). Activists also set fire to cars, motorcycles, tires, and cartons arranged in piles and devastated public and private property (Lyon 2015). Law enforcement officers answered the violent behavior by using water cannons and tear gas (AFP/A.P. 2015; Ls/sms, AP, dpa 2015; La Tribune 2014). As a result of confrontations, the most active participants were detained, arrested, and injured. Wounded in the protest policing were also police officers (20 Minutes avec AFP 2014; RT en français 2015).

In Belgium, the combination of hard and soft power approaches occurred (Figure 2.3: B″) as the blend of mental, and active and passive physical political violence. Frequent struggles were a direct reason for locating the case close to the hard power approach on the continuum. Belgium had this property in common with the other militant patterns that entered Finland, Germany, Portugal, Slovenia, Italy, Greece, Spain, and Ireland.

An obstreperously militant culture of political violence is the pattern that emerged in Belgium. Its properties are: (1) both representatives of a state apparatus and movement participants use political violence; (2) a low extent of mutual legitimation to commit political violence; (3) the modes of the legitimation of the use of political violence are authorization, rationalization, and moralization; (4) the intensity of physical political violence is on the continuum between the maximally intense active type and the threat, very close to the former; and (5) the mental, and active and passive physical forms of political violence contribute to the blend of soft and hard power approaches.

Germany: "Capitalism Kills"

The German pan-European and anti-austerity movement called the Blockupy (BBC 2015a; Eckardt and Angerer 2015; News24 2015) was less active than the Greek or Spanish movement (Radio Stimme Russlands 2012; Spiegel 2012). The most violent confrontation between anti-austerity protesters and representatives of the state apparatus took place ahead of the inauguration ceremony for the European Central Bank's (ECB) new headquarters in Frankfurt (Associated Press 2015; McHugh 2015). Demonstrators chose this place because they held economic elites culpable for the social and economic consequences of austerity measures.

In Germany, representatives of the state apparatus and movement participants used physical political violence. Authorities built the barbed wire barricades around the ECB for extra security (AFP/The Local 2015). Police officers had riot gear (AP 2015) and fired rubber bullets at the aggressive protesters (Dreier and Lantier 2015). They deployed police bats, pepper spray, tear gas, and water cannons to disperse protesters after the attacks on officers, firefighters, a police station, and the Old Opera House (BBC 2015a; Onyanga-Omara 2015; Spiegel 2015b; Wessel and Ewing 2015; Yan 2015). Political subjects fought (Onyanga-Omara 2015) despite declaring peaceful attitudes (Reuters 2015). The police cars, private vehicles, bikes, furniture, tires, garbage bins, trash, billboards, fences, and flammable objects on the streets were set on fire (AP 2015; Healy 2015; McHugh 2015; Il Messaggero 2015; Wessel and Ewing 2015; Yan 2015). Windows, waste bins, planters, and police cars were smashed (BBC 2015a; Fidler 2015; Healy 2015; Spiegel 2015c) and road signs torn out of the roads. The private and public property was severely damaged (Black *et al.* 2015; Sky News 2015).

Movement participants often dressed up as clowns (Fidler 2015; Weaver 2015), manifested vulgar non-verbal signs (BBC 2015a), and threw smoke flares, concrete slabs, cobblestones, paving stones, stones, rocks, bottles, and metal objects at the public property and representatives of the state apparatus, including firefighters (AP 2015; Associated Press 2015; BBC 2015a; Dailymail 2015; Kleeman 2015; Spiegel 2015a; Yan 2015). They also attacked police officers with an unidentified irritating substance similar to pepper spray (News24 2015; Yan 2015). Protesters blocked traffic (CBS News 2015). Some local schools, shops, restaurants, and trams stopped working (Capon 2015; CBC News 2015).

The intensity of physical political violence situates Germany on the continuum between the maximally intense active type and the threat, very close to the former (Figure 2.2: A′~). Its value was indeed very high. As in Belgium, Greece, Spain, Ireland, Portugal, Slovenia, and Italy, in Germany, movement participants and representatives of the state apparatus made use of excessive active physical political violence.

Political subjects decided to apply authorization, rationalization, and moralization to legitimate the deployment of political violence, just as in all the hector-led and other militant types. The major mode of the legitimation of the use of political violence was the authorization by law, regardless of a political role. Politicians and activists used mass media to express and disseminate the arguments for and against austerity measures respectively. In Germany, as in Austria, Belgium, Finland, France, the Netherlands, and Ireland, movement participants strongly emphasized the solidarity with Greece (Defencenet.gr 2015; Iefimerida 2015; Newsbomb 2015; Pavlou 2015). They waved Greek flags and held banners stating "#thisisacoup" and "*Οχι*" which means "No" in Greek (Le Blond 2015). The "No" sign manifested opposition to austerity policy in the European Union. Activists also evoked people as a general value they fought for over protests. Movement participants used the moral evaluation to legitimate the use of political violence as the values of solidarity and people were explicitly brought out.

Representatives of the state apparatus stressed that they guarded, maintained, and restored public order. As they argued, their role was to provide citizens, denizens, and numerous foreigners engaged in protests with safety and security. Then, representatives of the anti-austerity movement proclaimed the protests to be loud but peaceful (Reuters 2015). They highlighted they were eligible to organize protests to make their point. Thus, anti-austerity event participants referred to the authorization by law when taking advantage of political violence.

The third mode of the legitimation of using political violence was the goal-, effect-, and means-oriented instrumental rationalization. Stakeholders of the movement presented their arguments succinctly. They asserted they deployed political violence because of the socially adverse outcome of austerity measures and to manifest their strong opposition to the policy. Protesters displayed homogenous slogans; from among the most popular were: "People over banks, people over markets, humanity before profit" (Associated Press 2015), "E.C.B./B.C.E. [in English: the European Central Bank (ECB)/in French: Banque centrale européenne (BCE) – J.R.] stop your diktats," "Capitalism kills" (in German:

Kapitalismus tötet) (Black *et al.* 2015; Sky News 2015), "Thanks for nothing" (in German: *Danke für nichts*) (Dpa 2015), and "Free caviar for everyone" (teleSUR/md-TP-cm 2015). Activists also chanted "Anti-capitalism" (in German: *Anti-Kapitalismus*), which was coherent with the banners (CBC News 2015).

As a result of clashes, the people involved were detained, arrested, and injured (Associated Press 2015; CBS News 2015; Kleeman 2015; McHugh 2015; Yan 2015). In Germany, just as in Belgium, Portugal, Slovenia, and Italy, the extent of mutual legitimation to use political violence was low (Sky News 2015; Weaver 2015) (Figure 2.1: D). Indeed, those who attended clashes deplored the use of excessive active physical force. Political subjects labeled others as non-legitimated to behave in a violent way and for the purpose they did. As in Belgium, in Germany, the discrepancy between political subjects' actual usage of political violence and agreement on the use took on a high value.

The means used by political subjects over anti-austerity events indicated the occurrence of the blend of soft and hard power approaches (Figure 2.3: B″). The case was on the continuum close to the latter. Indeed, in Germany, just as in Finland, Belgium, Portugal, Slovenia, Italy, Greece, Spain, and Ireland, anti-austerity event participants used mental, and active and passive physical political violence.

In Germany, just as in Belgium, the hallmarks of an obstreperously militant culture of political violence are: (1) both representatives of a state apparatus and movement participants use political violence; (2) a low extent of mutual legitimation to use political violence; (3) the modes of the legitimation of the use of political violence are authorization, rationalization, and moralization; (4) the intensity of physical political violence is on the continuum between the maximally intense active type and the threat, very close to the former; and (5) the mental, and active and passive physical forms of political violence create the blend of soft and hard power approaches.

Portugal: "Fuck the Troika! We Want Our Lives!"

The Portuguese anti-austerity movement is called the 12 March Movement (in Portuguese: *Movimento 12 de Março*) (the name comes from the gathering staged on March 12, 2011, considered to be the beginning of the movement in Portugal) or the Portuguese for Struggling Generation (in Portuguese: *Geração à Rasca*). In Portugal, both representatives of the state apparatus and movement participants deployed political violence when acted for or against austerity measures respectively. Anti-austerity event attendees legitimated the use of political violence by employing authorization, rationalization, and moralization, not unlike in Austria, Belgium, Finland, France, Greece, Spain, the Netherlands, Ireland, Germany, Slovenia, and Italy.

The 12 March Movement organized one of the biggest waves of massive protests in the history of the state (Accornero and Ramos Pinto 2015; de Notícias 2013; Redação 2011) and commonly used both mental and physical political violence. During anti-austerity events, activists played music, carried Portuguese flags and banners to express anti-austerity stances and, according to event organizers, to create political awareness (Accornero and Ramos Pinto 2015; Al Jazeera and agencies 2012; Euronews 2013; 2014; Giunta 2015; McCauley 2015; Staff 2013). The most famous slogans: "Fuck the Troika! We want our lives!" (in Portuguese: *Que se Lixe a Troika! Queremos as nossas vidas*, also just "Fuck the Troika!": *Que se Lixe a Troika!* (QSLT)) (the so-called Troika consists of the International Monetary Fund, the European Central Bank, and the European Commission) (Baumgarten and Carmo Duarte 2015); "The Troika only gives unemployment" (in Portuguese: *Troika só dá desemprego*); "Out, out of here, hunger and misery IMF [the International Monetary Fund – J.R.]" (in Portuguese: *Fora, fora daqui, a fome a miséria e o FMI*); "Merkel does not rule here!" (in Portuguese: *A Merkel não manda aqui!*) (Esquerda 2012); "Saving banks kill the people" (in Portuguese: *Salvam bancos matam o povo*) (Baumgarten 2013); and "For professional dignity and people's security" (Queally 2013). Dignity, human safety and security, and human lives constructed the basis for the moral evaluation and abstraction applied to moralize the deployment of political violence.

The remarkable employment of music as a tool of political violence characterized Portuguese movement (NPR 2013). Activists wrote and sang the protest songs, which are thought to be a traditional tool of protest in Portugal (Baumgarten 2017), in a tone similar to the banners: "Fuck the government," "Fuck off back to Eton," and "Bullshit lies. Revolting, revolting!" (for more see: Giunta 2015). Protesters chanted over marches "Government, Merkel, and IMF out of here" (in Portuguese: *Governo, Merkel e FMI fora daqui*) (Esquerda 2012), and "General Strike" (in Portuguese: *Greve Geral*) (de Souza 2012). They legitimated the use of political violence by the goal-, means-, and effect-oriented instrumental rationalization (Sousa and Santos 2014). The structure of this mode of legitimation did not differ from those adopted in the already discussed countries.

In spite of declaring peaceful attitudes, movement participants clashed seriously with representatives of the state apparatus (Santos-Moura 2012). Protesters held flares (Telegraph 2013), set litter baskets and piled up litter on fire, jumped over the fire, attempted to set themselves on fire (BBC 2012a; Santos-Moura 2012), removed pavement, and deployed paving stones as a weapon (Santos-Moura 2012). They threw stones, rocks, metal objects, garbage, and burning objects at police officers. Some of the protesters were naked, others showed buttocks and wore masks (Santos-Moura 2012). Public institutions were closed, and their workers struck (Wise *et al.* 2012). Riot police in riot gear were armed with coercive measures and took advantage of them over clashes (Queally 2013; Santos-Moura 2012). The threat more than often transformed into active physical political violence.

Anti-austerity event participants legitimated the employment of political violence by law. Representatives of the state apparatus made the threat and permitted it as a response to protesters' attacks. The authorization to act aggressively came from their political rights and duties. Activists, on the other hand, considered force to be a necessary device to achieve their political goals. They claimed that they made use of their rights and duties within the political structure.

A very high extent of the intensity of physical political violence by stakeholders of anti-austerity movement situated Portugal between a maximally intense active type and the threat, very close to the former (Figure 2.2: A′~). As in Belgium, Greece, Spain, Ireland, Germany, Slovenia, and Italy, in Portugal, movement participants and representatives of the state apparatus employed political violence nearly maximally intensively.

Within the Portuguese culture of political violence, an extent of mutual legitimation to the deployment of political violence was low (Figure 2.1: D). Representatives of the state apparatus did not misuse political violence. Police officers had to intervene to restore public order, safety, and security in a public sphere because movement participants abused active physical force. The deployment of excessive physical political violence was not accepted by the attendees of clashes and politicians. The political subjects engaged in clashes recognized each other as non-legitimated to act in the way and for the purposes they did. In Portugal, as in Belgium, Germany, Slovenia, and Italy, the discrepancy between political subjects' actual usage of political violence and agreement on the use was high.

Furthermore, the employment of political violence was the combination of soft and hard power approaches (Figure 2.3: B″). On the continuum, the case was close to the latter because stakeholders of the movement made use of mental, passive and active physical political violence. The feature took on this value also in Finland, Belgium, Germany, Slovenia, Italy, Greece, Spain, and Ireland.

In Portugal, as in Belgium and Germany, an obstreperously militant culture of political violence is characterized by: (i) both representatives of a state apparatus and movement participants use political violence; (ii) a low extent of mutual legitimation to use political violence; (iii) the modes of the legitimation of the use of political violence are authorization, rationalization, and moralization; (iv) the intensity of physical political violence is on the continuum between the maximally intense active type and the threat, very close to the former; and (v) the mental, and active and passive physical forms of political violence constitute the blend of soft and hard power approaches.

Slovenia: "Do Not Wait for Spring – Spring Is Already Here"

In Slovenia, the anti-austerity movement, called the All-Slovenian Popular Uprising (Toplišek 2017; Kirn 2013a), was multi-generational, heterogeneous, and demonstrated the widespread nature of the dissatisfaction with political and economic elites, corruption, social inequality, and the austerity way the establishment responded to the crisis (Maza 2013b; Rushton 2013; The Slovenia Times 2012b). They heavily manufactured and underlined the distinction between "they, the corrupted" and "we, the good" (RT 2013a; Toplišek 2017). Its rallying call was "They are finished!" (in Slovene: *Gotovi so!)* (Toplišek 2017). Activists held numerous protests across the state (Euronews 2012; STA 2012; Mekina 2012; Zerdin 2013). Even the public institutions stopped working for a few days (Zerdin 2013).

The Slovene anti-austerity movement was, however, noted from staging "Protestival" (Novak 2013). It was the set of cultural-social events organized in Ljubljana since December 2012 under the slogan "Do not wait for spring – spring is already here," derived from the refrain of the popular Slovenian song (Maza 2013a; Nowak 2013). According to the manifesto, " 'Protestival' articulates protests against all political and economic measures that increasingly degrade human lives of Slovenians. They are specifically oriented towards the cultural expression of the people" (Maza 2013a). Movement participants assumed that "The 'Protestival' is a calling for a social renaissance and a return to the human while rejecting the manipulations of capital" and "It is connecting people through their cultural expression, via musical performances, physical theatre, puppets, poetry, as well as giving a voice to the protesters themselves, thus creating a unique people's forum" (Novak 2013). People gave flowers to police officers and carried candles and the banners with the white zombie masks against the background of blackboards, made zombie masks, wore zombie masks, and disguised themselves as white-face zombies since the Prime Minister had called protesters "communist zombies" (Dakskobler 2012; Novak 2013). Many of them dressed up as diverse monsters to make reference to the zombie style and brought stage props, such as coffins and burning broomsticks (Dakskobler 2012; Gracner 2013). Some of the protesters were black-clothed (Mekina 2014). Due to the zombie style (Ramos 2014), the protests organized by the Slovenian movement are known as the "Zombie Uprising" (Gracner 2013; Korsika 2015).

In Slovenia, both representatives of the state apparatus and movement participants used political violence, mainly over protests (Dr/jr *et al.* 2012). They legitimated violent behavior by applying authorization, rationalization, and moralization, just as in other states of the militant and hector-led patterns. Movement participants fiercely clashed with police officers (Arbutina and glb 2012). They threw rocks, stones, bottles, metal objects, flares (CBC News 2012; Maza 2013a; RT 2012c), fireworks, firecrackers (Novak *et al.* 2012), torches, and home-made explosives at representatives of the state apparatus (Mekina 2014). As a result of numerous exchanges, rioters were injured, detained, and arrested (CBC News 2012; Kirn 2013a; Maza 2013a; RT 2012c).

Protesters burnt the pictures of Maribor's (the city where some protests took place) Mayor Franc Kangler, litter baskets, and flammable objects (RT 2012c), and they severely damaged public and private property (Kirn 2013b). Police officers responded with the deployment of cavalry, water cannons, and tear gas to disperse the crowd and provide social safety and security. They also called air support (Durić and Žibret 2017; Kirn 2013b; Maza 2013a, 2013b; RT 2012c). The intensity of physical political violence was very high, which situated the case extremely close to the maximum extent. On the continuum, it was indeed between the maximally intense active type and the threat, very near to the former (Figure 2.2: A′~). Not unlike in Belgium, Greece, Spain, Ireland, Germany, Portugal, and Italy, in Slovenia, movement participants and representatives of the state apparatus made use of political violence almost maximally intensively.

Apart from physical political violence, the mental type was committed. Whistles and vulgar non-verbal signs such as giving somebody the finger were eagerly used (Dakskobler 2012). Movement participants chanted in front of the administrative building, "Thieves" (Maza 2013b), and on the streets, "It is enough!," "It is over with them, they are done!" (in Slovene: *gotov je, gotovi so!*), "They are all crooks!," and "We give the Parliament, but not the street!" (Kirn 2013b). The demand for "The spring to come, and Janša [the contemporaneous state's Prime Minister, Janez Jananša] the political class to leave" was also popular (Kirn 2013b). It appeared on banners as "Janša go home" as well (Santopadre 2012). Nonetheless, it was not the only slogan. Equally popular were: "I feel rEVOLt" [original spelling: with the marked inverted writing "LOVE"] (Wita 2013), "Power to the people," "Let's fire the troika, not the people" (RT 2013a), "Against EU servants" (Mekina 2014), "Dictatorship" (in Slovene: *Diktatura*), "End" (in Slovene: *Do konca*) (Dakskobler 2012), "No to destructive policies" (PanARMENIAN 2012), "Austere Austerity Leads to Even More Debt," "You Can Take Everything I Have, But the Economy Still Won't Grow," "Stop to Social Inequality," "Slovenia Is Most Competitive in Corruption" (The Slovenia Times 2012a), "All-Slovenian Revolt," "Parliament is a criminal nest," "Today is the new day," "You are flexibly fired," "You should walk among the people not over them," "Thieves," "Our city is not for sale," "Fuck you, loan rates," and "Direct democracy!" (APA Azeri Press Agency 2012; Tomaselli 2013). Thus, the protesters used, moralized, and rationalized the deployment of political violence (AFP 2012b; AP 2012; Dr/jr; Reuters; Vobič *et al.* 2014).

Movement participants referred to an abstraction such as the people, society, social well-being, social equality, direct democracy, and independence to justify and account for the use of political violence. They also argued against austerity policy by showing its deleterious results, introducing goals of political mobilization, and proposing means to solve the problems they turned against. Just as in other states, in Slovenia, the authorization by law was the dominant means of the legitimation of the deployment of political violence.

In Slovenia, as in Belgium, Germany, Portugal, and Italy, the mutual legitimation of stakeholders of the anti-austerity movement to deploy political violence was low (Figure 2.1: D). The Slovene case was marked with the use of excessive physical political violence that was unaccepted by clash attendees. Also, the political subjects engaged in anti-austerity events viewed each other as non-legitimated to act in the way and for the purposes they did. In sum, the discrepancy between political subjects' actual usage of political violence and agreement on the use took on a high value.

Although political subjects used the blend of soft and hard power approaches, the latter was ascendant (Figure 2.3: B″). Indeed, in Slovenia, just as in Finland,

Belgium, Germany, Portugal, Italy, Greece, Spain, and Ireland, mental, passive, and active kinds of physical political violence were in use. Hence, the case was on the continuum in a larger distance to the soft mode than to the hard one.

Not unlike in Belgium, Germany, and Portugal, in Slovenia, an obstreperously militant culture of political violence originated. This pattern is marked by (i) both representatives of a state apparatus and movement participants use political violence; (ii) a low extent of mutual legitimation to use political violence; (iii) the modes of the legitimation of the use of political violence are authorization, rationalization, and moralization; (iv) the intensity of physical political violence is on the continuum between the maximally intense active type and the threat, very close to the former; and (v) the mental, and active and passive physical forms of political violence contribute to the blend of soft and hard power approaches.

Italy: "Nobody Represents Us"

The Italian anti-austerity movement, called the Pitchforks (in Italian: *Forconi*), was heterogeneous and consisted of the employees of public and private sectors and students mobilized in the Anomalous Wave (in Italian: *Onda Anomala*) under the slogan "We won't pay for the crisis" (in Italian: *Noi la crisi non la paghiamo*) (AFP 2012a; BBC 2010b; Cullura 2013; Davies 2013; Gazzellanera 2012; Mauro 2012; RT 2013b; Staff 2015; VWArticles 2013; Zamponi 2013). They opposed the activities of economic and political elites, including Silvio Berlusconi at the head (Arens 2014). The name of the Pitchforks comes from the movement's roots among struggling farmers in Sicily, who in 2011 and 2012 staged strikes and roadblocks to demand more support from the government (Cullura 2013). Italians decided against austerity measures and expressed solidarity with Spain, just like activists in Austria, Belgium, Finland, France, the Netherlands, Ireland, and Germany. Their anti-austerity activities took place across the state (AP 2012).

Representatives of the state apparatus and movement participants used political violence regularly. They legitimated it by employing authorization, rationalization, and moralization, not unlike in Austria, Belgium, Finland, France, Greece, Spain, the Netherlands, Ireland, Germany, Portugal, and Slovenia. Moreover, in Italy, as in Belgium, Germany, Portugal, and Slovenia, the extent of cohesion between political subjects' actual usage of political violence and agreement on its use was low (Avvenire 2012; Gazzellanera 2012) (Figure 2.1: D). Political subjects made use of excessive physical political violence but saw each other as non-legitimated to behave violently. As a result, the discrepancy between political subjects' actual usage of political violence and agreement on the use was high.

Over anti-austerity events, some activists wore Italian flag masks and white nooses around their necks (AFP 2013b; RT 2013b). They carried flags, danced, played music (Saviano and Scacchioli 2013), and fought with police officers (Agencies 2014; Elgot 2012; O'Leary 2013; Odd Stuff 2012; Tanglao 2014).

Protesters threw paint bombs, stones, rocks, smoke flares, smoke bombs, bottles, eggs, oranges, and firecrackers at government buildings and police officers (Agencies 2014; AFP 2013b; BBC 2010b; Chiariello 2012; O'Leary 2013; Repubblica 2015; RT 2013b; The World Post 2013). In spite of declaring peaceful attitudes (Marchetti 2013), they also attacked police officers in riot gear by using clubs, sticks, and home-made bombs (Agencies 2014; La Stampa 2012; Lampugnani 2013; O'Leary 2013; Saviano and Scacchioli 2013). They turned over litter bins, set garbage on fire (O'Leary 2013; Repubblica 2015), devastated private and public property (Bacchi 2012a; Cilluffo 2014; O'Leary 2013; Odd Stuff 2012; Saviano and Scacchioli 2013), including police cars (Saviano and Scacchioli 2013). The road traffic and public communication were stopped, flights were canceled, and access to tourist attractions were blockaded (BBC 2010b; Davies 2013; Iannò 2013; Red.MM/mrj 2013; RT 2013b; Zamponi 2013). Public and private institutions stopped working (Bacchi 2012b; CBC News 2013; DAC 2014). Representatives of the state apparatus recognized the violent activities as non-legitimated.

Then, law enforcement officers deployed coercive measures, mostly batons and tear gas (AFP 2013b; Agencies 2014; Bacchi 2012a; The World Post 2013; Wire services 2014). They also made use of armored vehicles (Bacchi 2012a). Movement participants considered riot police actions to be the misuse of political violence (Bacchi 2012a; 2012b; Odd Stuff 2012). Accordingly, those engaged in violent clashes were detained, arrested, and injured (AFP 2013b; Avvenire 2012; Agencies 2014; O'Leary 2013; Redazione Barlettaviva 2013; RQuotidiano 2012; Tanglao 2014; Wire services 2014).

Overall, the intensity of physical political violence was very high, considerably near to the highest level (Figure 2.2: A′~). It was on the continuum between the maximally intense active type and the threat, very close to the former. Just like Belgium, Greece, Spain, Ireland, Germany, Portugal, and Slovenia, in Italy, movement participants and representatives of the state apparatus applied political violence almost maximally intensively.

The authorization by law was the major mode of the legitimation of the use of political violence in Italy. Not unlike political subjects in the above cases, Italians also employed the effect-, means- and goal-oriented instrumental rationalization. Movement participants deployed the moral evaluation by making references to the value of solidarity between the states most suffering from austerity policies. They also referred to abstraction by calling the political representation question, rights to work, security, safety, and dignity.

Buzzing, often chanted, and manifested on banners were the following slogans: "We will block the reform," (BBC 2010b) "#fuckausterity," "We won't pay for the crisis," "Nobody represents us" (in Italian: *Non ci rappresenta nessuno*) (Zamponi 2013), "No cuts, no profit!," "Their reform will not pass" (BBC 2010b), "No to the Crisis and Austerity! Let's take back our Schools and Cities!" (AFP 2012a), "Enough!" (Cullura 2013), "Austerity kills dignity. Reclaim Europe!" (Michael 2014), "One great work: home and income for all" (in Italian: *Una sola grande opera: casa e reddito per tutti*), "Fight against insecurity" (in Italian: *Lotta alla precarietà*), "Siege to power" (in Italian: *Assedio al potere*), "Stop austerity" (in Italian: *Smettere di austerità*) (Sarra 2013), and "We are the security hostages" (in Italian: *Noi ostaggio della sicurezza*) (Iannò 2013). The stock graffiti predicated "Usurious loan sharks" (in Italian: *Usurai strozzini*) (Gazzellanera 2012).

Political subjects employed the combination of soft and hard power approaches (Figure 2.3: B″). On the continuum of the forms of political violence, the Italian case was close to the latter because of the blend of mental, and active and passive physical political violence in use, just like in Finland, Belgium, Germany, Portugal, Slovenia, Greece, Spain, and Ireland.

In Italy, as in Belgium, Germany, Portugal, and Slovenia an obstreperously militant culture of political violence made an appearance. Its characteristics are: (i) both representatives of a state apparatus and movement participants use political violence; (ii) a low extent of mutual legitimation to use political violence; (iii) the modes of the legitimation of the use of political violence are authorization, rationalization, and moralization; (iv) the intensity of physical political violence is on the continuum between the maximally intense active type and the threat, very close to the former; and (v) the mental, and active and passive physical forms of political violence create the blend of soft and hard power approaches.

Greece: "Fight! They Are Drinking Our Blood"

In Greece, both representatives of the state apparatus and movement participants known as the Greek indignados or the Indignant Citizens Movement took advantage of political violence (Kanellopoulos *et al.* 2017; Nez 2016a, 178). However, the extent of cohesion between the political subjects' actual usage of political violence and agreement on the use was very low (Amnesty International – Greek Section 2011) (Figure 2.1: E). Riot police and activists used tear gas and other expired and carcinogenic chemical substances during violent protests (Phillips 2011; Radio Gamma 2015). Notably, police officers arrested movement participants before violent clashes and justified it by the need for averting aggressive confrontations, which met with strong public outcry (TVXS 2012). Activists claimed that representatives of the state apparatus committed an excess named the unlawful detention. Political subjects denounced the excessive use of physical force and recognized each other as non-legitimated to behave aggressively. Therefore, the discrepancy between political subjects' actual usage of political violence and agreement on the use was very high. The Greek pattern had this quality of mutual legitimation in common with Spain and Ireland.

In Greece, just as in Austria, Belgium, Finland, France, Spain, the Netherlands, Ireland, Germany, Portugal, Slovenia, and Italy, authorization, rationalization, and moralization legitimated the use of political violence. Representatives of the state apparatus were geared to make use of coercive measures in the period of mass political mobilization (RT 2012a; Salonicanews 2011; TVXS 2015c). Indeed, they deployed specialized less-than-lethal weapons, mainly pepper spray, tear gas, flash bombs, chemicals, stun grenades, smoke bombs, the rifles that fire rubber bullets, batons, and Long Range Acoustic Devices (Becatoros and Gatopoulos 2015; Euronews 2015b; The Huffington Post 2015; McHugh 2015b; Maltezou and Papadimas 2013; Reuters 2011). The use of political violence was instrumentally rationalized by introducing goals, means, and effects of violent behavior in a public sphere by politicians and police officers (Newsroom ΔΟΛ 2011).

Political subjects used authorization as the mode of legitimation of using political violence. Representatives of the state apparatus highlighted their duty of protecting public order, safety, and security. Movement participants justified and accounted for its usage by the references to the right to express their thought freely. They also used the exaggerated rhetoric of rights and freedoms to act against austerity. The dominant ways of explaining the motives of undertaking violent means to manifest opposition to the so-called Troika, Angela Merkel, and austerity measures (Kousi 2016; Manolis 2013; Nallu 2015; Nellas 2011; Radio Gamma 2015; Strupczewski 2012) put on the banners were: "These measures are killing us little by little and lawmakers in there don't give a damn" (Maltezou and Papadimas 2013) and "They are rich, they have everything and we have nothing and are fighting for crumbs, for survival" (Maltezou and Papadimas 2013). The very idea of general opposition fueled an anti-austerity campaign (Kanellopoulos *et al.* 2017). People who joined the anti-austerity movement manifested profound incomprehension of the implementation of austerity policies (Nooz 2015; Stokokkino 2015; The TOC 2015).

Protest participants hung flags and banners (Tagaris 2015). The most famous slogans were: "Thieves – hustlers – bankers" (in Greek: *Κλέφτες – απατεώνες – τραπεζίτες*), "You got the disease, we got the solution – revolution," "We are not commodities in the hands of bankers and politicians," "We don't owe, we don't sell, we don't pay" (Georgiopoulos 2011), "Cancel the bailout!" (in Greek: *Ακυρώστε το σχέδιο διάσωσης*), "No to the policies of the European Union, the European Central Bank, and the International Monetary Fund" (Triandafyllou and Tagaris 2015), "No to the euro" (in Greek: *Όχι στο ευρώ*), "The People will not be blackmailed," "The country's not for sale" (Tagaris 2015), "We have been betrayed!", "No" (in Greek: *Οχι*), "We said 'No', we meant 'No' " (Ide and Szeftel 2015), "Unfuck Greece" (TVXS 2015a; Zougla 2015a), "We live in Europe" (in Greek: *Μένουμε Ευρώπη*), and "Greek – Europe – Democracy" (in Greek: *Ελλάδα – Ευρώπη – Δημοκρατία*) (In.gr 2015). Sometimes satiric cartoons were displayed in public places to lampoon the politics deemed guilty for the results of austerity policy (Kaitatzi-Whitlock 2014; Kutz-Flamenbaum 2014; Radio Gamma 2015).

Activists rationalized the use of political violence by showing how damaging influence the austerity measures had on social existence, what to do, and how it should be done. The instrumental rationalization was goal-, effect-, and means-oriented. In turn, moralization made use of the references to abstraction. Movement participants invoked the state, the people, and democracy as the values which incentivized and fueled them to fight the austerity policy embodied by representatives of the state apparatus and the European Union. They often pleaded the international solidarity and mental support for Greece from other European countries.

When the movement acted, the Greek airplane, train, and ferry traffic in and out of the state stopped. Public buildings, such as schools, statehouses, banks, hospitals, and numerous private businesses were closed (Real.gr 2015). Parliament was stormed. Garbage piled up on the streets (Maltezou and Papadimas 2013). Access to tourist attractions was blocked. Movement participants used sticks and pipes as the tools to fight with police officers (AP 2011) and threw Molotov cocktails, firebombs, petrol bombs, rocks, stones, bottles, flares, smoke flares, pieces of marble, metal objects, and eggs at their opponents and public and private property (AP 2011; The Best News 2015; The Huffington Post 2015; Ide and Szeftel 2015; McHugh 2015b; Triandafyllou and Tagaris 2015). They caused enormous damage. Trash bins, cars, and some buildings, including, the finance ministry building and the Bank of Greece were set on fire (Euronews 2015b; McHugh 2015b; Maltezou and Papadimas 2013; Triandafyllou and Tagaris 2015). Local shops were looted (The Best News 2015; McHugh 2015b). Activists often chanted to warm up each other to act, "Fight! They're drinking our blood" (Maltezou and Papadimas 2013). People put bags on their heads to simulate suicides. Those activities resulted in people's death and more or less severe injuries (Guardian 2015; Phillips 2011). Law enforcement officers arrested and detained some of the protesters for questioning (Becatoros and Gatopoulos 2015).

In Greece, the extent of the intensity of the physical political violence used by the stakeholders of the movement engaged in protests was very close to the extremely high strength (Figure 2.2: A'~). As in Belgium, Spain, Ireland, Germany, Portugal, Slovenia, and Italy, it took on a very high value. Movement participants and representatives of the state apparatus made use of political violence almost maximally intensively. They had a close shave with its transposition into the extreme point on the continuum.

The configuration of mental, and active and passive physical political violence entered Greece, just like Finland, Belgium, Germany, Portugal, Slovenia, Italy, Spain, and Ireland. The measures used by political subjects over anti-austerity events located the Greek case on the continuum between soft and hard power approaches, close to the latter (Figure 2.3: B"). This location was the result of the deployment of excessive physical force for the duration of the Greek anti-austerity movement.

In Greece, an aggressively militant culture of political violence showed up. Symptomatic of this pattern are: (i) both representatives of a state apparatus and movement participants use political violence; (ii) a very low extent of mutual legitimation to use political violence; (iii) the modes of the legitimation of the use of political violence are authorization, rationalization, and moralization; (iv) the intensity of physical political violence is on the continuum between the maximally intense active type and the threat, very close to the former; and (v) the mental, and active and passive physical forms of political violence constitute the blend of soft and hard power approaches.

Spain: "Not Enough Bread for so Much Chorizo"

The Spanish anti-austerity movement is called the 15-M Movement (in Spanish: *Movimiento 15-M*) because it began with the protest launched with the gathering on May 15, 2011, one week before local elections (May 22) (Beas 2011), the Indignados Movement (the Outraged), and the Take the Square (Taibo 2013). In turn, its participants are known as the indignados. The 15-M Movement was as heterogeneous as the Italian Pitchforks and actively functioned in the whole state, often by organizing mass protests (Galais and Lorenzini 2017; Nez 2016b).

Representatives of the state apparatus and movement participants inflicted political violence (BBC 2014b; Day and Cobos 2012), which was of daily occurrence. They used authorization, rationalization, and moralization to legitimate the deployment of political violence, not unlike Austria, Belgium, Finland, France, Greece, the Netherlands, Ireland, Germany, Portugal, Slovenia, and Italy. In turn, as in Greece, in Spain, the extent of cohesion between political subjects' actual usage of political violence and agreement on its use was very low (Figure 2.1: E). Not only were police officers ready to deploy coercive measures, but they also deployed and misused them (The Journal.ie 2012; Mail Foreign Service 2012; Telegraph 2012a). They beat the protesters with batons, forced people into riot police vans, and fired plastic and rubber bullets to disperse the gathered in public places (BBC 2012b; Gates 2013; Tremlett and Traynor 2012; The World Post 2013). In social media, many users suggested the possibility that the secret police, infiltrated to cause violence, started most of the numerous violent clashes (Lopez 2012). In Spain, just like Greece and Ireland, the discrepancy between political subjects' actual usage of political violence and agreement on the use achieved a very high level. Political subjects did not accept how each other fulfilled their rights and duties arising out of political roles.

Protesters occupied public buildings and threw bottles, rocks, stones, flares, firecrackers, smoke bombs, and metal objects at policemen, and used sticks as a weapon (BBC 2014b; Gates 2013; Guardian 2014; RT 2014a; Telegraph 2012b). They set rubbish bins on fire and burnt police cars and makeshift coffins labeled "public services" (BBC 2012b; Gates 2013; Hedgecoe 2012). Also, they punctured the tires of riot police vans (Tremlett and Traynor 2012), smashed shop windows, and vandalized cash machines (AFP 2012b; Keating 2014). The participants of clashes were detained, arrested, and injured (CNN Wire Staff 2012; Guardian 2011; Heckle 2014; Sanz 2014). Private and public businesses stopped working because of strikes (The World Post 2013). Flights and trains were canceled. Metro and train stations were closed (The World Post 2013). People blocked traffic and access to tourist attractions. The extent of the intensity of physical political violence was, therefore, high and very close to the greatest point (Figure 2.2: A′~). The value of the intensity took on a very high value and had a transposition potential to change into the extreme type. Just as in Belgium, Greece, Ireland, Germany, Portugal, Slovenia, and Italy, the Spanish movement participants and representatives of the state apparatus deployed political violence almost maximally intensively.

The modes of the legitimation of the use of political violence were the authorization by law, moralization by moral evaluation, and instrumental goal-, effect-, and means-oriented rationalization. Police officers asserted that acted to provide the society with public order, security, and safety. They declared aiming at prevention, maintenance and, where appropriate, re-establishment of public order (Horsman 2017). Politicians supported this argument widely by utilizing mass media. The immoderate use of physical political violence was rationalized as the necessary tool to achieve those purposes (Lopez 2012).

In turn, movement participants claimed that they were also authorized to commit political violence by the right to manifest their opinion and the freedom of speech. Protesters often used the references to dignity to moralize the use of political violence. They even called their marches the "Marches of Dignity" (in Spanish: *Marchas de la dignidad*) (BBC 2014a). Movement participants carried flags and banners with cartoons and slogans such as "No votes yet" (in Spanish: *No les votes*), "That we are governed by whores, their children have already failed us" (in Spanish: *Que nos gobiernen las putas, sus hijos ya nos han fallado*), "Real Democracy Now" (in Spanish: *Democracia Real Ya*) (Rioja2 2011), "Revolt now," "Tax the rich," "Fighting or Slavery. Social Uprising" (Maltezou 2012), "Massive unemployment is violence" (JR/HJL/HRB 2015), "Bread, work and ceiling with DIGNITY. Walking towards the General Strike" (in Spanish: *Pan, trabajo y techo con DIGNIDAD. Caminando hacia la Huelga General*) (Agencies 2015), "Work, bread, and a roof (in Spanish: *Trabajo, pan y techo*) (RT 2015b), "Enough!" (in Spanish: *Basta!*) (Campos and Plandolit 2015), "No more cuts!" (RT 2014a), "Regime of the 1%, Crisis for 99%" (in Spanish: *Régimen del 1%, Crisis para el 99%*), "We are 99%" (in Spanish: *Somos el 99%*) "1984 G. Orwell" (RT 2012b), "We can change the history" (in Spanish: *Podemos cambiar la historia*) (McHugh 2015a), "Rise up European People," "No" and the sign of scissors (RT 2014b), "No to debt budgets" (in Spanish: *No a los presupuestos de la deuda*) (La Nación 2012), "It's not a crisis, it's the system," "It's not a crisis, I just don't love you anymore" (RT 2012b; Goodman 2015), and "The Troika go home" (Heckle 2013).

Activists beat drums and chanted "Yes, it can be done" (in Spanish: *Sí, se puede*) (RT 2012b; Goodman 2015), "They do not represent us" (in Spanish: *No nos representan*), "More education, less police" (in Spanish: *Más educación, menos policía*), "Do not look at us, join us" (in Spanish: *No nos mires, únete*), and "Resignation" (in Spanish: *Dimisión*) (La Nación 2012). Their argumentation introduced the aim to be achieved, the ways to perform them, and the expected effects. Mental political violence was dignity-driven because movement participants eagerly evoked this umbrella moral value to justify and explain their aggressive behavior.

Laying the consequences of austerity policies at the political and economic elites' door was popular in Spain (Asara 2016; Font *et al.* 2015). The blame was fixed mainly on the members of Spanish parliament and bankers, who, on the other hand, rationalized their politics. Then, the involvement in the 15-M Movement against the government and EU policy as well as broadly understood political elites was justified by their harmful acts: "We are here because we continue to be angry over the austerity policies which an economic elite is imposing on us" (RT 2012b). Graffiti saying "Guilty!" (in Spanish: *Culpable!*), and "Chorizo" on the statehouses and buildings owned by political and economic elites mirrored the major arguments (Tremlett and Roberts 2012). Furthermore, a poster used in the protests read "Not enough bread for so much chorizo" (chorizo is a type of traditional Spanish sausage made with pork) (in Spanish: *No hay pan para tanto chorizo*). It was the reference to political corruption because "chorizo" is the term employed to call somebody a "thief" (Palabraspormadrid 2013). Corrupt practices and austerity measures were tightly connected as the sources of social hardship in the argumentation.

In Spain, the violent measures used over anti-austerity events indicated the occurrence of the blend of soft and hard power approaches (Figure 2.3: B″). On the continuum set by these extreme values, the forms were closer to the latter due to the use of excessive mental, and active and passive physical political violence over protests. This value of the feature of a culture of political violence also entered Finland, Belgium, Germany, Portugal, Slovenia, Italy, Greece, and Ireland.

Just as in Greece, in Spain, an aggressively militant culture of political violence appeared. Typical of this pattern are: (i) both representatives of a state apparatus and movement participants use political violence; (ii) a very low extent of mutual legitimation to use political violence; (iii) the modes of the legitimation of the use of political violence are authorization, rationalization, and moralization; (iv) the intensity of physical political violence is on the continuum between the maximally intense active type and the threat, very close to the former; and (v) the mental, and active and passive physical forms of political violence create the blend of soft and hard power approaches.

Ireland: "Not Even Our Waters Run Free"

In Ireland, both representatives of the state apparatus and participants of the Irish heterogeneous anti-austerity movement deployed political violence. Political subjects made use of authorization, rationalization, and moralization to legitimate the employment of political violence, not unlike in the hector-led and the other militant patterns. Activists organized numerous protests against austerity measures, social politics, brutality of An Garda Síochána (commonly referred to as the Gardaí or "the guards"; An Garda Síochána means: the Guardian of the Peace, the Police Force of Ireland) (Anti Austerity Alliance 2017b; Duncan 2010), and to express the solidarity with and support for Greece and Spain (TVXS 2015b). As in Austria, Belgium, Finland, France, and the Netherlands, in Ireland, activists manifested the solidarity by displaying Greek and Spanish flags and banners with the slogans: "Ireland stands with Greece" and "Solidarity" (TVXS 2015b). The will of supporting the most suffering states was a kind of the moral evaluation (Desbos and Royal 2016) that legitimated taking advantage of political violence.

Worth underlining is that the extent of police officers' brutality was so high that it became the source of further angry protests (Shea 2015). The Guardian of the Peace went beyond the use of the threat and deployed coercive measures to restore the public order and to increase the level of safety and security. Law enforcement officers and politicians legitimated the use of physical force by the authorization by law. Movement participants, nonetheless, thoroughly denounced police officers' violent behavior and described them as unlawful. Officers acted, in the line of the opposite narration, in the scope of their rights and to carry out their fundamental duties (The Nationalist 2015). In Ireland, not unlike in Greece and Spain, the extent of cohesion between political subjects' actual usage of political violence and agreement on its use was very low (Figure 2.1: E). Active physical political violence was misused by stakeholders of the anti-austerity movement. Political subjects did not accept how others fulfilled their rights and duties within political roles. They refused to acknowledge each other as not contravening the boundaries of the law.

Authorization was also the mode of legitimation of the use of political violence selected by activists. They alleged the right to freedom of expression and freedom of assembly on the "public highway" (GuestPost 2015; Shea 2015) when they were acting aggressively (Adl 2015; BBC 2015b). Protest participants abruptly broke police barricades, which contributed to fierce clashes with representatives of the state apparatus (Brennan 2014; Galway Bay FM 2012; Piggot 2015). Police officers reacted to those activities by using pepper spray (Daniels 2012), which enraged the crowd (AP 2013). As a result, protesters blocked the traffic, but police did not resort to physical force to disperse them (AP 2013). Rarely did the protesters throw at representatives of the state apparatus eggs and accidentally found objects (Tuite 2012). Political subjects often fought (Irish Examiner 2012). Some of the protesters were detained, arrested, and wounded (Brennan 2014; Preston and Silke 2014; RTÉ 2015; Tuite 2012).

Rationalization and moralization also legitimated the use of political violence (Dublin 15 Anti Austerity Alliance 2017; Anti-Austerity Anti-Corruption Ireland 2017). Protesters used a coffin draped in an Irish flag as a battering ram, and they chanted "They say cut back, we say fight back" (Irish Examiner 2012; Osiris 2012). They torched flammable materials with the Irish political party symbols to express animosity towards the ruling class (Irish Examiner 2012). According to a popular narrative, "I'm here because I want to fight for my future" and "I want to be able to go to college, but Eamon Gilmore won't let that happen" (Eamon Gilmore served as Tánaiste and Minister for Foreign Affairs and Trade from 2011 to 2014 and the Leader of the Labour Party from 2007 to 2014) (Irish Examiner 2012). Children held banners "My generation has no future in Ireland thanks to Fine Gael, Labour & austerity" (Murphy 2012). They moralized the use of political violence and employed it by using the abstraction reference. According to this discursive creation, they fought for their future and rights to education and self-realization. Simultaneously, they declared against representatives of the state apparatus who sought to deprive them of the values by implementing austerity measures.

Protesters stopped traffic and blocked access to tourist attractions, sang protest songs (Brennan 2014), carried Irish flags, and displayed banners with slogans (Bardon 2015; Dublin Bay North Anti Austerity Alliance 2017; Irish Examiner 2012) such as "Not even our waters run free" (Daniels 2012), "No way, we won't pay" (Costello 2014), "Enda [Enda Kenny – the politician blamed for the results of austerity measures implementation]: stop punishing the poor for the sins of the rich," "Reject fear – austerity stops here – fight the property tax," "Fight for every job, resist every cut, people before profit," "Fight austerity, boycott property tax," "Austerity out, Labour out now, shame on ICTU [The Irish Congress of Trade Unions]" (Murphy 2012), "Jail the banksters" (Pattison 2015), and "Don't register [to the party politics which supported and imposed austerity measures], don't pay" (Humphries 2014). They carried the placards presenting pictures of the Labour Party founder and the 1916 martyr James Connolly and the message: "Shame on you, Labour working-class traitors" (De Breadun 2012). The underscored values that contributed to the moralization mode were the people and rights to work and water. Rationalization drew on the opposition to the consequences of austerity measures. Activists claimed they employed political violence to make politicians both stop following the destructive policy and punish political and economic elites rather than citizens. They also strived to restore the social conditions from before the implementation of austerity measures.

Hence, the instrumental rationalization of the use of political violence was the combination of goal-, effect-, and means-oriented argumentation against austerity. Not unlike the other states, in Ireland, the hard core of moralization inspired rationalization by fueling the strong-worded argumentation. The modes of the legitimation were tightly interlinked. There, just as in the other cases, the arguments applied to account for and justify the use of political violence were simultaneously its vehicle.

The intensity of physical political violence in Ireland was between the maximally intense active type and the threat, very close to the former (Figure 2.2: A′~). It achieved a very high value. Not unlike in Belgium, Greece, Spain, Germany, Portugal, Slovenia, and Italy, in Ireland, movement participants and representatives of the state apparatus employed political violence nearly maximally intensively.

In Ireland, not unlike Finland, Belgium, Germany, Portugal, Slovenia, Italy, Greece, and Spain, the blend of mental, and active and passive physical political violence stemmed. Then, the forms of political violence were on the continuum between hard and soft power approaches, close to the former (Figure 2.3: B″).

Like Greece and Spain, in Ireland, an aggressively-militant culture of political violence made an appearance. The following features are characteristic of this pattern: (i) both representatives of a state apparatus and movement participants use political violence; (ii) a very low extent of mutual legitimation to use political violence; (iii) the modes of the legitimation of the use of political violence are authorization, rationalization, and moralization; (iv) the intensity of physical political violence is on the continuum between the maximally intense active type and the threat, very close to the former; and (v) the mental, and active and passive physical forms of political violence constitute the blend of soft and hard power approaches.

Typologies of Cultures of Political Violence in Times of Austerity

The application of the conceptual framework of a culture of political violence to the empirical study allows us to verify the hypothesis. When the post-2008 anti-austerity movements acted, the patterns of a culture of political violence were undifferentiated in relation to a type of the political subject that employed violence to achieve political goals over the duration of the movements. Nonetheless, they richly differed in the values of its remaining four essential features: mutual legitimation to the use, modes of the legitimation of the use, the intensity of physical political violence, and forms of political violence.

Similarities and differences between the patterns are apparent when we delve analytically into the details of the hypothesis. Once again, the cultures of political violence were the same in terms of the stakeholders of anti-austerity movements that made use of political violence. In Austria, Belgium, Estonia, Finland, France, Greece, Spain, the Netherlands, Ireland, Germany, Portugal, Slovakia, Slovenia, and Italy, both movement participants and representatives of the state apparatuses committed political violence. The activities of the former drew the latter in contention. Nowhere was one of them the only perpetrator.

The cases were widely varied in the mutual legitimation to use political violence. The highest extent occurred in Estonia and Slovakia where the confrontation of strength did not take place with political subjects' consent. Participants of the Estonian movement avoided organizing protests. The Estonian and Slovak movements did not engage representatives of the state apparatuses in their activities directly. Instead, they held the discourses about austerity that were co-produced by their state opponents. The action and non-action of political subjects gained complete mutual legitimation. In turn, in Austria and the Netherlands, the mutual legitimation took on a value very close to the maximum extent. Admittedly, it was very high but lower than in Estonia and Slovakia. Movement participants organized events in a public sphere and used mental political violence to express their opinion in a commonly accepted manner. They neither used nor provoked the use of active physical political violence. Representatives of the state apparatuses participated in proceedings, but the protest policing benefited from the threat in the way accepted by the movements. The actions of activists were considered to be the potentially and presumptively dangerous threat against public order, safety, and security. As such, violent behavior was not fully approved. The cohesion did not take on the greatest value in those cases. A high extent of mutual legitimation in Finland and France located them close to the largest level. The incidents of the use of physical political violence occurred, and they were not legitimated by their participants. Political subjects approved others in the political structures and agreed upon the modes and purposes of applying political violence. A disagreement appeared over eminently violent incidents that, however, were not very frequent. Therefore, the discrepancy between political subjects' actual usage of political violence and agreement on the use was moderate. A low extent characterized Belgium, Germany, Portugal, Slovenia, and Italy. The use of excessive physical political violence was unaccepted by clash participants. Political subjects recognized others as non-legitimated to act in the way and for the purposes they did. Hence, the discrepancy between political subjects' actual deployment of political violence and agreement on the use took on a high value. A very low extent was in Greece, Spain, and Ireland. Spain was the only state where representatives of the state apparatus were accused in social media of initiating violent clashes in plain-clothes. In Greece, the police officers arrested movement participants before violent clashes and justified it by the need for preventing violent confrontations, which met with public outcry. Both in Greece and Spain, active physical political violence was misused by stakeholders of the anti-austerity movements. The violent actions of Irish police officers incentivized further angry protests. In Spanish, Greek, and Irish contexts, a full discrepancy occurred between political subjects' real employment of political violence and agreement on its use. Opponents lacked mutual acceptance on fulfilling their roles in the political structures in using political violence. In no state, nonetheless, did clashes transform into a militant conflict, and thus nowhere a complete absence of the cohesion occurred.

All the modes of the legitimation of the use of political violence made an appearance in the analyzed states, but they were slightly differently configured. The set of authorization, rationalization, and moralization occurred in most states: Austria, Belgium, Finland, France, Greece, Spain, the Netherlands, Ireland, Germany, Portugal, Slovenia, and Italy. The configuration of authorization and rationalization entered Slovakia. In Estonia, authorization, rationalization, and mythopoesis were in usage. It means that in each case, stakeholders of the anti-austerity movements applied authorization by law to explain and justify turning to political violence to achieve political goals. Not less popular was the goal-, means-, and effect-oriented instrumental rationalization that paved ways for the argument-based political violence. Political subjects also leaped at the moralization by moral evaluation and abstraction. The moralization was solidarity-, political-, and social-values-driven. Just in the Estonian case, the movement made use of mythopoesis to spin the cautionary tale supporting the employment of political violence. The arguments throw light on the relative uniformity of the cases in the modes of the legitimation of resorting to political violence.

The diversity of the cultures of political violence is mirrored by the variety of the values of the intensity of physical political violence that occurred in the European states. On the continuum, the first value of that feature located between the threat and the abandonment in the cases of Austria, France, and the Netherlands where the intensity was low. Then, between the maximally intense active physical political violence and the threat, close to the former was Finland. An extent of intensity was moderately high in the Finnish case. In Belgium, Greece,

Spain, Ireland, Germany, Portugal, Slovenia, and Italy, an extent of intensity located between the maximally intense active physical political violence and the threat, very close to the former. There, the use of the active force was much more frequent than the passive one, and the latter often transformed into the former. The abandonment of using physical political violence entered both Estonia and Slovakia.

The analysis neatly divides the cultures of political violence into three types according to the criterion of the forms of political violence. The first type characterizes Estonia and Slovakia. There, mental political violence originated, creating the purely soft power approach. Austria, France, and the Netherlands were on the continuum in a larger distance to the hard point than to the soft one. Active physical political violence did not originate there. Thereby, the second type draws on the soft power approach which was the blend of mental and passive physical political violence. The last value of the feature was the most frequent and consisted in intertwining soft and hard power approaches. It entered Finland, Belgium, Germany, Portugal, Slovenia, Italy, Greece, Spain, and Ireland which combined mental, and active and passive physical political violence. The cases were on the continuum between the extreme types close to a hard power approach.

The research results shed considerable light on the similarities and differences between the cultures of political violence which originated in the 14 member states of the Eurozone. The added value of the hypothesis verification is the construction of the five already introduced typologies. Each one has been constructed according to one and homogeneous criterion. They form, however, the basis for a more informative typology of a higher exploratory value. When we apply those five criteria concomitantly and simultaneously to categorize the patterns of a culture of political violence, we identify seven types of a culture of political violence among the Eurozone cases.

The first two types are of a placid nature. Whereas the placidly observing culture of political violence emerged in Estonia, the placidly rationalizing pattern entered Slovakia. Political subjects won hearts and minds by using an unmixed soft power approach. The types slightly differed but just in the modes of the legitimation of the use of political violence. In the Estonian pattern, mythopoesis occurred apart from the Slovak set of authorization and rationalization. The third type, the hector-consenting culture of political violence, entered Austria and the Netherlands. France was the location of the fourth type, the hector-acknowledgment pattern. Those two patterns were hector-led but approached hectoring differently. They slightly varied in an extent of cohesion between political subjects' actual usage of political violence and agreement on its use. Whereas the extent was very high in Austria and the Netherlands where the hector-consenting culture of political violence made an appearance, in France, where the hector-acknowledgment pattern occurred, it was just high. The indulgingly militant pattern, the fifth type, occurred just in Finland. In turn, the multitudinously represented obstreperously militant was the sixth pattern which occurred in Belgium, Germany, Portugal, Slovenia, and Italy. The last pattern, the aggressively militant type showed up in Greece, Spain, and Ireland. It was the most violent culture from among those that entered the Eurozone.

The similarities and dissimilarities between the patterns have already been discussed. Here, however, it should be highlighted that the most significant difference between the last three types of cultures of political violence on the one hand, and the placid and the hector-led on the other, were forms of political violence. The placid patterns were based on the purely soft power approach in the form of mental political violence. Then, the hector-led patterns drew on the soft power approach in the shape of the blend of mental and passive physical political violence. The militant types took advantage of the blend of soft and hard power approaches. There, political subjects made use of the combination of mental, and active and passive physical political violence. Nonetheless, the militant patterns varied in an extent of cohesion between political subjects' actual usage of political violence and agreement on the use. It was high in Finland (indulgingly militant), low in Belgium, Germany, Portugal, Slovenia, and Italy (obstreperously militant), and very low in Greece, Spain, and Ireland (aggressively militant).

The simultaneous and joint application of the five criteria allowed us to formulate the seven-type typology which consists of the seven patterns of a culture of political violence: placidly observing, placidly rationalizing, hector consenting, hector acknowledgment, indulgingly militant, obstreperously militant, and aggressively militant. It reveals the diversity of the cultures of political violence among stakeholders of the anti-austerity movements in the member states of the Eurozone. Not less importantly, it introduces what values the variable of the post-2008 patterns of a culture of political violence take on for the 14 cases.

In the next chapters, the research puts into work the variable in different meanings on account of its roles in an explaining process. Chapter 3 makes use of a culture of political violence as a dependent variable because it tests the explanatory frameworks that consider it to be a thing to be explained. Independent variables are theory-driven parts of the explanatory frameworks and thought to have explanatory power to account for why the different patterns of a culture of political violence entered the member states of the Eurozone in the times of austerity. Then, Chapter 4 utilizes a culture of political violence as an independent variable. Thus, it tests the explanatory frameworks that present it as an explaining indicator. Dependent variables derive from the theories and are claimed to explain the results of the variety of the post-2008 cultures of political violence.

Bibliography

20 Minutes avec AFP. 2014. "Manifestation monstre contre l'austérité et le gouvernement de droite en Belgique." *20 Minutes*, November 6. Accessed February 1, 2017. www.20minutes.fr/monde/1476651-20141106-manifestation-monstre-contre-austerite-gouvernement-droite-belgique.

Accornero, Guya and Pedro Ramos Pinto. 2015. "Patterns of Protest in Portugal Show the Relationship between the 'Old' Politics of Labour and 'New' Anti-Austerity Movements."

Democratic Audit UK, June 5. Accessed February 9, 2017. www.democraticaudit.com/2015/06/05/patterns-of-protest-in-portugal-show-the-relationship-between-the-old-politics-of-labour-and-new-anti-austerity-movements/.

Ad'ha Aljunied, Syed Mohammed. 2011. "Countering Terrorism in Maritime Southeast Asia: Soft and Hard Power Approaches." *Journal of Asian and African Studies* 47(6): 652–665.

Adl, Carol. 2015. "Arrests of Irish Anti-Austerity Activists Sparks London Solidarity Protest." *YourNewsWire*, February 11. Accessed February 7, 2017. http://yournews-wire.com/arrests-of-irish-anti-austerity-activists-sparks-london-solidarity-protest/.

AFP. 2012a. "Thousands of Italian Students Hold Anti-Austerity Protests." *Asia One*, October 5. Accessed February 12, 2017. http://news.asiaone.com/News/Latest+News/World/Story/A1Story20121005-375908.html.

AFP. 2012b. "Wave of Anti-Austerity Anger Breaks." *Jamaica Observer*, November 14. Accessed February 7, 2017. www.jamaicaobserver.com/news/Wave-of-anti-austerity-anger-breaks_12987649.

AFP. 2013a. "Austerity Opera to Be Performed in Estonian Capital." *Telegraph*, January 16. Accessed February 19, 2017. www.telegraph.co.uk/finance/financialcrisis/9806495/Austerity-opera-to-be-performed-in-Estonian-capital.html.

AFP. 2013b. "Clashes Break Out at Italy Anti-Austerity Protests." *The Local*, December 15. Accessed February 12, 2017. www.thelocal.it/20131215/clashes-break-out-at-italy-anti-austerity-protests.

AFP. 2014. "Manifestation anti-austérité massive à Bruxelles." *Le Point International*, April 4. Accessed February 1, 2017. www.lepoint.fr/monde/manifestation-anti-austerite-massive-a-bruxelles-04-04-2014-1809141_24.php.

AFP. 2015. "Après les violences à Air France, les syndicats face à un procès en illégitimité." *RTBF*, October 12. Accessed February 4, 2017. www.rtbf.be/info/economie/detail_apres-les-violences-a-air-france-les-syndicats-face-a-un-proces-en-illegitimite?id=9106658.

AFP/A.P. 2015. "Enorme manifestation anti-austérité à Bruxelles." *Le Quotidien*, October 7. Accessed February 1, 2017. www.lequotidien.lu/international/enorme-manifestation-anti-austerite-a-bruxelles/.

AFP/The Local. 2015. "Frankfurt Police Prepare for Anti-Austerity Demo." *The Local*, March 17. Accessed February 9, 2017. www.thelocal.de/20150317/police-prepare-for-ecb-demo.

Agencies. 2014. "Anti-Austerity Protest in Italy Turns Violent." *Al Jazeera*, April 13. Accessed February 12, 2017. www.aljazeera.com/news/europe/2014/04/anti-austerity-protest-italy-turns-violent-20144122357869885.html.

Agencies. 2015. "Thousands Rally in Spanish Anti-Austerity Protest." *Al Jazeera*, March 21. Accessed February 5, 2017. www.aljazeera.com/news/2015/03/thousands-rally-spanish-anti-austerity-protest-150321200719255.html.

Al Jazeera and Agencies. 2012. "Anti-Austerity Rallies Hit Spain and Portugal." *Al Jazeera*, September 30. Accessed February 10, 2017. www.aljazeera.com/news/europe/2012/09/2012929231237412237.html.

Alimi, Eitan Y., Chares Demetriou, and Lorenzo Bosi. 2015. *The Dynamics of Radicalization. A Relational and Comparative Perspective*. New York: Oxford University Press.

Alter Summit. 2015. "Week of Action 'With the Greeks against Austerity': 20–26th of June." *Alter Summit*, No date. Accessed February 18, 2017. www.altersummit.eu/accueil/article/week-of-action-with-the-greeks?lang=en.

Amenta, Edwin. 2016. "Neoliberal Globalization, Democratization, and Movement Responses." *Mobilization: An International Quarterly* 21(4): 389–391.

Ames, Paul. 2012. "Estonia Uses the Euro, and the Economy is Booming." *CNBC*, June 5. Accessed February 19, 2017. www.cnbc.com/id/47691090.

Amnesty International – Greek Section. 2011. "Ριψη δακρυγονων κατα τη συγκρουση της ελληνικης αστυνομιας με τους διαδηλωτες στην αθηνα." Amnesty International – Greek Section, June 29. Accessed February 6, 2017. www.amnesty.gr/news/articles/article/8435/ripsi-dakrygonon-kata-ti-sygkroysi-tis-ellinikis-astynomias-me-toys.

Amundsen, Michael. 2013. "Estonian Austerity, Paul Krugman, and Twitter: All the Elements of an Opera?" *The Christian Science Monitor*, March 13. Accessed February 19, 2017. www.csmonitor.com/World/Europe/2013/0313/Estonian-austerity-Paul-Krugman-and-Twitter-All-the-elements-of-an-opera.

Andretta, Massimiliano. 2017. "Neoliberalism and Its Discontents in Italy: Protests Without Movement?" In *Late Neoliberalism and its Discontents in the Economic Crisis: Comparing Social Movements in the European Periphery*, edited by Donatella della Porta, Massimiliano Andretta, Tiago Fernandes, Francis O'Connor, Eduardo Romanos, and Markos Vogiatzoglou, 201–242. Cham: Palgrave Macmillan.

Anfara, Jr., Vincent A. and Norma T. Mertz. 2015. "Setting the Stage." In *Theoretical Frameworks in Qualitative Research*, edited by Vincent A. Anfara, Jr. and Norma T. Mertz, 1–20. 2nd edition. London: Sage.

Anti Austerity Alliance Galway. 2017. "Anti Austerity Alliance Galway." *Facebook*, No date. Accessed February 17, 2017. www.facebook.com/AntiAusterityAllianceGalway/?fref=ts.

Anti Austerity Alliance. 2017a. "Anti Austerity Alliance." *Facebook*, No date. Accessed February 17, 2017. www.facebook.com/AntiAusterityAlliance/?fref=ts.

Anti Austerity Alliance. 2017b. "What We Stand For." *The Official Website of Anti Austerity Alliance*, No date. Accessed February 17, 2017. http://antiausterityalliance.ie/category/what-we-stand-for/.

Anti-Austerity Anti-Corruption Ireland. 2017. "Anti-Austerity Anti-Corruption Ireland." *Facebook*, No date. Accessed February 17, 2017. www.facebook.com/Anti-Austerity-Anti-Corruption-Ireland-786089538128788/?ref=br_rs.

AP. 2011. "Athens, Greece – In Photos: Greek Anti-Austerity Protesters Clash with Police." *Vos Iz Neias?*, June 15. Accessed February 4, 2017. www.vosizneias.com/85532/2011/06/15/athens-greece-in-photos-greek-anti-austerity-protesters-clash-with-police/.

AP. 2012. "Cortei e proteste, Europa in piazza Guerriglia e feriti a Roma e Torino Cancellieri: bene l'operato dalla Polizia." *La Stampa Italia*, November 15. Accessed February 12, 2017. www.lastampa.it/2012/11/14/italia/cronache/eurostrike-cortei-in-citta-JniHxYLuO6EWHhqY4i66FK/pagina.html.

AP. 2013. "Irish Anti-Austerity Protesters Clash with Police." *USA Today*, September 18. Accessed February 7, 2017. www.usatoday.com/story/news/world/2013/09/18/irish-austerity-protesters-police/2833511/.

AP. 2015. "German Activists Riot at Austerity Protest in Frankfurt." *Al Jazeera*, March 19. Accessed February 7, 2017. www.aljazeera.com/news/2015/03/german-activists-riot-austerity-protest-frankfurt-150318073001242.html.

APA Azeri Press Agency. 2012. "Thousands of Slovenians Hold Anti-Austerity Protest in Ljubljana." *APA*, December 22. Accessed February 18, 2017. http://en.apa.az/print/184966.

Arbutina, Zoran and glb. 2012. "Slovenia – Back to Reality, Forth to Austerity." *DW*, December 17. Accessed February 11, 2017. www.dw.com/en/slovenia-back-to-reality-forth-to-austerity/a-16459181.

Arens, Marianne. 2014. "Aumentano le proteste contro le politiche di austerità." *World Socialist Website*, November 22. Accessed February 13, 2017. www.wsws.org/it/2014/nov2014/ital-n22.shtml.

Asara, Viviana. 2016. "The Indignados as a Socio-Environmental Movement: Framing the Crisis and Democracy." *Environmental Policy and Governance* 26(6): 527–542.

Associated Press. 2015. "Police Cars Torched at Anti-Austerity Protest in Germany." *Dailymail*, March 18. Accessed February 8, 2017. www.dailymail.co.uk/wires/ap/article-3000180/Police-cars-set-afire-austerity-protest-Germany.html.

Avvenire. 2012. "Manifestazioni in Tutta Europa. Sciopero anti-austerity Scontri a Milano 16 feriti a Roma." November 14. Accessed February 13, 2017. www.avvenire.it/economia/pagine/sciopero-europeo-contro-austerity.

Bacchi, Umberto. 2012a. "Anti-Austerity Protests: Italian Police Club Unarmed Demonstrator." *International Business Times*, November 14. Accessed February 12, 2017. www.ibtimes.co.uk/italy-police-club-protester-hit-rome-404948.

Bacchi, Umberto. 2012b. "Anti-Austerity Protests in Europe: 'Guerrila Warfare' in Rome, 80 Arrests in Spain." *International Business Times*, November 14. Accessed February 12, 2017. www.ibtimes.co.uk/spain-italy-police-protest-clash-photos-404919.

Balogová, Beata. 2010. "Unions Rally against Austerity Package." *The Slovak Spectator*, October 18. Accessed February 18, 2017. https://spectator.sme.sk/c/20037746/unions-rally-against-austerity-package.html.

Bandow, Doug. 2013. "The Triumph of Good Economics: 'Austere' Baltic States Outgrow Their European Neighbors." *Forbes*, April 15. Accessed February 19, 2017. www.forbes.com/sites/dougbandow/2013/04/15/the-triumph-of-good-economics-austere-baltic-states-outgrow-their-european-neighbors/#56afa11c7ac5.

Banjo. 2015. "Anti-Austerity Protest in Finland." *Banjo*, 22 August. Accessed February 2, 2017. http://ban.jo/News/Europe/20150822/Anti-Austerity-Protest-In-Finland-Helsinki/.

Bardon, Sarah. 2015. "Anti-Austerity Protesters March in Dublin City Centre." *The Irish Times*, December 8, Accessed February 7, 2017. www.irishtimes.com/news/politics/anti-austerity-protesters-march-in-dublin-city-centre-1.2458772.

Baumgarten, Britta and Mariana Carmo Duarte. 2015. "Portugal: The Crisis and New Actors against Austerity." *Green European Journal*, No date. Accessed February 9, 2017. www.greeneuropeanjournal.eu/portugal-the-crisis-and-new-actors-against-austerity/.

Baumgarten, Britta. 2013. "Anti-austerity Protests in Portugal." *CritCom*, October 2. Accessed February 9, 2017. http://councilforeuropeanstudies.org/critcom/anti-austerity-protests-in-portugal/.

BBC. 2010a. "European Cities Hit by Anti-Austerity Protests." *BBC*, September 29. Accessed February 3, 2017. www.bbc.com/news/world-europe-11432579.

BBC. 2010b. "Italian Student Protesters Occupy Leaning Tower of Pisa." *BBC*, November 25. Accessed February 12, 2017. www.bbc.com/news/world-europe-11841199.

BBC. 2012a. "Spain and Portugal See Big Anti-Austerity Rallies." *BBC*, September 15. Accessed February 10, 2017. www.bbc.com/news/world-europe-19611375.

BBC. 2012b. "Violent Clashes as Austerity Protests Grip EU Cities." *BBC*, November 15. Accessed February 3, 2017. www.bbc.com/news/world-europe-20320993.

BBC. 2014a. "Disturbios en protestas contra austeridad en España." *BBC*, March 22. Accessed February 22, 2017. www.bbc.com/mundo/ultimas_noticias/2014/03/140322_ultnot_espana_protestas_austeridad_az.

BBC. 2014b. "Spain Austerity: Huge Madrid Protest Turns Violent." *BBC*, March 23. Accessed February 5, 2017. www.bbc.com/news/world-europe-26703528.

BBC. 2015a. "Germany Riot Targets New ECB Headquarters in Frankfurt." *BBC*, March 18. Accessed February 9, 2017. www.bbc.com/news/world-europe-31938592.

BBC. 2015b. "Thousands Attend Anti-Austerity Rallies across UK." *BBC*, June 20. Accessed February 8, 2017. www.bbc.com/news/uk-politics-33210014.

Beas, Diego. 2011. "How Spain's 15-M Movement Is Redefining Politics." *Guardian*, October 15. Accessed February 7, 2017. www.theguardian.com/commentisfree/2011/oct/15/spain-15-m-movement-activism.

Becatoros, Elena and Derek Gatopoulos. 2015. "Greece Austerity Bill Triggers Riots, Political Revolt." *The Huffington Post*, July 15. Accessed February 4, 2017. www.huffingtonpost.ca/2015/07/16/greece-seeks-relief-from-_n_7807136.html.

Bernal, Victoria. 2017. "Diaspora and the Afterlife of Violence: Eritrean National Narratives and What Goes Without Saying." *American Anthropologist* 119(1): 23–34.

Betz, Frederick. 2016. *Stability in International Finance: Applications of Price Disequilibrium Theory*. London: Springer.

Black, Jeff, Richard Weiss, and Alessandro Speciale. 2015. "Violent Anti-Austerity Protests Mar Opening of New ECB Headquarters in Germany." *Financial Post*, March 18. Accessed February 9, 2017. http://business.financialpost.com/news/economy/violent-anti-austerity-protests-mar-opening-of-new-ecb-headquarters-in-germany.

Bloomberg/Hahn. 2012. "Die Anti-Spar-Bewegung gewinnt an Dynamik." *Trend*, May 23. Accessed June 8, 2017. www.trend.at/news/die-anti-spar-bewegung-dynamik-328641.

Borooah, Vani K. 2014. *Europe in an Age of Austerity*. New York: Palgrave Macmillan.

Bosi, Lorenzo, Chares Demetriou, and Stefan Malthaner. 2014. "A Contentious Politics Approach to the Explanation of Radicalization." In *Dynamics of Political Violence: A Process-Oriented Perspective on Radicalization and the Escalation of Political Conflict*, edited by Lorenzo Bosi, Chares Demetriou, and Stefan Malthaner, 1–23. Farnham and Burlington, VT: Ashgate.

Bosi, Lorenzo, Marco Giugni, and Katrin Uba. 2016. "The Consequences of Social Movements: Taking Stock and Looking Forward." In *The Consequences of Social Movements*, edited by Lorenzo Bosi, Marco Giugni, and Katrin Uba, 1–37. Cambridge: Cambridge University Press.

Bourdieu, Pierre. 1991. *Language and Symbolic Power*. Cambridge: Polity Press.

Boyd, John. 2010a. "Breweries: Government Tax Hike Will Bury Us." *The Daily.SK*, October 13. Accessed March 4, 2017. www.thedaily.sk/brewers-say-government-hike-in-excise-tax-will-bury-them/.

Boyd, John. 2010b. "Metal Unions Spark Up Protests." *The Daily.SK*, September 23. Accessed March 4, 2017. www.thedaily.sk/metal-unions-spark-up-protests/.

Boyd, John. 2010c. "Trade Unions Storm Out of Labour Ministry Talks." *The Daily.SK*, December 16. Accessed March 4, 2017. www.thedaily.sk/trade-unions-storm-out-of-labour-ministry-talks/.

Brennan, Colin. 2014. "Watch Anti-Water Charge Protesters and Gardai Clash after March Brings Dublin to a Standstill." *Irish Mirror*, December 11. Accessed February 7, 2017. www.irishmirror.ie/news/irish-news/watch-anti-water-charge-protesters-gardai-4787391.

Bruter, Michael. 2013. "Measuring the Immeasurable? Capturing Citizens' European Identity." In *Political Science Research: Methods in Action*, edited by Michael Bruter and Martin Lodge, 25–46. New York: Palgrave Macmillan.

Campos, Pedro García and Medir Plandolit. 2015. "Wave of Anti-Austerity Protests Begin in Spain with Thousands Marching on Streets of Madrid." *Vice News*, March 21. Accessed February 5, 2017. https://news.vice.com/article/wave-of-anti-austerity-protests-begin-in-spain-with-thousands-marching-on-streets-of-madrid.

Capon, Felicity. 2015. "350 Arrested as Frankfurt Anti-Austerity Protests Turn Violent." *Newsweek*, March 18. Accessed February 9, 2017. http://europe.newsweek.com/350-arrested-frankfurt-anti-austerity-protests-turn-violent-314794?rm=eu.

CBC News. 2012. "Anti-Austerity Slovenia Protesters Clash with Police: Has Worst Recession of 17 Eurozone Countries." *CBC News*, December 1. Accessed February 11, 2017. www.cbc.ca/news/world/anti-austerity-slovenia-protesters-clash-with-police-1.1298756.

CBC News. 2013. "Italy Anti-Austerity Protests Draw Thousands to Rome: Transit Workers Stage Nationwide Strike." *CBC News*, October 19. Accessed February 12, 2017. www.cbc.ca/news/world/italy-anti-austerity-protests-draw-thousands-to-rome-1.2126917.

CBC News. 2015. "Frankfurt Police Confront Anti-Austerity Protesters: 350 People Detained as Officers Pursued What They Said Was a Minority of Violence-Minded Activists." *CBC News*, March 18. Accessed February 9, 2017. www.cbc.ca/news/world/frankfurt-police-confront-anti-austerity-protesters-1.2999940.

CBS News. 2015. "Anti-Austerity Protests Turn Violent in Germany." *CBS News*, March 18. Accessed February 9, 2017. www.cbsnews.com/news/germany-protests-mar-opening-european-central-bank-headquarters-frankfurt/.

Chabanet, Didier and Arnaud Lacher. 2016. "The Occupy Movement in France: Why Protests Have Not Taken Off." In *Street Politics in the Age of Austerity: From the Indignados to Occupy*, edited by Marcos Ancelovici, Pascale Dufour, and Héloïse Nez, 279–294. Amsterdam: Amsterdam University Press.

Chiariello, Biagio. 2012. "#14n, l'Europa scende in piazza contro l'austerity: scene di guerriglia a Roma." *Fanpage.it*, November 14. Accessed February 13, 2017. www.fanpage.it/14n-l-europa-scende-in-piazza-contro-l-austerity-in-italia-protesta-anche-la-scuola-diretta/.

Cilluffo, Selene. 2014. "Manifestazione Roma 12 aprile: movimenti in piazza, il problema è a sinistra." *Cronaca*, April 12. Accessed February 13, 2017. www.today.it/cronaca/manifestazione-roma-12-aprile-2014.html.

CNN Wire Staff. 2012. "Protesters, Police Clash in Madrid." *CNN*, September 26. Accessed February 6, 2017. http://edition.cnn.com/2012/09/25/world/europe/spain-protests/.

Connolly, Kate and Angelique Chrisafis. 2012. "Anti-Austerity Movements Gaining Momentum across Europe." *Guardian*, April 27. Accessed February 7, 2017. www.theguardian.com/world/2012/apr/27/anti-austerity-movements-europe.

Cooper, Victoria. 2016. "Austerity, Harm and Victimisation." In *A Companion to Crime, Harm and Victimization*, edited by Karen Corteen, Sharon Morley, Paul Taylor, and Joanne Turner, 11–14. Croydon: Policy Press.

Copeland, Caroline. 2017a. Respond to query 2/17/2017: Garda Research Unit. Register: 17/02/2017 [in the author's records].

Copeland, Caroline. 2017b. Respond to query 3/3/2017: Garda Research Unit. Register: 3/03/2017 [in the author's records].

Costello, Norma. 2014. "Irish People Are Finally Taking to the Streets Against Austerity." *Vice*, November 4. Accessed February 8, 2017. www.vice.com/en_us/article/the-tide-is-turning-against-austerity-in-ireland-488.

Craddock, Emma. 2017. "Caring About and For the Cuts: A Case Study of the Gendered Dimension of Austerity and Anti-Austerity Activism." *Gender, Work & Organization* 24(1): 69–82.

Cullen, Pauline and Mary P. Murphy. 2017. "Gendered Mobilizations against Austerity in Ireland." *Gender, Work & Organization* 24(1): 83–97.

Cullura, Santo. 2013. "'Pitchfork' Protests Rattle Italian Government." *BBC*, December 13. Accessed February 12, 2017. www.bbc.com/news/world-europe-25368433.

Cutler, David. 2010. "Factbox: European Workers Stage Anti-Austerity Protests." *Reuters*, October 12. Accessed February 18, 2017. www.reuters.com/article/us-europe-protests-factbox-idUSTRE69B21220101012?mod=related&channelName=worldNews.

DAC. 2014. "Art. 18, scontri durante proteste contro governo e austerità." *Wall Street Italia*, December 12. Accessed February 13, 2017. www.wallstreetitalia.com/art-18-scontri-durante-proteste-contro-governo-e-austerit/.

Dailymail. 2015. "Frankfurt in Flames: Anti-Austerity Protesters Burn Police Cars and Clash with Riot Cops at Opening of European Central Bank's New HQ." *Dailymail*, March 18. Accessed February 9, 2017. www.dailymail.co.uk/news/article-3000398/Frankfurt-flames-Anti-austerity-protesters-burn-police-cars-clash-riot-cops-opening-European-Central-Bank-s-new-HQ.html.

Dakskobler, Luka. 2012. "Slovenia's Anti-Government Protests 2012." *Luka Dakskobler*, No date. Accessed February 11, 2017. www.lukadakskobler.com/stories/anti-government-protests/.

Daniels, Mick. 2012. "Demonstration at Labour Conference Galway." *YouTube*, April 14. Accessed February 7, 2017. www.youtube.com/watch?v=as3gpx8yUV4&feature=relmfu.

Davies, Lizzy. 2013. "Italy Hit by Wave of Pitchfork Protests as Austerity Unites Disparate Groups." *Guardian*, December 13. Accessed February 12, 2017. www.theguardian.com/world/2013/dec/13/italy-pitchfork-protests-austerity-unites-groups.

Davies, Thomas, Holly Eva Ryan, and Alejandro Milcíades Peña (eds.). 2016. *Protest, Social Movements and Global Democracy Since 2011: New Perspectives*. Bingley: Emerald Group.

Day, Paul and Tomás Cobos. 2012. "Spain Protests Labor Reforms as Hundreds of Thousands Take to Streets." *The World Post*, February 19. Accessed February 5, 2017. www.huffingtonpost.com/2012/02/19/spain-protests-labor-reforms_n_1287491.html.

De Breadun, Deaglan. 2012. "Protestors Disrupt Labour Conference." *The Irish Times*, April 14. Accessed February 7, 2017. www.irishtimes.com/news/protestors-disrupt-labour-conference-1.709384.

de Notícias, Diário. 2012. "Portugal: Major Anti-Austerity March in Lisbon." *Vox Europ*, February 13. Accessed February 10, 2017. www.voxeurop.eu/en/content/news-brief/1505451-major-anti-austerity-march-lisbon.

de Souza, Gilberto. 2012. "Protestos contra o capitalismo paralisam Lisboa, Atenas, Madri e Bruxelas." *Correio do Brasil*, February 29. Accessed February 10, 2017. www.correiodobrasil.com.br/protestos-contra-o-capitalismo-paralisam-lisboa-atenas-madri-e-bruxelas/392165/.

Defencenet.gr. 2015. "Διαδηλώσεις σε όλη την Ευρώπη υπέρ της Ελλάδας και κατά της λιτότητας – Μόνο στην Ελλάδα θα γίνει διαδήλωση υπέρ των απαιτήσεων των δανειστών!" *Pro News*, June 21. Accessed February 5, 2017. http://tiny.pl/g1cjp.

della Porta, Donatella. 2017. "Late Neoliberalism and Its Discontents: A Comparative Conclusion." In *Late Neoliberalism and its Discontents in the Economic Crisis: Comparing Social Movements in the European Periphery*, edited by Donatella della Porta, Massimiliano Andretta, Tiago Fernandes, Francis O'Connor, Eduardo Romanos, and Markos Vogiatzoglou, 261–296. Cham: Palgrave Macmillan.

della Porta, Donatella, Abby Peterson, and Herbert Reiter. 2006. "Policing Transnational Protest: An Introduction." In *The Policing of Transnational Protest*, edited by Donatella della Porta, Abby Peterson, and Herbert Reiter, 1–12. Hampshire and Burlington, VT: Ashgate.

Desbos, Clément and Frédéric Royal. 2016. "Camps as the Sole Symbolic Expression of Protest: The Difficulties of Occupy in Ireland." In *Street Politics in the Age of Austerity: From the Indignados to Occupy*, edited by Marcos Ancelovici, Pascale Dufour, and Héloïse Nez, 253–278. Amsterdam: Amsterdam University Press.

Dpa. 2016. "Sparmaßnahmen der Landesregierung Proteste gegen Einschnitte bei Landesbeamten." *Höchster Kreisblatt: Frankfurter Neue Presse*, January 22. Accessed

February 9, 2017. www.kreisblatt.de/rhein-main/Proteste-gegen-Einschnitte-bei-Landesbeamten;art1491,1227982.

Dr/jr, AFP, Reuters, AP. 2012. "Thousands Protest against Austerity in Slovenia." *DW*, November 18. Accessed February 18, 2017. www.dw.com/en/thousands-protest-against-austerity-in-slovenia/a-16387391.

Dreier, Christoph and Alex Lantier. 2015. "Massive Police Mobilization against Anti-Austerity Protest in Frankfurt, Germany." *World Socialist Website*, March 19. Accessed February 17, 2017. www.wsws.org/en/articles/2015/03/19/prot-m19.html.

Dublin 15 Anti Austerity Alliance. 2017. "Dublin 15 Anti Austerity Alliance." *Facebook*, No date. Accessed February 17, 2017. www.facebook.com/D15AntiAusterityAlliance/?ref=br_rs.

Dublin Bay North Anti Austerity Alliance. 2017. "Dublin Bay North Anti Austerity Alliance." *Facebook*, No date. Accessed February 17, 2017. www.facebook.com/DublinBayNorthAAA/?ref=br_rs.

Duncan, Pamela. 2010. "Up to 500 Students Protest over Garda Behaviour." *The Irish Times*, November 11. Accessed February 7, 2017. www.irishtimes.com/news/up-to-500-students-protest-over-garda-behaviour-1.675042.

Dunn, Bill. 2015. "Making Sense of Austerity: The Rationality in an Irrational System." *The Economic and Labour Relations Review* 25(3): 417–434.

Durić, Džemal and Danijel Žibret. 2017. Respond to query 630–36/2017/4: Slovenian National Police. Register: 630–36/2017/4(262–03) [in the author's records].

DW. 2016. "Police in Belgium Fire Water Cannon at Anti-Austerity Protesters." *DW*, May 24. Accessed February 4, 2017. www.dw.com/en/police-in-belgium-fire-water-cannon-at-anti-austerity-protesters/a-19280167.

Eckardt, Andy and Carlo Angerer. 2015. "Frankfurt Anti-Austerity Protesters Clash with Police, Torch Cop Cars." *NBC News*, March 18. Accessed February 9, 2017. www.nbcnews.com/news/world/german-blockupy-anti-austerity-ecb-protest-sees-cop-cars-torched-n325506.

Ei leikata. 2015. "Is this Finland." *Twitter*, December 17. Accessed February 2, 2017. https://twitter.com/eileikata.

Elgot, Jessica. 2012. "Europe Anti-Austerity Protests: Anger in Spain, Italy, Greece, Portugal Spreads to Brussels." *The Huffington Post*, November 14. Accessed February 12, 2017. www.huffingtonpost.co.uk/2012/11/14/europe-anti-austerity-protests_n_2129669.html.

Esquerda. 2012. "Centenas de pessoas em protesto nas ruas de Lisboa contra visita de Merkel." *Esquerda.net*, November 12. Accessed February 10, 2017. www.esquerda.net/artigo/centenas-de-pessoas-em-protesto-nas-ruas-de-lisboa-contra-visita-de-merkel/25423.

Euronews. 2012. "Slovenia the Latest to Feel Anti-Austerity Protests." *Euronews*, December 3. Accessed February 11, 2017. www.euronews.com/2012/12/03/slovenia-the-latest-to-feel-anti-austerity-protests.

Euronews. 2013. "Lisbon Littered with Anti-Austerity Protest." *Euronews*, March 27. Accessed February 10, 2017. www.euronews.com/2013/03/27/lisbon-littered-with-anti-austerity-protest.

Euronews. 2014. "Lisbon: Thousands Join Anti-Austerity March over 2014 Budget." *Euronews*, February 2. Accessed February 10, 2017. www.euronews.com/2014/02/02/lisbon-thousands-join-anti-austerity-march-over-2014-budget.

Euronews. 2015a. "Anti-Austerity, Anti-Macron Law: Thousands Protest on Streets of France." *Euronews*, April 9. Accessed February 3, 2017. www.euronews.com/2015/04/09/anti-austerity-anti-macron-law-thousands-protest-on-streets-of-france.

Euronews. 2015b. "Hooded Anarchists Clash with Greek Riot Police in Athens." *Euronews*, March 18. Accessed February 4, 2017. www.euronews.com/2015/03/18/hooded-anarchists-clash-with-greek-riot-police-in-athens.

Euronews. 2015c. "Thousands Rally in Support of Greece's Anti-Austerity Government Ahead of Bailout Talks in Brussels." *Euronews*, February 15. Accessed February 4, 2017. www.euronews.com/2015/02/15/thousands-rally-in-support-of-greece-s-anti-austerity-government-ahead-of-.

Europe says OXI. 2015. "#THISISACOUP-Protest: OXI Means OXI, NO to Financial Blackmail, Solidarity with the Greek People!" *Facebook*, July 15. Accessed February 18, 2017. www.facebook.com/events/968923229795124/.

Fernandes, Tiago. 2017. "Late Neoliberalism and Its Discontents: The Case of Portugal." In *Late Neoliberalism and its Discontents in the Economic Crisis: Comparing Social Movements in the European Periphery*, edited by Donatella della Porta, Massimiliano Andretta, Tiago Fernandes, Francis O'Connor, Eduardo Romanos, and Markos Vogiatzoglou, 169–200. Cham: Palgrave Macmillan.

Fidler, Matt. 2015. "Blockupy: Anti-ECB Protest in Frankfurt – in Pictures." *Guardian*, March 18. Accessed February 9, 2017. www.theguardian.com/world/gallery/2015/mar/18/blockupy-anti-ecb-protest-in-frankfurt-in-pictures.

Finland Times. 2014. "Police Use Pepper Spray to Quell Demonstration in Helsinki: Huge Protest against Govt's Austerity Policy." *Finland Times*, April 26. Accessed February 2, 2017. www.finlandtimes.fi/national/2014/04/26/6436/Huge-protest-against-govt%E2%80%99s-austerity-policy.

Finlay, Christopher J. 2017. "The Concept of Violence in International Theory: A Double-Intent Account." *International Theory* 9(1): 67–100.

Flesher Fominaya, Cristina. 2017. "European Anti-Austerity and Pro-Democracy Protests in the Wake of the Global Financial Crisis." *Social Movement Studies* 16(1): 1–20.

Font, Joan, Magdalena Wojcieszak, and Clemente J. Navarro. 2015. "Participation, Representation and Expertise: Citizen Preferences for Political Decision-Making Processes." *Political Studies* 63(S1): 153–172.

France TV Info. 2014. "Belgique: manifestation monstre à Bruxelles contre l'austérité." *Gauche Anticapitaliste*, November 9. Accessed February 1, 2017. www.gauche-anticapitaliste.ch/?p=862.

Freitas, Jorge. 2017. Respond to query no 271/JF: Polícia de Segurança Pública. Register: 3F05–2017 [in the author's records].

Fulton, Deirdre. 2016. "Anti-Austerity Leftist Announces Challenge to French President Hollande." *Popular Resistance*, August 22. Accessed February 4, 2017. https://popular-resistance.org/anti-austerity-leftist-announces-challenge-to-french-president-hollande/.

Galais, Carol and Jasmine Lorenzini. 2017. "Half a Loaf Is (Not) Better than None: How Austerity-Related Grievances and Emotions Triggered Protests in Spain." *Mobilization: An International Quarterly* 22(1): 77–95.

Galway Bay FM. 2012. "Protestors Break through Garda Lines at Labour Party Conference." *Galway News*, April 14. Accessed February 7, 2017. https://web.archive.org/web/20120415121406/www.galwaynews.ie:80/25311-protestors-break-through-garda-lines-labour-party-conference.

Gates, Sara. 2013. "Firefighters Clash with Riot Police in Spain during Austerity Protest." *The World Post*, May 29. Accessed February 5, 2017. www.huffingtonpost.com/2013/05/29/firefighters-riot-police-austerity-protest_n_3353851.html.

Gazzellanera. 2012. "Scioperi anti-austerity in Italia. Tensione e corteo a Roma. Manifestazioni in tutto il paese e nell'Europa del Sud." *Gazzellanera*, November 14.

Accessed February 13, 2017. http://gazzellanera.altervista.org/scioperi-anti-austerity-in-italia-tensione-e-corteo-a-roma-manifestazioni-in-tutto-il-paese-e-nelleuropa-del-sud/.

General Policing Division. 2017. Respond to query 2/13/2017: Hellenic Police Headquarters. Register: 13/02/2017 [in the author's records].

Georgiopoulos, George. 2011. "Greece Austerity Protests Grow." *The Huffington Post*, August 5. Accessed February 4, 2017. www.huffingtonpost.com/2011/06/05/greece-austerity-protests_n_871531.html.

Gerbaudo, Paolo. 2017. "The Indignant Citizen: Anti-Austerity Movements in Southern Europe and the Anti-Oligarchic Reclaiming of Citizenship." *Social Movement Studies* 16(1): 26–50.

Giunta, Carrie. 2015. "Do Protest Songs Work? Ten Inspiring Songs for the Fight against Austerity." *Stop the War Coalition*, June 27. Accessed February 9, 2017. www.stopwar.org.uk/news-comment/870-do-protest-songs-work-ten-inspiring-songs-for-the-fight-against-austerity.

Gleize, Pauline. 2015. "Mouvement de grève en France contre l'austérité économique." *Les Voix Du Monde*, April 9. Accessed February 4, 2017. www.rfi.fr/france/20150409-mouvement-greve-france-contre-austerite-economique.

Goodman, Al. 2015. "Tens of Thousands Fill Madrid Square for Anti-Austerity Rally." *CNN*, January 31. Accessed February 5, 2017. http://edition.cnn.com/2015/01/31/world/spain-madrid-podemos-rally/.

Gracner, Brigita. 2013. "Eastern Europe: Mass Protests Topple Bulgarian Government, Zombie Uprising in Slovenia." *Links*, March 15. Accessed February 11, 2017. http://links.org.au/node/3258.

Guardian. 2011. "Spanish Riot Police Clash in Madrid with Anti-Austerity Protesters." *Guardian*, August 5. Accessed February 5, 2017. www.theguardian.com/world/2011/aug/05/spanish-police-clash-austerity-protesters.

Guardian. 2014. "Spanish Riot Police Arrest 12 in Clashes with Anti-Austerity Protesters." *Guardian*, March 22. Accessed February 5, 2017. www.theguardian.com/world/2014/mar/22/spain-austerity-march-riot-police-clash.

Guardian. 2015. "Guardian: Οι 20 σταθμοί της ελληνικής κρίσης." *Iefimerida*, July 25. Accessed February 20, 2017. www.iefimerida.gr/news/213858/guardian-oi-20-stathmoi-tis-ellinikis-krisis.

GuestPost. 2015. "The Criminalisation of Social Protest in Ireland: The Jobstown Aftermath and the ECHR." *Human Rights in Ireland*, February 16. Accessed February 8, 2017. http://humanrights.ie/international-lawinternational-human-rights/the-criminalisation-of-social-protest-in-ireland-the-jobstown-aftermath-and-the-echr/.

Guralnik, Clara. 2017. Respond to query 1.1–14/368–2: Police and Border Guard Board. Register: 70008747 [in the author's records].

Healy, Blathnaid. 2015. "Riot in Germany as Blockupy Anti-Austerity Protest Turns Violent." *Mashable*, March 18. Accessed February 8, 2017. http://mashable.com/2015/03/18/frankfurt-protests-ecb-germany/#T3Q92pyJIaqF.

Heckle, Harold. 2013. "Thousands of Anti-Austerity Protesters March in Madrid, Frankfurt, Lisbon." *CTV News*, June 1. Accessed February 8, 2017. www.ctvnews.ca/business/thousands-of-anti-austerity-protesters-march-in-madrid-frankfurt-lisbon-1.1306955.

Heckle, Harold. 2014. "Spain Anti-Austerity Protesters Clash with Cops." *USA Today*, March 22. Accessed February 6, 2017. www.usatoday.com/story/money/business/2014/03/22/spain-anti-austerity-protesters-clash-with-police/6744225/.

Hedgecoe, Guy. 2012. "Spain Austerity Protesters in Clash with Riot Police." *The Irish Times*, September 26. Accessed February 6, 2017. www.irishtimes.com/news/spain-austerity-protesters-in-clash-with-riot-police-1.538360.

Horsman, Marjolein. 2017. Respond to query 2017.00000005: Railpol on behalf of the Spanish National Police. Register: 2017.00000005 [in the author's records].

Huff, Connor and Dominika Kruszewska. 2016. "Banners, Barricades, and Bombs: The Tactical Choices of Social Movements and Public Opinion." *Comparative Political Studies* 49(13): 1774–1808.

Humphries, Conor. 2014. "Largest Irish Anti-Austerity March in Years Targets Qater Charges." *Reuters*, October 11. Accessed February 7, 2017. http://uk.reuters.com/article/uk-ireland-politics-protests-idUKKCN0I00O020141011.

Iannò, Santo. 2013. "Roma blindata nel giorno della protesta. I cittadini: 'Noi ostaggio della sicurezza'." *lFattoQuotidiano.it*, October 19. Accessed February 13, 2017. www.ilfattoquotidiano.it/2013/10/19/roma-blindata-nel-giorno-della-protesta-4mila-agenti-e-cittadini-ostaggio-della/748905/.

Ide, Ella and Eve Szeftel. 2015. "'We have been betrayed!' Protest Turns Violent as Greece Votes." *Yahoo! News*, July 15. Accessed February 4, 2017. www.yahoo.com/news/betrayed-protest-turns-violent-greece-votes-213451062.html?ref=gs.

Iefimerida. 2015. "Διαδήλωση την Τετάρτη στη Γερμανία κατά της λιτότητας στην Ελλάδα." *Iefimerida*, March 3. Accessed February 5, 2017. www.iefimerida.gr/news/196331/diadilosi-tin-tetarti-sti-germania-kata-tis-litotitas-stin-ellada.

IFES. 2017a. "Europe." *The International Foundation for Electoral Systems*, No date. Accessed March 10, 2017. www.ifes.org/europe.

IFES. 2017b. "Electoral Violence." *The International Foundation for Electoral Systems*, No date. Accessed March 10, 2017. www.ifes.org/issues/electoral-violence.

Il Messaggero. 2015. "Francoforte, proteste anti-austerity: scontri all'inaugurazione della nuova sede Bce." *Il Messaggero*, March 19. Accessed February 13, 2017. www.ilmessaggero.it/index.php?p=articolo&id_old=1245544&start=5.

In.gr. 2015. "Μεγάλη συγκέντρωση κατά της λιτότητας στο Σύνταγμα." *In.gr*, June 21. Accessed February 6, 2017. http://news.in.gr/greece/article/?aid=1500006512.

Irish Examiner. 2012. "Protesters Break through Garda Lines at Labour Conference." *Irish Examiner*, April 14. Accessed February 7, 2017. www.irishexaminer.com/breakingnews/ireland/protesters-break-through-garda-lines-at-labour-conference-547506.html.

ISP. 2016. "Top International Publisher List." Accessed June 9, 2016. www.scijournal.org/top-international-journal-publisher.shtml.

Jabareen, Yosef. 2009. "Building a Conceptual Framework: Philosophy, Definitions, and Procedure." *International Journal of Qualitative Methods* 8(4): 49–62.

Jedelsky, Peter. 2017. Respond to query 35049/17: Federal Police. Register: 0003506 [in the author's records].

John, Mark, Louise Ireland, and Mark Heinrich. 2015. "Thousands Protest Amid Strikes Against Cutbacks in France." *The World Post*, April 9. Accessed February 3, 2017. www.huffingtonpost.com/2015/04/09/france-protests-strikes-auserity_n_7032070.html.

Jordà, Òscar and Alan M. Taylor. 2016. "Time for Austerity: Estimating the Average Treatment Effect of Fiscal Policy." *The Economic Journal* 126(590): 219–255.

JR/HJL/HRB. 2015. "Spain Anti-Austerity Party Leads in Opinion Poll." *Press TV*, January 26. Accessed February 6, 2017. www.presstv.ir/Detail/2015/01/26/394797/Spain-antiausterity-party-leads-in-opinion-pol.

Julian, Sébastien. 2012. "Le mouvement anti-austérité peut-il avoir gain de cause?" *L'Express L'Expansion*, November 14. Accessed February 4, 2017. http://lexpansion.lexpress.fr/actualite-economique/le-mouvement-anti-austerite-peut-il-avoir-gain-de-cause_1357183.html.

Kamdar, Mira. 2016. "In Paris, a Protest Movement Awakens." *New York Times*, April 14. Accessed February 4, 2017. www.nytimes.com/2016/04/14/opinion/in-paris-a-protest-movement-awakens.html?_r=0.

Kanellopoulos, Kostas, Konstantinos Kostopoulos, Dimitris Papanikolopoulos, and Vasileios Rongas. 2017. "Competing Modes of Coordination in the Greek Anti-Austerity Campaign, 2010–2012." *Social Movement Studies* 16(1): 101–118.

Katsambekis, Giorgos. 2016. "Radical Left Populism in Contemporary Greece: Syriza's Trajectory from Minoritarian Opposition to Power." *Constellations* 23(3): 391–403.

Kavanagh, Gerry. 2017. Respond to query 2017–02–13: An Garda Síochána. Register: 2017–02–13 [in the author's records].

Keating, Fiona. 2014. "Spanish Police Fire Rubber Bullets as Anti-Austerity Protest Turns Violent." *International Business Times*, March 23. Accessed February 6, 2017. www.ibtimes.co.uk/spanish-police-fire-rubber-bullets-anti-austerity-protest-turns-violent-1441453.

Keller, Berndt. 2014. "The Continuation of Early Austerity Measures: The Special Case of Germany." *Transfer: European Review of Labour and Research* 20(3): 387–402.

Kirn, Gal. 2013a. "A Ghost Is Haunting Slovenia, the Ghost of Revolution!" *New Socialist*, February 16. Accessed February 11, 2017. www.newsocialist.org/679-a-ghost-is-haunting-slovenia-the-ghost-of-revolution.

Kirn, Gal. 2013b. "Social Uprising in Slovenia against Neoliberal Austerity Measures." *Global Research*, February 25. Accessed February 11, 2017. www.globalresearch.ca/social-uprising-in-slovenia-against-neoliberal-austerity-measures/5324218.

Klandermans, Bert and Jacquelien van Stekelenburg. 2016. "Taking Austerity to the Streets: Fighting Austerity Measures or Austerity States." *Mobilization: An International Quarterly* 21(4): 431–448.

Klandermans, Bert, Jacquelien van Stekelenburg, and Marie-Louise Damen. 2015. "Beneficiary and Conscience Constituencies: On Interests and Solidarity." In *Austerity and Protest: Popular Contention in Times of Economic Crisis*, edited by Marco Giugni and Maria Grasso, 155–170. London and New York: Routledge.

Kleeman, Sophie. 2015. "13 Powerful Photos Show the Anti-Austerity Protests Rocking Germany." *World.Mic*, March 18. Accessed February 8, 2017. https://mic.com/articles/113158/13-powerful-photos-show-the-massive-anti-austerity-protests-rocking-germany#.1ePiBgfEJ.

Konak, Nahide and Rasim Özgür Dönmez (eds.). 2017. *Waves of Social Movement Mobilizations in the Twenty-First Century: Challenges to the Neo-Liberal World Order and Democracy*. London: Lexington Books.

Konwicki, Piotr. 2013. "Estonia Has Much to Teach Us about How Real Austerity Works in Practice." *City A. M.*, March 15. Accessed February 19, 2017. www.cityam.com/article/estonia-has-much-teach-us-about-how-real-austerity-works-practice.

Koorits, Vahur. 2012. "2012 – A Year of Discontent in Estonia." *VahurKoortis* December 31. Accessed March 5, 2017. http://vahurkoorits.blogspot.com/2012/12/2012-year-of-discontent-in-estonia.html.

Korsika, Anej. 2015. "The Fight for Socialism in Slovenia." *Scriboman: Mercenary Writer*, March 29. Accessed February 11, 2017. https://anejkorsika.wordpress.com/2015/03/29/the-fight-for-socialism-in-slovenia/.

Kubišová, Lubica. 2011. "Úsporné opatrenia môžu znamenať zánik oddelení." *Náš Mikuláš* March 15. Accessed February 15, 2017. https://nasmikulas.sme.sk/c/5807293/usporne-opatrenia-mozu-znamenat-zanik-oddeleni.html.

L'obs. 2014. "Belgique: manifestation monstre, émaillée d'incidents, contre l'austérité." *L'obs*, November 6. Accessed February 1, 2017. http://tempsreel.nouvelobs.com/monde/20141106.AFP0128/belgique-100-000-manifestants-contre-le-gouvernement-de-droite.html.

La Nación. 2012. "Manifestaciones contra la austeridad en Madrid al grito de 'dimisión'." La Nación, October 27. Accessed February 21, 2017. www.nacion.com/mundo/Manifestaciones-austeridad-Madrid-grito-dimision_0_1301669884.html.

La Stampa. 2012. "Cortei e proteste, Europa in piazza Guerriglia e feriti a Roma e Torino Cancellieri: bene l'operato dalla Polizia." *La Stampa*, November 14. Accessed February 13, 2017. www.lastampa.it/2012/11/14/italia/cronache/eurostrike-cortei-in-citta-JniHxYLuO6EWHhqY4i66FK/pagina.html.

La Tribune. 2014. "Manifestations anti-austérité monstres à Bruxelles." *La Tribune.fr*, April 4. Accessed February 1, 2017. www.latribune.fr/actualites/economie/union-europeenne/20140404trib000823719/manifestations-anti-austerite-monstres-a-bruxelles.html.

Lampugnani, Luca. 2013. "Manifestazione #19O, antagonisti in piazza contro l''austerità a senso unico': tensioni a Roma. Tende a Porta Pia, presidio fino a martedì." *International Business Times*, October 20. Accessed February 13, 2017. http://it.ibtimes.com/manifestazione-19o-antagonisti-piazza-contro-lausterita-senso-unico-tensioni-roma-tende-porta-pia.

Lane, Ruth. 2016. "Sartori's Challenge: Political Models from the Bottom Up." *Comparative Political Studies* 49(8): 1128–1160.

Le Blond, Josie. 2015. "Radical Left Protests in Germany over Bailout Deal 'Coup' against Greeks." *Guardian*, July 15. Accessed February 9, 2017. www.theguardian.com/world/2015/jul/15/radical-left-protests-across-germany-over-bailout-deal-coup-against-greeks.

Le Monde. 2014. "'Hollande ça suffit': l'extrême-gauche manifeste à Paris." *Le Monde.fr*, April 12. Accessed February 4, 2017. www.lemonde.fr/politique/article/2014/04/12/manifestation-anti-austerite-a-paris_4400339_823448.html.

Le Monde. 2015. "En Belgique, une immense manifestation contre l'austérité." *Le Monde.fr*, October 7. Accessed February 1, 2017. www.lemonde.fr/international/article/2015/10/07/en-belgique-une-immense-manifestation-contre-l-austerite_4784562_3210.html.

Le Roux, Gaëlle. 2012. "Manifestation anti-austérité à Paris: 'Hollande, c'est du Sarko light!'." *France 24*, October 1. Accessed February 3, 2017. www.france24.com/fr/20120930-france-manifestation-traite-budgetaire-europeen-austerite-gauche-melenchon-europe-finances.

Lombardo, Emanuela. 2017. "The Spanish Gender Regime in the EU Context: Changes and Struggles in Times of Austerity." *Gender, Work & Organization* 24(1): 20–33.

Lopez, Alejandro. 2012. "Spain's Anti-Cuts Protests Violently Broken up by Police." *World Socialist Website*, September 27. Accessed February 6, 2017. http://projectcensored.org/riot-police-violently-break-up-anti-austerity-protests-in-spain/.

Ls/sms, AP, dpa. 2015. "Anti-Austerity March Draws 80,000 Protesters to Belgium's Streets." *DW*, October 7. Accessed February 18, 2017. www.dw.com/en/anti-austerity-march-draws-80000-protesters-to-belgiums-streets/a-18767021.

Lyon, Carole. 2015. Belgique. A Bruxelles, 'la colère de la rue' contre l'austérité." *Currier International*, November 7. Accessed February 1, 2017. www.courrierinternational.com/article/2014/11/07/bruxelles-la-colere-de-la-rue-contre-l-austerite.

Mail Foreign Service. 2012. "Riot Police Clash with Anti-Austerity Demonstrators in Madrid after Thousands Take to the Streets to Protest against Cuts." *Dailymail*, September 25. Accessed February 7, 2017. www.dailymail.co.uk/news/article-2208557/Riot-police-clash-anti-austerity-demonstrators-Madrid-thousands-streets-protest-cuts.html#ixzz4Y0AMAx8v.

Mailand, Mikkel. 2014. "Austerity Measures and Municipalities: The Case of Denmark." *Transfer: European Review of Labour and Research* 20(3): 417–430.

Major, Aaron. 2014. *Architects of Austerity: International Finance and the Politics of Growth*. Stanford, CA: Stanford University Press.

Maltezou, Renee and Lefteris Papadimas. 2013. "Greece Protests Turn Violent." *The World Post*, January 7. Accessed February 4, 2017. www.huffingtonpost.com/2012/11/07/greece-protests_n_2088775.html.

Maltezou, Renee. 2012. "Europeans Protest Austerity at May Day Rallies." *Reuters*, May 1. Accessed February 5, 2017. www.reuters.com/article/us-protests-greece-idUSBRE8400CL20120501.

Manolis, Gasparakis. 2013. "Ευρωπαϊκή διαδήλωση κατά της λιτότητας και της φασιστικής απειλής απόψε στην Αθήνα (ανανέωση)." *Η ΑΥΓΗ Α.Ε*, June 20. Accessed February 6, 2017. www.avgi.gr/article/430332/europaiki-diadilosi-kata-tis-litotitas-kai-tis-fasistikis-apeilis-apopse-stin-athina-ananeosi-.

Marchetti, Vinicio. 2013. "Anti-austerità, le dimostrazioni odierne riempiono Piazza del Popolo a Roma." *Mondo Forex*, December 18. Accessed February 13, 2017. www.mondo-forex.com/anti-austerita-le-dimostrazioni-odierne-riempiono-piazza-del-popolo-a-roma/.

Mauro, Angela. 2012. "In piazza la nuova generazione di movimento: gli studenti medi anti-Monti. Grillo li punta ma non li ha." *L'Huffington Post*, November 14. Accessed February 13, 2017. www.huffingtonpost.it/2012/11/14/in-piazza-la-nuova-generazione_n_2130679.html.

Maza, Cristina. 2013a. "Rough Guide to Slovenian Protests, 2012/2013." *Cafebabel*, February 4. Accessed February 11, 2017. www.cafebabel.co.uk/society/article/rough-guide-to-slovenian-protests-20122013.html.

Maza, Cristina. 2013b. "Slovenia Joins Euro Zone Anti-Austerity Protests." *Policy.Mic* February 10. Accessed February 11, 2017. https://mic.com/articles/25332/slovenia-joins-euro-zone-anti-austerity-protests#.bVS7ZwHT0.

McCauley, Lauren. 2015. "Portugal Rejoices as Anti-Austerity Left Coalition Forms to Oust Right Wing: Socialists, Communists, and Left Bloc Unite in 'Unprecedented' Coalition to End Years of Punishing Cuts." *Common Dreams*, November 10. Accessed February 9, 2017. www.commondreams.org/news/2015/11/10/portugal-rejoices-anti-austerity-left-coalition-forms-oust-right-wing.

McHugh, David. 2015. "Police Cars Burn at Anti-Austerity Protest in Germany." *Global News*, March 18. Accessed February 8, 2017. http://globalnews.ca/news/1888780/police-cars-set-afire-at-austerity-protest-in-germany/.

McHugh, Jess. 2015a. "European Anti-Austerity 2015: Podemos, Spain's Protest Party, Looks to an Uncertain Future after Tsipras Resignation, Dips in the Polls." *International Business Times*, February 9. Accessed February 5, 2017. www.ibtimes.com/european-anti-austerity-2015-podemos-spains-protest-party-looks-uncertain-future-2079500.

McHugh, Jess. 2015b. "Greece Anti-Austerity Protests 2015 Video, Photos: In Athens, Riots Break Out, Tear Gas and Molotov Cocktails Exchanged during Greek Strike." *International Business Times*, December 11. Accessed February 4, 2017. www.ibtimes.com/greece-anti-austerity-protests-2015-video-photos-athens-riots-break-out-tear-gas-2181485.

McPartland, Ben. 2015. "Anti-Austerity Protests Sweep across France." *The Local*, April 9. Accessed February 3, 2017. www.thelocal.fr/20150409/anti-austerity-strike-closes-eiffel-tower-in-paris.

Mekina, Borut. 2012. "Slovenia: The Placid People's Revolt." *Vox Europ*, December 14. Accessed February 11, 2017. www.voxeurop.eu/en/content/article/3163301-placid-people-s-revolt.

Mekina, Borut. 2014. "EU Elections to Test Slovenia's Handling of Crisis." *EUobserver*, February 26. Accessed February 11, 2017. https://euobserver.com/eu-elections/123150.

Michael, Anna. 2014. "Italy Anti-Austerity Demonstration Leads to Violent Clashes." *Pakistan Press Club*, No date. Accessed February 12, 2017. http://pakistanpressclub.com/italy-anti-austerity-demonstration-leads-to-violent-clashes/7354/.

Miles, Matthew B., A. Michael Huberman, and Johnny Saldana. 2013. *Qualitative Data Analysis: A Methods Sourcebook*. 3rd edition. London: Sage.

Mitchell, Daniel J. 2012. "Estonia and Austerity: Another Exploding Cigar for Paul Krugman." *Forbes*, June 7. Accessed February 19, 2017. www.forbes.com/sites/danielmitchell/2012/06/07/estonia-and-austerity-another-exploding-cigar-for-paul-krugman/#5daf5af776ae.

Moulds, Josephine. 2012. "Estonia and Latvia: Europe's Champions of Austerity?" *Guardian*, June 8. Accessed February 2, 2017. www.theguardian.com/world/2012/jun/08/estonia-latvia-eurozone-champions-austerity.

Moustaki, Irini. 2000. "A Latent Variable Model for Ordinal Variables." *Applied Psychological Measurement* 24(3): 211–223.

Murphy, William. 2012. "Anti-Austerity Protest in Dublin (Ireland) – 24 November 2012." *Flickr*, November 24. Accessed February 7, 2017. www.flickr.com/photos/infomatique/8215132626.

Müsgen, Hanne. 2017. Respond to query O3–12007/1#1. Federal Police. Register: 170213 [in the author's records].

Nallu, Preethi. 2015. "Anti-Austerity Forces Grow in Italy after Greece Vote." *Al Jazeera*, February 7. Accessed February 12, 2017. www.aljazeera.com/indepth/features/2015/02/anti-austerity-forces-grow-italy-greece-vote-150207073012952.html.

Nellas, Demetris. 2011. "Anti-Austerity Protest in Greece Draws 5,000." *Deseret News Utah*, June 18. Accessed February 4, 2017. www.deseretnews.com/article/700145163/Anti-austerity-protest-in-Greece-draws-5000.html.

Neugera, James G. 2012. "EU-Gipfel konfrontiert Merkel mit der Forderung 'Keine Tabus'." *Welt*, May 23. Accessed June 8, 2017. www.welt.de/newsticker/bloomberg/article106365904/EU-Gipfel-konfrontiert-Merkel-mit-der-Forderung-Keine-Tabus.html.

News24. 2015. "Police Cars Torched at Anti-Austerity Protest in Germany." *News24*, March 18. Accessed February 9, 2017. www.news24.com/World/News/Police-cars-torched-at-anti-austerity-protest-in-Germany-20150318.

News247. 2015. "Μεγάλες διαδηλώσεις σε Παρίσι και Αγγλία: Υπέρ της Ελλάδας, κατά της λιτότητας." *Madala.gr*, June 20. Accessed February 5, 2017. www.madata.gr/epikairotita/world/423574.html.

Newsbomb. 2015. "Γερμανία: Διαδήλωση κατά της λιτότητας στην Ελλάδα με... ελληνική εκπροσώπηση." *Newsbomb*, June 20. Accessed February 5, 2017. www.newsbomb.gr/kosmos/news/story/598577/germania-diadilosi-yper-ton-prosfygon-kai-kata-tis-litotitas-stin-ellada.

Newsroom ΔΟΛ. 2011. "Χιλιάδες κόσμου διαδήλωσαν κατά των μέτρων λιτότητας, λένε τα ξένα πρακτορεία ειδήσεων." *In.gr*, June 6. Accessed February 21, 2017. http://news.in.gr/greece/article/?aid=1231112037.

Nez, Héloïse. 2016a. "Social Movements Facing the Crisis: Indignados and Occupiers in Europe." In *Social Movement Studies in Europe: The State of the Art*, edited by Olivier Fillieule, and Guya Accornero, 173–187. New York: Berghahn Books.

Nez, Héloïse. 2016b. "'We Must Register a Victory to Continue Fighting': Locating the Action of the Indignados in Madrid." In *Street Politics in the Age of Austerity: From the Indignados to Occupy*, edited by Marcos Ancelovici, Pascale Dufour, and Héloïse Nez, 121–146. Amsterdam: Amsterdam University Press.

Nooz. 2015. "Διαδηλώσεις κατά της λιτότητας σε όλη τη χώρα." *Nooz*, June 17. Accessed February 6, 2017. www.nooz.gr/greece/sintagma-diadilonoun-kata-tis-litotitas.

Novak, Marjeta. 2013. "Slovenia Rises in Artful 'Protestivals'" *Waging Non-violence: People-Powered News & Analysis*, March 21. Accessed February 11, 2017. http://wagingnonviolence.org/feature/slovenia-rises-in-artful-protest/.

Novak, Marja, Zoran Radosavljevic, and Mark Heinrich. 2012. "Slovenia Police Arrest 141 in Violent Anti-Austerity Protests." *Reuters*, December 4. Accessed February 11, 2017. www.reuters.com/article/us-slovenia-arrests-idUSBRE8B30QM20121204.

NPR. 2013. "Opera Singer Becomes (Soprano) Voice of Protest in Portugal." *NPR*, July 18. Accessed February 10, 2017. www.npr.org/sections/parallels/2013/07/18/202626305/Opera-Singer-Becomes-Soprano-Voice-Of-Protest-In-Portugal.

Nye, Joseph S., Jr. 2004. *Soft Power: The Means to Success in World Politics*. New York: Public Affairs.

O'Connor, Francis. 2017. "The Presence and Absence of Protest in Austerity Ireland." In *Late Neoliberalism and its Discontents in the Economic Crisis: Comparing Social Movements in the European Periphery*, edited by Donatella della Porta, Massimiliano Andretta, Tiago Fernandes, Francis O'Connor, Eduardo Romanos, and Markos Vogiatzoglou, 65–98. Cham: Palgrave Macmillan.

O'Leary, Naomi. 2013. "Italian Anti-Austerity Protesters Clash with Police." *Reuters*, October 20. Accessed February 12, 2017. http://uk.reuters.com/article/uk-italy-demonstration-idUKBRE99I06L20131019.

Odd Stuff. 2012. "Students and Riot Police Clash during Anti-Austerity Protests Italy." *Odd Stuff Magazine*, October 8. Accessed February 12, 2017. http://oddstuffmagazine.com/students-and-riot-police-clash-during-anti-austerity-protests-italy.html.

Oddo, John. 2011. "War Legitimation Discourse: Representing 'Us' and 'Them' in Four US Presidential Addresses." *Discourse & Society* 22(3): 287–314.

Onyanga-Omara, Jane. 2015. "Anti-Austerity Protest Turns Violent in Germany." *USA Today*, March 18. Accessed February 8, 2017. www.usatoday.com/story/news/world/2015/03/18/frankfurt-ecb-headquarters-anti-austerity-protests/24946425/.

Osiris, Lita. 2012. "Dublin Anti-Austerity Protest 24/11/12." *YouTube*, November 26. Accessed February 7, 2017. www.youtube.com/watch?v=H9oU_JsRkQQ.

Ouest France Justice et Liberté. 2015. "Bruxelles. Incidents en marge d'une manifestation massive anti-austérité." *Ouest France Justice et Liberté*, October 7. Accessed February 1, 2017. www.ouest-france.fr/monde/bruxelles-incidents-en-marge-dune-manifestation-massive-anti-austerite-3746555.

Palabraspormadrid. 2013. "No hay pan para tanto chorizo." *Palabraspormadrid*, March 20. Accessed February 6, 2017. https://palabraspormadrid.blogspot.com/2013/03/no-hay-pan-para-tanto-chorizo.html.

PanARMENIAN. 2012. "Thousands Gather for Anti-Austerity Rally in Slovenia." *PanARMENIAN*, November 17. Accessed February 11, 2017. www.panarmenian.net/eng/news/133004/.

Pattison, Brynmor. 2015. "Irish Water and Anti-Austerity Demonstrators Enter Bank of Ireland Branch in Dublin Protest." *Irish Mirror*, December 8. Accessed February 8, 2017. www.irishmirror.ie/news/irish-news/irish-water-anti-austerity-demonstrators-6975987.

Pavlou, Eleni. 2015. "Anti-Austerity Protesters Clash with Police in Frankfurt." *Sigma-live*, March 18. Accessed February 9, 2017. www.sigmalive.com/en/news/international/128484/antiausterity-protesters-clash-with-police-in-frankfurt#.

Pelagidis, Theodore and Michael Mitsopoulos. 2016. *Who's to Blame for Greece?: Austerity in Charge of Saving a Broken Economy*. New York: Palgrave Macmillan.

Phillips, Leigh. 2011. "Amnesty Condemns Greek Crackdown on Anti-Austerity Protests." *EUobserver*, June 30. Accessed February 4, 2017. https://euobserver.com/economic/32571.

Pickerill, Jenny, John Krinsky, Graeme Hayes, Kevin Gillan, and Brian Doherty. 2015. *Occupy! A Global Movement*. London and New York: Routledge.

Piggott, Mark. 2015. "Ireland: 80,000 March in Protest at Austerity Linked New Water Charges." *International Business Times*, August 30. Accessed February 7, 2017. www.ibtimes.co.uk/ireland-80000-march-protest-austerity-linked-new-water-charges-1517706.

Politie. 2017. Respond to query 170207–00391234534: Politie. Register: 170207–00391234534 [in the author's records].

Press TV Videos. 2013. "Austrians Protest against Austerity Measures." *YouTube*, December 19. Accessed February 18, 2017. www.youtube.com/watch?v=3O-he7QhNUY.

Press TV. 2015. "30,000 People Protest against Austerity Cuts in Finland." *Press TV*, September 18. Accessed February 2, 2017. http://presstv.ir/Detail/2015/09/18/429767/Finland-protest-Helsinki-austerity-Juha-Sipila.

Protothema.gr. 2015. "Βρυξέλλες: Διαδήλωση υπέρ της Ελλάδας και κατά της λιτότητας." *Protothema.gr*, June 21. Accessed February 5, 2017. www.protothema.gr/world/article/486524/diadilosi-uper-tis-elladas-stis-vruxelles/.

Punch, Keith F. 2014. *Introduction to Social Research: Quantitative and Qualitative Approaches*. 3rd edition. London: Sage.

Queally, Jon. 2013. "Anti-Austerity Cops Face Off against Riot Police in Portugal." *Popular Resistance*, November 23. Accessed February 10, 2017. https://popularresistance.org/anti-austerity-cops-face-off-against-riot-police-in-portugal/.

Radio Gamma. 2015. "Μεγάλες συγκεντρώσεις σε όλη τη χώρα ενόψει Eurogroup (ΦΩΤΟ)." *Radio Gamma*, February 16. Accessed February 6, 2017. http://tiny.pl/g1cjj.

Radio Stimme Russlands. 2012. "Frankfurt am Main: über 20.000 Teilnehmer 'marschierten' gegen Sparmaßnahmen." Radio Stimme Russlands, May 20. Accessed February 9, 2017. https://de.sputniknews.com/german.ruvr.ru/2012_05_20/75323899/.

Ramos, Jhun. 2014. "Anti-Corruption Religious Group, 'Zombie Church' Expands in Slovenia." *Christian Today*, December 27. Accessed February 11, 2017. www.christiantoday.com.au/article/anti.corruption.religious.group.zombie.church.expands.in.slovenia/18825.htm.

Raun, Alo and Oliver Kund. 2012. "ACTA meeleavaldus jäi oodatust kesisemaks." *Postimees*, February 11. Accessed March 5, 2017. www.postimees.ee/735944/acta-meeleavaldus-jaei-oodatust-kesisemaks.

Real.gr. 2015. "Με μεγάλη συμμετοχή η γενική απεργία κατά της λιτότητας." *Euro2Day*, February 16. Accessed February 6, 2017. www.euro2day.gr/news/highlights/article-news/1375668/me-megalh-symmetohh-h-genikh-apergia-kata-ths.html.

Red.MM/mrj. 2013. "Manifestazioni anti-austerità a Roma: Migliaia di persone sono scese in piazza." *RSI*, May 13. Accessed February 13, 2017. www.rsi.ch/news/mondo/cronaca/Manifestazioni-anti-austerit%C3%A0-a-Roma-434579.html.

Redação. 2011. "Lisboa junta-se hoje a protesto mundial anti-austeridade." *TVI 24*, October 15. Accessed February 10, 2017. www.tvi24.iol.pt/economia/protestos/lisboa-junta-se-hoje-a-protesto-mundial-anti-austeridade.

Redazione Barlettaviva. 2013. "Manifestazione anti-austerity a Roma, un barlettano tra i fermata: 15 persone sottoposte a fermo dalle forze dell'ordine dopo gli scontri nella Capitale." *Barlettaviva*, October 19. Accessed February 12, 2017. www.barlettaviva.it/notizie/manifestazione-anti-austerity-a-roma-un-barlettano-tra-i-fermati/.

Repečkaitė, Daiva. 2015. "Why Are Baltic States Posing as Anti-Greece?" *New Internationalist Magazine: People, Ideas and Action for Global Justice*, July 1. Accessed February 2, 2017. https://newint.org/features/web-exclusive/2015/07/01/baltic-states-anti-greece/.

Repubblica. 2015. "Corteo anti-austerity, antagonisti lanciano fumogeni e uova contro sede Ue." *Repubblica*, February 14. Accessed February 13, 2017. http://video.repubblica.it/politica/corteo-anti-austerity-antagonisti-lanciano-fumogeni-e-uova-contro-sede-ue/192088/191050.

Reuters. 2011. "Επεισόδια στις διαδηλώσεις κατά των μέτρων λιτότητας." *Ναυτεμπορική*, July 28. Accessed February 21, 2017. www.naftemporiki.gr/video/414939/epeisodia-stis-diadiloseis-kata-ton-metron-litotitas.

Reuters. 2015. "Protesters Clash with Police Near New European Bank HQ in Frankfurt." *Newsweek*, March 18. Accessed February 9, 2017. http://europe.newsweek.com/protesters-clash-police-near-new-european-bank-hq-frankfurt-314692.

Rioja2. 2011. "No hay pan para tanto chorizo." *Rioja2*, May 19. Accessed February 5, 2017. www.rioja2.com/n-80730-2-para_tanto_chorizo/.

Romanos, Eduardo. 2017. "Late Neoliberalism and Its Indignados: Contention in Austerity Spain." In *Late Neoliberalism and its Discontents in the Economic Crisis: Comparing Social Movements in the European Periphery*, edited by Donatella della Porta, Massimiliano Andretta, Tiago Fernandes, Francis O'Connor, Eduardo Romanos, and Markos Vogiatzoglou, 131–168. Cham: Palgrave Macmillan.

Rosenberg, M. Michael. 2016. "The Conceptual Articulation of the Reality of Life: Max Weber's Theoretical Constitution of Sociological Ideal Types." *Journal of Classical Sociology* 16(1): 84–101.

RQuotidiano. 2012. "L'Europa in piazza contro l'austerity. Scontri a Roma: 8 arresti e 50 fermi." *IlFattoQuotidiano.it*, November 14. Accessed February 12, 2017. www.ilfattoquotidiano.it/2012/11/14/spagna-italia-grecia-irlanda-e-portogallo-piigs-in-piazza-contro-lausterity/413340/.

RT en français. 2015. "La police utilise des canons à eau lors d'une manifestation anti-austérité à Bruxelles." *RT en français*, October 7. Accessed February 1, 2017. https://francais.rt.com/international/7960-belgique-bruxelles-austerite-manifestation.

RT. 2012a. "Greek Austerity: Path to Recovery, or Path to Violence?" *RT*, May 11. Accessed February 5, 2017. www.rt.com/news/greece-austerity-recovery-violence-970/.

RT. 2012b. "Mass Anti-Austerity Protests Weep through Spain." *RT*, May 13. Accessed February 5, 2017. www.rt.com/news/mass-protests-spain-madrid-118/.

RT. 2012c. "Scores Injured in Anti-Austerity Slovenia Clashes." *RT*, December 4. Accessed February 11, 2017. www.rt.com/news/slovenia-clashes-protesters-austerity-elites-198/.

RT. 2013a. "Anti-Austerity Protests Rock Slovenia as Fears of Bailout Grow." *RT*, 27 April. Accessed February 11, 2017. www.rt.com/news/austerity-protests-bail-out-504/.

RT. 2013b. "'Pitchfork' Protesters Clash with Police as Italy Hit by Week of Anti-Austerity Rallies." *RT*, December 15. Accessed February 12, 2017. www.rt.com/news/italy-pitchfork-protests-clashes-259/.

RT. 2014a. "101 Injured, 29 Arrested in Madrid as Anti-Austerity March Turns Violent." *RT*, March 24. Accessed February 6, 2017. www.rt.com/news/spain-protest-cuts-crisis-509/.

RT. 2014b. " 'No more cuts!' Thousands across Spain Stage Anti-Govt Protests (VIDEO, PHOTOS)." *RT*, April 4. Accessed February 6, 2017. www.rt.com/news/rally-spain-austerity-policies-321/.

RT. 2015a. "30k Finns Protest Govt-Planned Cuts, Nationwide Strike Grinds Country to a Halt." *RT*, September 18. Accessed February 2, 2017. www.rt.com/news/315843-finland-nationwide-strike-cuts/.

RT. 2015b. " 'Bread, jobs, dignity': Crowds Gather for Anti-Austerity March in Madrid." *RT*, March 21. Accessed February 5, 2017. www.rt.com/news/242885-spain-dignity-march-protest/.

RTÉ. 2015. "Thousands Take Part in Demonstrations against Jailed Protesters." *RTÉ*, February 23. Accessed February 7, 2017. www.rte.ie/news/2015/0221/681856-water-charge-protest/.

Rushton, Steve. 2013. "How Students Are Sparking a Direct Democracy Movement in Slovenia." *Occupy.com*, January 8. Accessed February 11, 2017. www.occupy.com/article/how-students-are-sparking-direct-democracy-movement-slovenia#sthash.A4j1BhF4.dpbs.

S2W. 2015. "Finland: Schools to Close, Rail Network to Shut Down in Austerity Protest." *Libcom.org*, September 13. Accessed February 2, 2017. https://libcom.org/news/finland-schools-close-rail-network-shut-down-austerity-protest-14092015.

Sahu, Amogh and Frederick Jordaan. 2013. "The Myth of Successful Eurozone Austerity: Estonia." *Economic Interests*, February 26. Accessed February 19, 2017. https://economicinterest.wordpress.com/2013/02/26/the-myth-of-successful-eurozone-austerity-estonia/.

Salonicanews. 2011. "Διαδήλωση κατά των σκληρών μέτρων λιτότητας." *Salonicanews.com*, December 1. Accessed February 21, 2017. http://tiny.pl/g1cjl.

Santopadre, Marco. 2012. "Slovenia: proteste antiausterity e scontri a Maribor e Lubiana." *Contropiano*, December 2. Accessed February 11, 2017. http://contropiano.org/news/internazionale-news/2012/12/01/slovenia-proteste-antiausterity-e-scontri-a-maribor-e-lubiana-012989.

Santos-Moura, Violeta. 2012. "Anti-Austerity Protests: Lisbon." *Violeta Moura*, October 15. Accessed February 10, 2017. www.violetamoura.eu/antiausterityprotestslisbon#2.

Sanz, Inmaculada. 2014. "Massive Anti-Austerity Protest in Spain." *Popular Resistance*, March 23. Accessed February 6, 2017. https://popularresistance.org/massive-anti-austerity-protest-in-spain/.

Sarra, Chiara. 2013. "Roma blindata per il corteo degli antagonisti. Bombe carta contro il ministero delle Finanze." *Il Giornale*, October 19. Accessed February 13, 2017. www.ilgiornale.it/news/cronache/tutto-pronto-manifestazione-contro-lausterity-si-temono-959897.html.

Saviano, Carmine and Michela Scacchioli. 2013. "Decine di migliaia di antagonisti a Roma. Bombe carta contro ministeri: 15 fermati." *Repubblica*, October 19. Accessed February 12, 2017. www.repubblica.it/cronaca/2013/10/19/news/corteo_a_roma_degli_antagonisti_altri_fermi_e_sequestri_delle_forze_dell_ordine-68925392/.

SENSE. 2009. "Ranking of Academic Publishers." Accessed June 9, 2016. www.sense.nl/gfx_content/documents/ABCDE-indeling%20Scientific%20Publishers%20SENSE_approved_May_2009.pdf.

Shea John O. 2015. "The Criminalisation of Social Protest in the Republic of Ireland: The Movement against Economic Austerity and Water Privatization. The Jobstown Aftermath and the ECHR." *Global Research*, February 27. Accessed February 8, 2017.

www.globalresearch.ca/the-criminalisation-of-social-protest-in-the-republic-of-ireland-the-movement-against-economic-austerity-and-water-privatization/5433673.

SITA, Plus JEDEN DEŇ/vip, ds, md. 2013. "Úsporné opatrenia si vybrali svoju daň: Padli prvé školy!" *Pluska*, November 21. Accessed February 16, 2017. www.pluska.sk/spravy/z-domova/tri-zakladne-skoly-septembri-skoncili-dalsie-budu-prepustat.html.

SITA. 2013. "KDH vyzýva vládu, aby zverejnila úsporné opatrenia." *Topsky.sk*, July 9. Accessed February 15, 2017. www.topky.sk/cl/100535/1355012/KDH-vyzyva-vladu—aby-zverejnila-usporne-opatreniav.

Sky News. 2015. "Scores Injured in Violent Frankfurt Clashes." *Sky News*, March 18. Accessed February 9, 2017. http://news.sky.com/story/scores-injured-in-violent-frankfurt-clashes-10367296.

Smith-Spark, Laura. 2012. "Anger at Austerity, Immigration Feeds Far Right's Rise in Europe." *CNN*, May 9. Accessed June 8, 2017. http://edition.cnn.com/2012/05/08/world/europe/europe-far-right-austerity/index.html.

Sousa, Helena and Luís António Santos. 2014. "Portugal at the Eye of the Storm: Crisis, Austerity and the Media." *Javnost – The Public* 21(4): 47–61.

Spanakos, Anthony Petros. 2016. "Conceptualising Comparative Politics: A Framework." In *Conceptualising Comparative Politics*, edited by Anthony Petros Spanakos and Francisco Panizza, 1–16. London and New York: Routledge.

Spangler, Scott. 2016. *Accelerating Discovery: Mining Unstructured Information for Hypothesis Generation*. London and New York: CRC Press.

Spiegel. 2012. "Einsatz in Frankfurt 'Blockupy' – Demonstranten protestieren friedlich." *Spiegel*, May 19. Accessed February 9, 2017. www.spiegel.de/wirtschaft/soziales/grossdemonstration-von-blockupy-in-frankfurt-verlaeuft-friedlich-a-833977.html.

Spiegel. 2015a. "Blockupy in Frankfurt am Main Ausnahmezustand rund um die EZB." *Spiegel*, March 18. Accessed February 9, 2017. www.spiegel.de/politik/deutschland/blockupy-protest-tausende-in-frankfurt-erwartet-a-1024115.html.

Spiegel. 2015b. "Blockupy-Proteste Am Abend kehrt in Frankfurt Ruhe ein." *Spiegel*, March 18. Accessed February 9, 2017. www.spiegel.de/politik/deutschland/blockupy-frankfurt-proteste-gegen-ezb-loesen-sich-langsam-auf-a-1024312.html.

Spiegel. 2015c. "Frankfurt am Main Krawalle bei Blockupy-Protesten rund um die EZB." *Spiegel*, March 18. Accessed February 9, 2017. www.spiegel.de/wirtschaft/soziales/blockupy-proteste-ausschreitungen-in-frankfurt-am-main-a-1024105.html.

STA. 2012. "Protests Not Letting up as Rallies Continue across Slovenia." *The Slovenia Times*, December 7. Accessed February 11, 2017. www.sloveniatimes.com/protests-not-letting-up-as-rallies-continue-across-slovenia/2.

Staff. 2013. "Portugal: Anti-Austerity Protesters Occupy Government Ministries." *Popular Resistance*, December 1. Accessed February 10, 2017. https://popularresistance.org/portugal-anti-austerity-protesters-occupy-government-ministries/.

Staff. 2015. "Italy: Thousands of Students Protest Education Reforms." *Popular Resistance*, March 29. Accessed February 12, 2017. https://popularresistance.org/italy-thousands-of-students-protest-against-education-reforms/.

Stokokkino. 2015. "Ογκώδεις απεργιακές διαδηλώσεις κατά της λιτότητας και των μνημονίων." *Stokokkino*, November 13. Accessed February 6, 2017. www.stokokkino.gr/article/1000000000019971/Ogkodeis-oi-apergiakes-diadiloseis-pou-oloklirothikan-to-mesimeri.

Strupczewski, Jan. 2012. "Greek Debt Crisis: EU/IMF Report Says Greece Needs to Keep Slashing Its Budget." *The Huffington Post*, May 13. Accessed February 4, 2017. www.huffingtonpost.com/2012/03/13/greek-debt-crisis_n_1341148.html.

Sulík, Richard. 2013. "Úsporné opatrenia – vojna ideológií." *Európska únia*, May 6. Accessed February 15, 2017. http://europskaunia.oldweb-sulik.sk/usporne-opatrenia-eu/.

Tagaris, Karolina. 2015. "Several Thousand Rally in Athens against Austerity." *Reuters*, June 21. Accessed February 4, 2017. www.reuters.com/article/us-eurozone-greece-protests-idUSKBN0P10VY20150621.

Taibo, Carlos. 2013. "The Spanish Indignados: A Movement with Two Souls." *European Urban and Regional Studies* 20(1): 155–158.

Tanglao, Leezel. 2014. "Clashes Erupt During Anti-Austerity Protests in Rome." *Vice News*, April 12. Accessed February 12, 2017. https://news.vice.com/article/clashes-erupt-during-anti-austerity-protests-in-rome.

Tarrow, Sidney. 2011. *Power in Movement: Social Movements and Contentious Politics*. 3rd edition. Cambridge and New York: Cambridge University Press.

Telegraph. 2012a. "Spain: Rubber Bullets Fired at Violent Anti-Austerity Protest." *Telegraph*, September 26. Accessed February 6, 2017. www.telegraph.co.uk/news/worldnews/europe/spain/9567090/Spain-rubber-bullets-fired-at-violent-anti-austerity-protest.html.

Telegraph. 2012b. "Spanish Police Battle Anti-Austerity Protesters." *Telegraph*, July 20. Accessed February 6, 2017. www.telegraph.co.uk/news/worldnews/europe/spain/9413804/Spanish-police-battle-anti-austerity-protesters.html.

Telegraph. 2013. "Debt Crisis: European Union Workers Stage Anti-Austerity Protests and Strikes." *Telegraph*, No date. Accessed February 10, 2017. www.telegraph.co.uk/news/picturegalleries/worldnews/9678346/Debt-crisis-European-Union-workers-stage-anti-austerity-protests-and-strikes.html?frame=2398622.

teleSUR/md-TP-cm. 2015. "Hundreds of Anti-Austerity Protesters Arrested in Frankfurt." *TeleSUR TV*, March 18. Accessed February 9, 2017. www.telesurtv.net/english/news/Hundreds-of-Anti-Austerity-Protesters-Arrested-in-Frankfurt-20150318-0012.html.

The Best News. 2015. "Χιλιάδες διαδηλωτές στους δρόμους κατά της λιτότητας-Επεισόδια στην Αθήνα." *The Best News*, November 13. Accessed February 5, 2017. https://translate.google.pl/translate?hl=pl&sl=el&u=www.thebest.gr/news/index/viewStory/363093&prev=search.

The Economist. 2013. "Not So Calvinist Any More: The Party of Freedom Benefits from Dutch Austerity Fatigue." *The Economist*, September 28. Accessed February 7, 2017. www.economist.com/news/europe/21586887-party-freedom-benefits-dutch-austerity-fatigue-not-so-calvinist-any-more.

The Globe and Mail. 2010. "Anti-Austerity Protests Hit France." *The Globe and Mail*, October 14. Accessed February 3, 2017. www.theglobeandmail.com/report-on-business/anti-austerity-protests-hit-france/article1370351/.

The Huffington Post. 2015. "Χιλιάδες πολίτες διαδήλωσαν κατά των νέων μέτρων λιτότητας – Επεισόδια και χημικά στο Σύνταγμα." *The Huffington Post*, December 11. Accessed February 5, 2017. www.huffingtonpost.gr/2015/11/12/koinwnia-liveblog-apergia-_n_8541298.html.

The Journal.ie. 2012. "Spanish Police Beat Protesters after Anti-Austerity Protest." *The Journal.ie*, September 25. Accessed February 7, 2017. www.thejournal.ie/protests-spain-609872-Sep2012/.

The Local staff. 2015. "Anti-Austerity Protests Weep across France." *Vancouver Ecosocialists*, April 12. Accessed February 3, 2017. www.ecosocialistsvancouver.org/article/anti-austerity-protests-sweep-across-france.

The Malaymail Online. 2015. "Finns Strike, Protest against Harsh Austerity Cuts." *The Malaymail Online*, September 18. Accessed February 2, 2017. www.themalaymail online.com/world/article/finns-strike-protest-against-harsh-austerity-cuts.

The Nationalist. 2015. "Anti-Austerity Protestors March to Bank of Ireland on College Green." *The Nationalist*, December 8. Accessed February 8, 2017. www.carlow-nationalist.ie/2015/12/08/anti-austerity-protestors-march-to-bank-of-ireland-on-college-green/.

The Slovenia Times. 2012a. "A Few Thousands Gathered to Oppose Austerity." *The Slovenia Times*, November 17. Accessed February 18, 2017. www.sloveniatimes.com/thousands-gather-in-ljubljana-to-oppose-austerity.

The Slovenia Times. 2012b. "Anti-Austerity Protests Announced for Saturday." *The Slovenia Times*, November 16. Accessed February 11, 2017. www.sloveniatimes.com/anti-austerity-protests-announced-for-saturday.

The TOC. 2015. "Μεγάλες συγκεντρώσεις με συνθήματα κατά της λιτότητας." *The Times of Change*, November 13. Accessed February 6, 2017. www.thetoc.gr/politiki/article/i-kubernisi-apenanti-sto-prwto-megalo-apergiako-test.

The World Post. 2013. "Europe Austerity Protests: Strikes Sweep Southern Europe in Response to Cuts." *The World Post*, January 14. Accessed February 3, 2017. www.huffingtonpost.com/2012/11/14/europe-austerity-protests-strikes-greece-italy-france_n_2129091.html.

Tomaselli, Emanuel. 2013. "Slovenia: The Government Falls. Mass Protests Continue." *In Defence of Marxism*, April 19. Accessed February 11, 2017. www.marxist.com/slovenia-government-falls-mass-protests-continue.htm.

Toplišek, Alen. 2017. "The Slovenian United Left: From Protest to Movement, and from Movement to Party." *Open Democracy*, January 19. Accessed February 11, 2017. www.opendemocracy.net/can-europe-make-it/alen-topli-ek/slovenian-united-left-from-protest-to-movement-and-from-movement-to.

Tremlett, Giles and Ian Traynor. 2012. "Spanish Take to Streets in Protest as MPs Pass €65bn Austerity Package." *Guardian*, July 19. Accessed February 5, 2017. www.theguardian.com/business/2012/jul/19/spain-austerity-protest-bank-bailout-bond.

Tremlett, Giles and Martin Roberts. 2012. "Spain's Cultural Fabric Tearing Apart as Austerity Takes its Toll." *Guardian*, September 28. Accessed June 8, 2017. www.theguardian.com/world/2012/sep/28/spain-cultural-fabric-tears-austerity-cuts.

Triandafyllou, Vassilis and Karolina Tagaris. 2015. "Greece Debt Crisis: Anti-Austerity Protests Turn Violent as Petrol Bombs Thrown at Police." *Mirror*, July 15. Accessed February 4, 2017. www.mirror.co.uk/news/world-news/greece-debt-crisis-anti-austerity-protests-6074666.

TRT World. 2015. "Finns Take to Streets for Anti-Austerity Strike in Helsinki." *TRT World*, September 19. Accessed February 2, 2017. www.trtworld.com/europe/finns-take-to-streets-for-anti-austerity-strike-in-helsinki-8121.

Tuite, Tom. 2012. "Jobless Man Charged after Egg Attack on Gilmore's Ministerial Car." *Independent*, October 5. Accessed February 7, 2017. www.independent.ie/irish-news/jobless-man-charged-after-egg-attack-on-gilmores-ministerial-car-28817835.html.

TVXS. 2012. "Χιλιάδες διαδηλωτές στους δρόμους της Θεσσαλονίκης κατά της λιτότητας." *TVXS*, September 8. Accessed February 21, 2017. http://tvxs.gr/news/ellada/epi-podos-astynomikoi-kai-ergazomenoi.

TVXS. 2015a. "Διαδηλώσεις κατά της λιτότητας σε Αθήνα, Άμστερνταμ και Βρυξέλλες." *TVXS*, June 21. Accessed February 21, 2017. http://tvxs.gr/news/ellada/diadiloseis-kata-tis-litotitas-se-athina-amsterntam-kai-brykselles.

TVXS. 2015b. "Διαδηλώσεις υπέρ Ελλάδας και κατά λιτότητας σε όλη την Ευρώπη [ΦΩΤΟ+ΒΙΝΤΕΟ]." *TVXS*, June 20. Accessed February 5, 2017. http://tvxs.gr/news/ellada/diadiloseis-yper-tis-elladas-kai-kata-tis-litotitas-se-parisi-kai-berolino.

TVXS. 2015c. "Μαζικές απεργιακές διαδηλώσεις κατά της λιτότητας σε όλη τη χώρα." *TVXS*, November 12. Accessed February 21, 2017. http://tvxs.gr/news/ellada/mazikes-apergiakes-diadiloseis-kata-tis-litotitas-se-oli-ti-xora.

Vaara, Eero. 2014. "Struggles over Legitimacy in the Eurozone Crisis: Discursive Legitimation Strategies and Their Ideological Underpinnings." *Discourse & Society* 25(4): 500–518.

Väisänen, Juha-Pekka. 2015. " 'Peoples Power' Anti-Austerity Protest in Finland." *Transform Europe*, August 25. Accessed February 2, 2017. www.transform-network.net/blog/blog-2015/news/detail/Blog/-6cd55f4bbb.html.

van den Broek, Hans-Peter. 2017. "Labelling and Legitimization: Justifying Political Violence in the Basque Country." *Terrorism and Political Violence* 29(1): 119–136.

van Leeuwen, Theo. 2007. "Legitimation in Discourse and Communication." *Discourse & Communication* 1(1): 91–112.

van Leeuwen, Theo. 2008. *Discourse and Practice: New Tools for Critical Discourse Analysis*. New York: Oxford University Press.

VanDusky-Allen, Julie. 2017. "Winners, Losers, and Protest Behavior in Parliamentary Systems." *The Social Science Journal* 54(1): 30–38.

Velmet, Aro. 2014. "Estonia: Not the Neoliberal Stronghold You've Been Sold." *Left East*, May 5. Accessed February 2, 2017. www.criticatac.ro/lefteast/estonia-not-the-neoliberal-stronghold-sold/.

Virta, Sirpa and Minna Branders. 2016. "Legitimate Security? Understanding the Contingencies of Security and Deliberation." *The British Journal of Criminology* 56(6): 1146–1164.

Vogiatzoglou, Markos. 2017. "Turbulent Flow: Anti-Austerity Mobilization in Greece." In *Late Neoliberalism and its Discontents in the Economic Crisis: Comparing Social Movements in the European Periphery*, edited by Donatella della Porta, Massimiliano Andretta, Tiago Fernandes, Francis O'Connor, Eduardo Romanos, and Markos Vogiatzoglou, 99–130. Cham: Palgrave Macmillan.

VWArticles. 2013. "Italy's Anti-Austerity 'Pitchfork Revolution' Grows." *Value Walk*, December 18. Accessed February 12, 2017. www.valuewalk.com/2013/12/italys-anti-austerity-pitchfork-revolution-grows/.

Wagstyl, Stefan. 2012. "Estonia: Path to Growth via Austerity Defies Eurozone Doubters." *Estonian World*, December 19. Accessed February 19, 2017. http://estonianworld.com/business/estonia-path-to-growth-via-austerity-defies-eurozone-doubters-and-krugman/.

Waites, Rosie. 2014. "Austrians Disillusioned with EU Austerity." *The Local*, May 20. Accessed February 18, 2017. www.thelocal.at/20140520/why-the-eu-elections-matter-to-austria.

Wearden, Graeme. 2012. "Europe's Day of Anti-Austerity Strikes and Protests Turn Violent – As It Happened." *Guardian*, November 14. Accessed January 31, 2017. www.theguardian.com/business/2012/nov/14/eurozone-crisis-general-strikes-protest-day-of-action.

Weaver, Matthew. 2015. "At Least 350 People Arrested in Protest at ECB HQ in Frankfurt." *Guardian*, March 18. Accessed February 9, 2017. www.theguardian.com/business/2015/mar/18/anti-capitalist-protesters-clash-police-ecb-frankfurt-hq.

Weber, Max. 2012. "The 'Objectivity' of Knowledge in Social Science and Social Policy." In *Max Weber: Collected Methodological Writings*, edited and translated by Hans Henrik Bruun and Sam Whimster, 100–138. London and New York: Routledge.

Wessel, Rhea and Jack Ewing. 2015. "Germans Protest European Austerity Measures." *New York Times*, March 18. Accessed February 8, 2017. www.nytimes.com/2015/03/19/business/european-central-bank-protests-frankfurt.html?_r=0.

Whitman, Elizabeth. 2015. "Finland Anti-Austerity Strike Shuts Down Public Transport, Flights as Recession Pits Labor Unions against Government." *International Business Times*, September 18. Accessed February 2, 2017. www.ibtimes.com/finland-anti-austerity-strike-shuts-down-public-transport-flights-recession-pits-2103573.

Wiener, Antje. 2014. *A Theory of Contestation*. London: Springer.

Wire services. 2014. "Thousands in Paris and Rome Protest Austerity Measures." *Al Jazeera America*, April 12. Accessed February 3, 2017. http://america.aljazeera.com/articles/2014/4/12/rome-paris-anti-austerityprotests.html.

Wise, Peter, Miles Johnson, Giulia Segreti, Tom Burgis, and Ben Fenton. 2012. "Anti-Austerity Protests Sweep Europe." *Financial Times*, November 14. Accessed February 18, 2017. www.ft.com/content/67fffbe2-2e3e-11e2-8bb3-00144feabdc0.

Wita, Pawel. 2013. "The Uprising in Slovenia: Europe's Latest Popular Challenge to Austerity and Corruption." *Occupy.com*, February 14. Accessed February 11, 2017. www.occupy.com/article/uprising-slovenia-europes-latest-popular-challenge-austerity-and-corruption#sthash.Zyjjvzoo.dpbs.

Wolff, Rick. 2010. "French Revolutions." *Yes! Magazine*, October 26. Accessed February 3, 2017. www.yesmagazine.org/people-power/french-revolutions.

Worldcrunch/Expatica. 2012. "Europe Hit by Anti-Austerity Protests and Strikes." *Expatica*, November 14. Accessed February 7, 2017. www.expatica.com/nl/news/Europe-hit-by-anti-austerity-protests-and-strikes_361543.html.

Yan, Holly. 2015. "Protest Turns Violent in Germany at European Central Bank Opening." *CNN*, March 18. Accessed February 8, 2017. http://edition.cnn.com/2015/03/18/europe/germany-european-central-bank-protest/.

YLE. 2015a. "Police Detain Nine Protesters at Anti-Austerity Demonstration." *YLE UUtiset*, September 22. Accessed February 2, 2017. http://yle.fi/uutiset/osasto/news/police_detain_nine_protesters_at_anti-austerity_demonstration/8247070.

YLE. 2015b. "Thursday's Papers: Anti-Austerity Protests, Academics Slam Gov't Plans, and 1000 Nicki Minaj Cut-Outs Flood Senate Square." *YLE UUtiset*, November 6. Accessed February 2, 2017. http://yle.fi/uutiset/osasto/news/thursdays_papers_anti-austerity_protests_academics_slam_govt_plans_and_1000_nicki_minaj_cut-outs_flood_senate_square/8065544.

Zamponi, Lorenzo. 2013. "Pre-Occupied and Dis-Occupied: Italian Movements and the Challenges of Anti-Austerity Protests." *CritCom*, November 26. Accessed February 12, 2017. http://councilforeuropeanstudies.org/critcom/pre-occupied-and-dis-occupied-italian-movements-and-the-challenges-of-anti-austerity-protests/.

Zerdin, Ali. 2013. "Thousands Strike amid Gov't Crisis in Slovenia." *Yahoo! Finance*, January 23. Accessed February 11, 2017. http://finance.yahoo.com/news/thousands-strike-amid-govt-crisis-slovenia-140348376-finance.html.

Zougla. 2015a. "Διαδήλωση κατά της λιτότητας στο Σύνταγμα." *Zougla*, June 17. Accessed February 5, 2017. www.zougla.gr/greece/article/live-diadilosi-kata-tis-litotitas-sto-sintagma.

Zougla. 2015b. "Παρίσι: Διαδήλωση υπέρ της Ελλάδας, κατά της λιτότητας." *Zougla*, June 28. Accessed February 5, 2017. www.zougla.gr/kosmos/article/parisi-diadilosi-iper-tis-eladas-kata-tis-litotitas.

3 Towards the Explanations of the Sources of Cultures of Political Violence

DOI: 10.4324/9781351205757-4

Uncovering the Sources of Cultures of Political Violence

Identification of distinctive and essential features of the cultures of political violence which occurred in the Eurozone was a necessary step towards the explanation of their sources. The objectives of the chapter are to test the empirical effectiveness of the current explanatory frameworks by working with the post-2008 incidents in which anti-austerity movements' stakeholders participated, to make a contribution to the development of an explanatory framework meeting the correctness criteria, and to verify if a developed model accounts for the cultures of political violence. The chapter evaluates empirically the explanatory frameworks, identified in the literature review, that treat cultures of political violence as the things to be explained.

Although it may seem to be potentially useful to make a theory generation-vs-verification contrast sharply to underline differences in research process stages, the distinction is not carried out so sharply in practice. Theory generation is highly dependent on proposing new explaining indicators and frameworks and progressive verification as well (Punch 2014, 134). Hence, the quest for the explanation of the patterns of a culture of political violence begins with verification. The process of testing is, however, led by methodological and theoretical effectiveness purposes on the one hand and the critical remarks formulated in the literature review on the other. A new approach is shaped and reshaped before proposing how to contribute to an explanatory framework useful to scrutinize the research subject field.

Methodology for Verification of the Theories that Consider a Culture of Political Violence as the Thing to be Explained

The chapter solves the second research problem of to what extent current explanatory frameworks explain why stakeholders of the post-2008 anti-austerity movements had particular patterns of a culture of political violence. To do so, it verifies the following hypothesis: current explanatory frameworks probably to a low extent explain why stakeholders of the post-2008 anti-austerity movements had particular patterns of a culture of political violence. The current explanatory frameworks are those identified in the literature review and already assessed in terms of correctness criteria and general applicability to empirical research. They undergo a test in spite of their drawbacks which are an insufficient reason for discarding the theories that prove problematic. Each theory in social science is controversial, and their development is accelerated only with theoretical, methodological, and empirical efforts rather than mere abandonment (Opp 2009, 8). The subsequent parts of the chapter formulate and test the specific theory-driven hypotheses.

The statistical analysis method serves the verification of the specific hypotheses. The Pearson correlation technique allows us to determine the type and strength of linear correlations between explaining indicators and indicators to be explained. The analysis computes Pearson linear correlation (r) separately for each set of indicators, and it interprets research results under a more detailed scale than a standard measuring instrument to provide us with conclusions as precise as possible. Values on a scale present the conditions of rejecting null hypotheses. For a good research practice purpose, let us introduce the instrument. It is as follows for positive coefficients:

$|r|=0$ – the absence of correlation
$0.0<|r|\leq 0.1$ – very small positive correlation
$0.1<|r|\leq 0.3$ – small positive correlation
$0.3<|r|\leq 0.5$ – medium positive correlation
$0.5<|r|\leq 0.7$ – strong positive correlation
$0.7<|r|\leq 0.9$ – very strong positive correlation
$0.9<|r|<1.0$ – almost full positive correlation
$|r|=1.0$ – full positive correlation

The research adopts a parallel scale for negative coefficients:

$|r|=0$ – the absence of correlation
$0.0>|r|\geq -0.1$ – very small negative correlation
$-0.1>|r|\geq -0.3$ – small negative correlation
$-0.3>|r|\geq -0.5$ – medium negative correlation
$-0.5>|r|\geq -0.7$ – strong negative correlation
$-0.7>|r|\geq -0.9$ – very strong negative correlation
$-0.9>|r|>-1.0$ – almost full negative correlation
and $|r|=-1.0$ – full negative correlation

The extreme values are often of asymptotic nature in social sciences.

The analysis also conducts a two-tail test to compute the statistical significance of the correlations, and it assesses them on a standard scale. The Pearson correlation is significant when the Sig. 2-tailed is at the 0.05 level or lower. In turn, it is not significant when the coefficient is at a level higher than 0.05.

In turn, when there is no need to calculate, the explanatory models undergo the causal-process observations that allow us to handle the data-set observations (Brady *et al.* 2006) or they are rejected by critical argumentation (Munck 2016; Paine 2016; Schneider 2016). The choice of a set of methods, techniques, and tools heavily depends on a type of data either qualitative or quantitative as well as on a quest for research process optimization.

A type of cultures of political violence is a dependent variable which carries three values of its patterns located on a simple ordinal scale: placid, hector-led, and militant. A placid type is aggressive narrowly (coded as 1), hector-led – moderately (coded as 2), and militant – sublimely (coded as 3). As the previous chapter has shown, whereas Estonia and Slovakia had placid cultures of political violence, Austria, the Netherlands, and France – hector-led patterns, and Finland, Belgium, Germany, Portugal, Slovenia, Italy, Greece, Spain, and Ireland – militant patterns (Figure 3.1). They were diversified in mutual legitimation to the use of political violence, modes of the legitimation of the use, the intensity of the use of physical force, and forms of political violence.

Independent variables come from the theories identified in the literature review. The research tests each explanatory framework to evaluate and compare its empirical effectiveness with others. Thus, the explaining indicators recognized as the potential contributors to a culture of political violence, whose validity is to be tested, are: intrastate elements of political violence involving vicious struggles for the pinnacle of political power by aspirants of collective political subjects such as ethnic groups or inhabitants of geographical entities, rivalry between regions, and colonization of the land (Ayele 2011), seminal experiences of war, revolution, and civil war (LaPorte and Worley 2008), structural indicators (Onslow 2011), noisy and turbulent politics of the street, the town square, and the factory, in which socioeconomic grievances, hostility to state authority, and new and recycled dreams of a purified community are expressed (Gerwarth

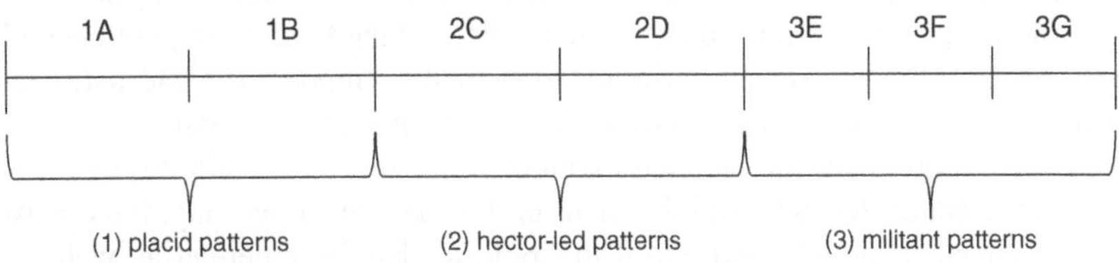

1: placid patterns

1A: placidly observing culture of political violence (Estonia)

1B: placidly rationalizing culture of political violence (Slovakia)

2: hector-led patterns

2C: hector-consenting culture of political violence (Austria and the Netherlands)

2D: hector-acknowledgment culture of political violence (France)

3: militant patterns

3F: indulgingly militant culture of political violence (Finland)

3G: obstreperously militant culture of political violence (Belgium, Germany, Portugal, Slovenia, and Italy)

3H: aggressively militant culture of political violence (Greece, Spain, and Ireland)

Figure 3.1 Post-2008 cultures of political violence in the Eurozone.

Source: Author's own study.

2011), the situation when the highly mobilized and urbanized civil society in the developed states with strong democratic traditions identified with the state does not confine its militaries to the narrowly constitutional role and ruthless and determined military governments threatens at length the civil society (Theobald 1999), repeated expressions of political violence (Eubank and Weinberg 2000), tribal and religious loyalties (Waldman 2007), non-political agencies of socialization (Kling 1963), youths' engagement in electoral violence (Okwong 2012), the fictions of political violence defined as novels, short stories, plays, movies, or parts thereof, where political processes and political views are reasonably close to the surface (Dexter and Guittet 2014), and the internationalist spirit of the 1960s (Pensado 2013). They are the explaining indicators derived from the theories which treat them as the sources of cultures of political violence.

The second type of independent variables relates to the temporal dimension of political reality. It is the time from the date of the explaining indicator's last occurrence (the independent variables of the first type) to the date of the first use of political violence by stakeholders of an anti-austerity movement. The time is determined by the simple subtraction expressible in the shape of the following straightforward algebraic expression: $a - b = c$. The period involved is the difference (c), and it forms a result of subtracting b from a. Whereas the date of the first use of political violence by stakeholders of an anti-austerity movement is the minuend (a), the date of a given indicator's last occurrence is the subtrahend (b).

Some general methodological assumptions are to be introduced here to shed light on the verification of the models' empirical effectiveness in explaining the diversity of cultures of political violence. The application of the conceptual framework of a culture of political violence to the empirical analysis in the previous chapter allowed us to establish the dates of the first use of political violence by stakeholders of anti-austerity movements. Importantly, the dates relevant to the research process indicate the beginning of objection to austerity. They were more than often in phase with the implementation of austerity measures in the states. Keeping in mind that, in the span under scrutiny, the opposition to social inequality and anti-democratic tendencies emerged as well, we made attempts to capture the very first violent behavior committed exactly against austerity. According to empirical evidence, stakeholders of the anti-austerity movements used political violence for the first time in 2010 in Belgium (BBC 2010a), France (The Globe and Mail 2010), Ireland (Duncan 2010), Slovakia (Balogová 2010), and Italy (BBC 2010b); in 2011 in Greece (Phillips 2011), Spain (Beas 2011), and Portugal (Redação 2011); in 2012 in Austria (Wearden 2012), Estonia (Guralnik 2017), the Netherlands (Connolly and Chrisafis 2012), Germany (Müsgen 2017), and Slovenia (Durić and Žibret 2017); and in 2014 in Finland (Finland Times 2014).

Due to the lack of databases containing the indicators determined in the literature review, the research employs a qualitative method of written sources analysis to gather data sufficient and necessary to test the specific hypotheses. The research technique of data collection is a content analysis of secondary sources, more strictly, secondary specialist literature concerning the indicators involved in the explanatory frameworks. It is crucial to establish what values are taken on by the indicators or the sets of indicators in particular states and to present them in the form of the data-set observations. These databases are the original contribution of this research to the studies on cultures of political violence. For the purpose of empowering the basis of arguments, the analysis makes use of theoretical sampling and adopts sources triangulation. The research tool is an instruction to review the secondary data.

The theory-based explanatory frameworks undergo tests in their existing, modified, and extended if necessary forms or are rejected if unmodifiable and unemployable to the case studies. The changes made in their content do not encroach upon the hard core of the models. The research verifies the central hypothesis by weighing up the arguments and counterarguments formulated throughout the chapter over the verification of the specific hypotheses concerning particular explanatory frameworks. The conclusions and proposals inform clues useful to develop new models.

Intrastate, Regional, and Colonial Explaining Indicators

The first explanatory framework considers the intrastate, regional, and colonial indicators to be the things accounting for the culture of political violence in Ethiopia between 1769 and 2009. It defines the culture as the use of extensive physical political violence in the state. The intrastate indicator is the element of political violence finding its expression in vicious struggles for the height of political power taken up by aspirants of collective political subjects such as ethnic groups or inhabitants of geographical entities. The regional indicator is the rivalry between regions. The colonial indicator is the colonization of the land (Ayele 2011, 216–217). Although Negussay Ayele's model is context-laden, a researcher acquires a universal explanatory framework after dropping the time and territory references from its design (Rak 2017a).

Ayele's explanatory framework informs the first set of specific hypotheses to be tested.

H_0: There might be no correlation between a fixed set of intrastate, regional, and colonial indicators and the time of its appearance in the history of a state and a pattern of a culture of political violence of stakeholders of an anti-austerity movement in the state.

H_A: If in the history of a state, a fixed set of intrastate, regional, and colonial indicators make an appearance, stakeholders of an anti-austerity movement in the state might have a militant culture of political violence, but the culture loses its militant value over time and the more time intervenes from the occurrence of the indicators, the more peaceful the culture gets.

While mindful of state contexts (Bosi *et al.* 2015), the verification of Ayele's model consists of three general stages set according to a subject matter criterion. On each stage, a different explaining indicator – out of the three – is submitted for analysis. The research checks carefully if the particular explaining indicator occurred in the history of a state, when it took place last time before or over the continuance of an anti-austerity movement, and what was the time from the date of the explaining indicator's last occurrence to the date of the first use of political violence by stakeholders of an anti-austerity movement. It determines the values of the indicators detachedly for each state. Then, the fixed set of the indicators and their configurations undergo a test as the components of the explanatory models.

The first part of the test takes into consideration the first component of Ayele's explanatory framework. In drawing on the secondary literature, it checks over whether the intrastate indicator occurred in the member states of the Eurozone. The model encompasses the active physical political violence expressed in brute struggles for the height of political power by aspirants of collective political subjects such as ethnic groups or inhabitants of geographical entities (Ayele 2011, 216). According to Ayele, the intrastate indicator occurs in a state when an ethnic group or inhabitants of a geographical entity pursue their claim to rule by deploying physical force. Making claims to rule is not associated with irredentism whose hard core are territorial claims. Rather, this approach concentrates on the endeavors made to change the relationships between political subjects in the relation of public power. Intervention in politics is not just an opposition to ruling elites, but it is organized to take their place (O'Kane 2015). Those who used to be the ruled subjects seek to become the ruling subjects. Furthermore, on the grounds of a more general statement, if a collective political subject employs physical political violence to pursue its claim to rule, the intrastate indicator makes an appearance.

The only state from among the 14 cases where the intrastate indicator did not emerge was Slovenia typified with the obstreperously militant culture of political violence. In the states with the placid patterns, the manifestations of the intrastate indicator were the following: Estonia – the 1924 Estonian *coup d'état* attempt finished in 1924 (Valge 2011) and Slovakia – the 1948 Czechoslovak *coup d'état* in 1948 (Lukes 2011). Note should be taken, the Prague Spring (1968) does not meet the critical criteria of the intrastate indicator introduced in the theoretical framework because it was not an intervention in politics organized by the ruled subject to take the place of the ruling subject. The time from the date of the intrastate indicator's last occurrence to the date of the first use of political violence by stakeholders of an anti-austerity movement was 88 years in Estonia and 62 in Slovakia.

In the states with hector-led cultures of political violence, the intrastate indicator took the form of the failed *coup d'état* attempt, the so-called July Putsch in Austria finished in 1934 (Klösch 2007), the failed *coup d'état* attempt, the so-called Troelstra's mistake in the Netherlands in 1918 (Verkade 1965), and the failed *coup d'état*, the Algiers putsch, also known as the Generals' putsch in France in 1961 (McCarthy *et al.* 2013). The time from the date of the intrastate indicator's last occurrence to the date of the first use of political violence by stakeholders of an anti-austerity movement was 78 years in Austria, 94 in the Netherlands, and 49 in France.

The intrastate indicator took on the variety of shapes also in the states with militant cultures of political violence. They were: the failed *coup d'état* attempt, the so-called Pyjamas Coup in Greece finished in 1975 (Thomopoulos 2011), the failed *coup d'état*, known as the 23-F in Spain in 1981 (Hill 2007), the Mäntsälä rebellion, the failed *coup d'état* attempt in Finland in 1932 (Ahlbäck 2016), the Easter Rising in Ireland in 1916 (Dhiarmada 2016), the failure of the members of the German resistance to assassinate Adolf Hitler and seize control in Germany in 1944 (Hart 2013), the organization by the Armed Forces Movement the Carnation Revolution, a military *coup d'état* in Portugal in 1974 (Fishman 2011), the Belgian Revolution in Belgium in 1830 (Church 1977), and the Golpe Borghese, the failed *coup d'état* attempt in Italy in 1970 (Tota and Luchetti 2016).

The time from the date of the intrastate indicator's last occurrence to the date of the first use of political violence by stakeholders of an anti-austerity movement was 36 years in Greece, 30 in Spain, 82 in Finland, 94 in Ireland, 68 in Germany, 37 in Portugal, 180 in Belgium, and 40 in Italy.

In the states with placid cultures of political violence, the intrastate time indicator ranged from 62 to 88. Then, the ends of the continuum of the states with hector-led patterns were 49 and 94. In the states with militant types, the values of the indicator ranged from 30 to 180. The exemplifications of the latter pattern took on both the lowest and the highest values. Among the hector-led cases was the state with a lower value than the states classified as the placid patterns. In turn, the placid cases assumed a higher value than one of the hector-led cases. Strictly speaking, no regularity has appeared in the data concerning the time factor.

The explaining indicator characterizes most of the states in the world, and it is of low explanatory power as the part of the model in its current form. The simple co-occurrence avoids providing any compelling explanation. Checking it for the dates of appearance, however, has failed to increase the model's value. The analysis has revealed no regularity between the intrastate indicators and the cultures of political violence. The correlations between the variables support that argument. The Pearson correlation between a type of a culture of political violence and the occurrence of the intrastate indicator coefficient equals 0.189, indicating a small positive linear correlation, and it points out that the coefficient is not significantly different from 0. The Sig. 2-tailed level is 0.517, which is considerably higher than 0.05. Noticeably, there is no statistically significant correlation between the explaining indicator and the indicator to be accounted for at the 0.05 level.

The time from the date of the intrastate indicator's last occurrence to the date of the first use of political violence by stakeholders of anti-austerity movements ranged from 30 years in Spain with the aggressively militant pattern to 180 in Belgium with the obstreperously militant culture. The analysis has shown no regularity in the relationships between the types of a culture of political violence and the period under scrutiny. The correlation between a type of a culture of political violence and the time from the date of the intrastate indicator's last occurrence to the date of the first use of political violence by stakeholders of an anti-austerity movement coefficient equals −0.043, indicating a very small negative correlation, and it states that the coefficient is not significantly different from 0. The Sig. 2-tailed level is 0.889, which is tremendously higher than 0.05. A statistically significant correlation does not exist between the variables at the 0.05 level. Furthermore, the coefficient is counted for 13 out of 14 cases because the intrastate indicator did not enter Slovenia, which indeed reduces the meaning of the indicator even more so. The intrastate indicator occurred in 92.86 percent of the cases.

In Ayele's model, the second explaining indicator is the rivalry between regions. When the rivalry makes an appearance, the regional indicator emerges. The rivalry meeting a critical criterion existed in four out of 14 cases, in Spain, Ireland, Belgium, and Italy. In Spain, the rivalry between Catalonia and other regions was present over the Spanish anti-austerity movement continuance (2011) (Vargas 2015). The Irish anti-austerity movement co-occurred with the rivalry between Irish republican and Ulster loyalties (2010) (Phillips 2015). Similarly, when the Belgian anti-austerity movement acted, the rivalry between the Flemish Region (Flanders), the Walloon Region (Wallonia), and Brussels-Capital Region entered Belgium (2010) (Collard 2014). Abruzzo (The Abruzzi), Basilicata, Calabria, Campania, Emilia-Romagna, Friuli-Venezia, Giulia, Lazio (Latium), Liguria, Lombardia (Lombardy), Marche (The Marches), Molise, Piemonte (Piedmont), Puglia (Apulia), Sardegna (Sardinia), Sicilia (Sicily), Toscana, (Tuscany), Trentino-Alto Adige, Umbria, Valle d'Aosta, and Veneto rivaled in Italy when the Italian anti-austerity movement functioned (2010) (Valeriano 2013). The time from the date of the regional indicator's last occurrence to the date of the first use of political violence by stakeholders of the anti-austerity movement was 0 in years, in each case.

Whereas stakeholders of the anti-austerity movements in Belgium and Italy epitomized the obstreperously militant culture of political violence, Spanish and Irish political subjects formed the aggressively militant pattern. The explaining indicator co-occurred only in 28.57 percent of the cases. In Finland, Germany, Portugal, Slovenia, and Greece with the militant cultures, regional rivalries were not present. Although the regional indicator entered many states with the militant patterns, we should not overstate its meaning and explanatory potential due to its absence in the history of other states with the placid, hector-led, and militant patterns. So, its role as the part of the explanatory framework is minor. However, the regional indicator did not co-occur in the states with the placid and hector-led types. It means that if a regional rivalry exists in a state, a militant pattern of a culture of political violence is more likely to originate there than placid or the hector-led patterns. More likely also is that if the rivalry does not emerge, a placid or hector-led pattern makes an appearance. Nevertheless, an extent of probability is not very high just because of the already discussed flaws.

The Pearson correlation between a type of a culture of political violence and the occurrence of the regional indicator coefficient equals −0.432, indicating a medium negative linear correlation, and it shows that the coefficient is not significantly different from 0. The Sig. 2-tailed level is 0.123, which is strikingly higher than 0.05. The results demonstrate that there is no statistically significant correlation at the 0.05 level.

Ayele defines the colonial indicator as the colonization of the land (Ayele 2011). The analysis strives to observe if the territory of a state was colonized, rather than if a state was a colonizer. The meaning taken on by the explaining category comes directly from Ayele's theory. It should not be, therefore, confused with other types of relations between an empire and the territories ancillary to the empire (Annus 2012; Loomba 2005). Additionally, the exclusion of the direct references to Ethiopia from the framework follows its replacement with another methodological assumption. The research dismisses the simplest approach of a colonizing Europe and a colonized Africa and Asia from the sixteenth century onwards because it obscures the details of the colonial history, and it fails to consider the experience of people in colonies (Cooper 2005). It also does not adopt the questionable premise that a colony ought to be an overseas territory of a colonizer. The predicate "overseas" is not a distinctive feature of the colonies in the review of the history of the states (Steinmetz 2014).

Instead, the institution of a colony in one territory by a ruling political subject from another territory, and the subsequent perpetuation, expansion, and exploitation of that colony are of the nature of colonialism. The act of the institution manufactures a set of unequal relationships between the colonial center and the colony and, thereby, also between the colonists and the indigenous peoples. A group of people who leave their native state to create in a new land, a settlement subject to or connected with the parent nation, creates a colony.

In the history of European states, colonialism was usually one of the types of dependency relations between territories, which emerged over time (Steinmetz 2014). Their appearance had either a concealed or overt form (Bäcker 2011, 123). In spite of the considerable moderation of the criteria of the colonial indicator distinction, it appeared only in three out of 14 cases. It means that the explaining indicator originated merely in 21.43 percent of the cases. It emerged in all the states with the placid cultures of political violence, that is, in Estonia, the colonial period finished in 1991 (Mertelsmann and Rahi-Tamm 2009) and 1989 in Slovakia (Myant 1992). Furthermore, in both cases, it took the form of Soviet colonialism, the occupation of the territories that later developed into a colonial rule (Annus 2012). The indicator existed pending the end of colonialism. The term is acknowledged as the date of the last occurrence of the indicator.

Surprisingly, the time from the date of the colonial indicator's last occurrence to the date of the first use of political violence by stakeholders of the anti-austerity movements was the same in both states, and it totaled exactly 21 years. The colonial indicator also entered Ireland, but the time was equal to 79 years. It was the Statute of Westminster 1931 (Hull 2015) which stopped the colonialism. In Ireland, in contrast to Estonia and Slovakia, the aggressively militant culture of political violence pattern emerged. Only one from among the nine states with the militant type was the colony. Furthermore, the colonial indicator did not enter the states with the hector-led patterns.

The Pearson correlation between a type of a culture of political violence and the appearance of the colonial indicator coefficient equals 0.595, indicating a strong positive linear correlation, and it points out that the coefficient is significantly different from 0. The Sig. 2-tailed level is 0.025, which is strikingly lower than 0.05. It reveals a statistically significant correlation at the 0.05 level. Its meaning should not be, however, overestimated for the explanatory framework. Contrary to Ayele, the colonial indicator typifies the more peaceful patterns of a culture of political violence.

On the one hand, the co-occurrence of the elements of the explanatory framework is indisputable when we consider strictly and only the states with the placid patterns. On the other hand, the framework should be tested in this scope by working with further examples to verify if the relations between the indicators are not casual deceptively. We put forward this caveat because the research has identified no regularity between the indicators in other cases. In contrast to Ayele's assumption, the colonial indicator did not precede the cultures of political violence that benefited from the use of excessive physical political violence. Ireland, representing the militant pattern, was the only exception to this statement, but the model in its current form does not introduce its potential derivation. Ultimately, although it cannot be foreclosed that the colonial explaining indicator comes in handy to account for the placid patterns, the model is of relatively low explanatory power to deal with the question of the European cultures of political violence.

The facts of simple occurrence explain little here. It would therefore be advisable to delve deeper into the very nature of the indicator. The history of colonization is worth scrutinizing in terms of how many times a state was colonized, how long it was a colony, what the proceedings of the dependency relation were, and how exactly the relationship ended. One may consider the rhetoric of the new capitalism as a "new colonial" power (Sartre 2001) to be an inspiring framework for a reconceptualization of Ayele's model in the semantic field of the colonial indicator. Finally, it would also be desirable to check whether a state has been in some other dependency relations and, if so, what essential features it has had. Note should be taken that much more time passed from the date of the colonial indicator's last occurrence to the date of the first use of political violence by stakeholders of the anti-austerity movement in the militant than the placid type. It suggests that in the former colonies which lost their colonial status a shorter time ago, it is more likely that a placid pattern occurs than in the colonies which lost it a long time ago.

Ayele argues for employing the intrastate, regional, and colonial indicators as the fixed explaining set (Ayele 2011). Nevertheless, all the explaining indicators occurred merely in Ireland, that is 7.14 percent of the cases. It means that the explanatory framework as a unified whole has not provided a researcher with the possibility to explain and compare the sources of the cultures of political violence. The Pearson correlation between a type of a culture of political violence and the full Ayele model coefficient equals −0.189, indicating a small negative linear correlation, and it shows that the coefficient is not significantly different from 0. The Sig. 2-tailed level is 0.517, which is measurably higher than 0.05. It means that the correlation is not statistically significant at the 0.05 level, in contrast to Ayele's assumption.

The test of significance does not allow us to reject the null hypothesis at the 0.05 level, which indicates that there is no significant correlation between the intrastate, regional, and colonial indicators and the time of their occurrence in the history of a state and a pattern of a culture of political violence of stakeholders of an anti-austerity movement in the state. It means that the alternative hypothesis cannot be assumed.

Apparently, the model has proved rather useless to approach the remaining 13 cases where the fixed set of the indicators have not emerged. Its applicability is, therefore, confined to account for the culture of political violence entering Ethiopia in the particular historical period, in the line of Ayele's original model. The verification of Ayele's framework fails to come across with arguments for considering the straightforward involvement of the indicators to the explanatory model under construction. Nonetheless, it informs the explanatory model which approaches the indicators in specific configurations.

It was much more useful to take the components of the explaining set as the elements of the arrays of diverse models which may emerge in various configurations and thus create distinct frameworks. Stronger is a relationship between the configurations of the sets of the explaining indicators and the cultures of political violence than the individual explaining indicators and the patterns. The Pearson correlation between a type of a culture of political violence and a configuration of the intrastate, regional, and colonial explaining indicators coefficient equals 0.651, indicating a strong positive linear correlation, and it points out that the coefficient is significantly different from 0. The Sig. 2-tailed level is 0.012, which is substantially lower than 0.05. It reveals notably a statistically significant correlation at the 0.05 level.

Notably, the configurations of the explaining indicators show that only and all the placid cultures of political violence typify with the occurrence of the intrastate and colonial indicators. The hector-led types, but not only they, are marked with the intrastate indicator. More diversified are the explanatory frameworks of the militant pattern. The mildest militant culture of political violence, the indulgingly militant type in Finland, shares the explanatory model with the hector-led patterns. The moderately militant types, the obstreperously militant patterns in Belgium, Germany, Portugal, Slovenia, and Italy, are broadly based. They are explained by the set of the intrastate and regional indicators (Belgium and Italy) and just the intrastate indicator (Portugal and Germany). The model is not useful to explain the Slovene culture of political violence. The sets of the explaining indicators of the most thuggish patterns, the aggressively militant culture of political violence in Greece, Spain, and Ireland, were fully diversified. They were: just the intrastate indicator, the set of the intrastate and regional indicators, and the configuration of the intrastate, colonial, and regional indicators respectively.

Undoubtedly, the full Ayele model encompassing the intrastate, colonial, and regional explaining indicators used as the fixed, united, and unchangeable set is of low applicability to explain the occurrence of cultures of political violence. It may, however, be effectively modified to boost its explanatory power in the already introduced directions but, obviously, they are not the only one.

Experiences of War, Revolution, and Civil War

Norman LaPorte and Matthew Worley presume that if German party militants' seminal experiences of war, revolution, and civil war take place, a culture of political violence occurs (2008, 246). Just as in Ayele, a culture of political violence is defined as the use of extensive physical political violence. The framework lacks assumption about its gradability. In contrast to Ayele, not Ethiopia but Germany is the territorial context of the phenomena involved in LaPorte and Worley's theoretical approach. The reference to the state makes the approach highly contextual and, thus, applicable to examine the research field severely restricted by the particular territorial boundaries. It may be, however, quickly removed from the explanatory model for the purpose of increasing the level of its applicability to empirical studies. The theory formulated by LaPorte and Worley informs the null and alternative hypotheses.

H_0: There might be no correlation between a fixed set of war, civil war, and revolution indicators and the time of their occurrence in the history of a state and a pattern of a culture of political violence of stakeholders of an anti-austerity movement in the state.

H_A: If in the history of a state, a fixed set of war, civil war, and revolution indicators occur, stakeholders of an anti-austerity movement in the state might have a militant culture of political violence, but the culture loses its militant value over time, and the more time intervenes from the occurrence of the indicators, the more peaceful the culture becomes.

LaPorte and Worley introduce a quite simplified but clear approach towards the explaining indicators (Carter *et al.* 2012; O'Kane 2015; Tarrow 2007). The straightforward occurrence of war, civil war, and revolution in a particular state is considered by them to be an explanation of the complex phenomenon of a culture of political violence. The predicate of "seminal" does not provide a researcher with additional aspects of conflicts as long as we assume that each of them always has socially important consequences. In fact, the model fails to cover the sources, course, and outcomes of warfare and revolutionary acts. The repertoire and intensity of contention, frequency, features, and dynamics of the indicators in the history of a particular state are omitted as well (McAdam 2014; Wada 2016).

Sue Onslow's case study of Zimbabwe shows that the distinctive features of war are worth taking into consideration in attempts to account for the most vicious cultures of political violence. Nevertheless, the researcher fails to produce any complete explanatory framework which would involve war. Onslow merely points out that some structural indicators may contribute to the occurrence of a culture of political violence (2011, 8). The category of a structural factor is broad, unspecified, and thus far from being applicable in its current shape to account for the European patterns.

By the time of testing the framework, the research verifies if, what, and when the explaining indicators entered the particular states. War is the first indicator under scrutiny, but it may be approached in at least two different ways. First, we can confirm the occurrence of the war explaining indicator if the authority of a state wages war. Second, we can verify the existence of the war explaining indicator when the war takes place on the territory of a state and, thus, afflicts its populace. LaPorte and Worley avoid operationalizing the category, so the methodological assumption to be made is not limited to the design properties. The first proposal concerns the war which might be somewhere beyond the interest of the state inhabitants. The questions of public advocacy of taking part in war and backlash against its making are outside the scope of the indicator features. Additionally, in general, they do not have to be taken into consideration by the ruling political subjects. The results of waging war are not necessarily socially noticeable and measurable. The second suggestion refers to a political structure as a whole to a higher extent. Denizens of a state are directly engaged in the warfare which is not recognized barely as a domain of political elites. Following the arguments, the research adopts the second variant form to deal with the values of the war indicator.

LaPorte and Worley present the use of extensive physical political violence as the very essence of a culture of political violence. The results of their model application to analysis provide arguments against and for its empirical effectiveness to explain dissimilarities between the patterns of a culture of political violence.

For the sake of clarity, the dates recognized as the occurrence of the war, civil war, and revolution indicators are equal to the closing caesurae of the warfare or revolutionary activities in a state. Each state involved in the research was in a state of war in the past, including those with the placid patterns. It means that the indicator made an appearance in 100 percent of the cases. Warfare took the form of the Guerrilla war in the Baltic states finished in 1956 in Estonia (Zaccor 1994), World War II in Slovakia, Austria, the Netherlands, France, Greece, Finland, Germany, Belgium, and Italy finished in 1944 in France and Greece, and in 1945 in the other states (Willmott 2008), the Peninsular War finished in 1814 in Spain (Daly 2016), the dissident Irish Republican campaign was lingering in 2010 when the Irish anti-austerity movement came into being (Tonge 2014), and the Ten-Day War, called the Slovenian Independence War or the Weekend War finished in 1991 in Slovenia (Prebilič and Guštin 2010). It points out solely the absolute co-occurrence of the facts, which is nothing to marvel over because the war left its mark on the history of Europe.

Note should be taken that the Spanish Civil War (1936–1939) is treated as a civil war rather than war, although foreign military entities engaged in the warfare. This methodological choice is justified by the relationships between the belligerents. In fact, the major political actors were internal. They were just supported by the external entities (Matthews 2014).

The sheer appearance of war in the history is not a forceful component of the explanatory framework proposed by LaPorte and Worley if we assess it out of some other indicators. Not more useful is the next aspect under scrutiny, the time from the end of a particular war to the violent behavior of an anti-austerity movement. The Pearson correlation between a type of a culture of political violence and the time from the date of the war indicator's last occurrence to the date of the first use of political violence by stakeholders of the anti-austerity movement coefficient equals 0.095, indicating a very small positive linear correlation, and it reveals that the coefficient is not significantly different from 0. The Sig. 2-tailed level is 0.747, which is higher than 0.05. It is not a statistically significant correlation at the 0.05 level. It means that it does not matter how many years have passed since the war finished when we aim to explain the European cultures of political violence.

The time, in years, from the date of the war indicator's last occurrence to the date of the first use of political violence by stakeholders of an anti-austerity movement was: 56 in Estonia, 65 in Slovakia, 67 in Austria, 67 in the Netherlands, 66 in France, 67 in Greece, 197 in Spain, 69 in Finland, 0 in Ireland, 67 in Germany, 93 in Portugal, 65 in Belgium, 21 in Slovenia, and 65 in Italy. In the states with the placid cultures of political violence, it ranges from 56 to 65. The extreme values of the cases with the hector-led patterns are 66 and 67. No meaningful regularity emerges between the indicators because the exemplifications of the militant types are on the continuum determined by 0 and 197. The values of all the cultures of political violence are localizable on the last continuum, which means that no regularity exists in the relationships between a pattern of a culture of political violence and the time from the date of the war indicator's last occurrence to the date of the first use of political violence by stakeholders of an anti-austerity movement.

The second part of the explanatory framework concentrates on the civil war indicator. Just like the war indicator, it fails to deal with the details of potentially useful properties to account for the diversity of the cultures of political violence (Hartzell 2009). The civil war emerged as the Austrian Civil War, also known as the February Uprising finished in 1934 in Austria (Jeffrey 1995), the Fronde in 1653 in France (Davies 1990), the Greek Civil War in 1949 in Greece (Christodoulakis 2016), the Spanish Civil War, known as The Civil War or The War in 1939 in Spain (Matthews 2014), the Finnish Civil War in 1918 in Finland (Arosalo 1998), the Irish Civil War in 1923 in Ireland (Kissane 2000), The German Peasants' War in 1525 in Germany (Scott and Scribner 1991), the brief civil war in 1919 in Portugal (Payne 2011), and the Italian Civil War in 1945 in Italy (Pavone 2014). It did not occur in Estonia, Slovakia, the Netherlands, Belgium, and Slovenia, which means that the indicator emerged in 64.29 percent of the cases.

It allows us to discern that civil war erupted in the states with the hector-led and militant cultures of political violence. Nevertheless, it did not erupt in all of those states, which inhibits detecting a considerably meaningful regularity in the relations between the indicators. Importantly, the civil war indicator did not make an appearance in the cases with the placid patterns. The Pearson correlation between a type of a culture of political violence and the occurrence of the civil war indicator coefficient equals −0.509, indicating a high negative linear correlation, and it points out that the coefficient is significantly different from 0. The Sig. 2-tailed level is 0.063, which is slightly higher than 0.05. Therefore, it is not a statistically significant correlation at the 0.05 level.

The time from the date of the civil war indicator's last occurrence to the date of the first use of political violence by stakeholders of an anti-austerity movement, in years, was: 78 in Austria, 357 in France, 62 in Greece, 72 in Spain, 96 in Finland, 87 in Ireland, 487 in Germany, 92 in Portugal, and 65 in Italy. The values ranged from 78 to 357, in the states with the hector-led cultures of political violence. The extreme values of the indicator in the states with the militant patterns were 62 and 487. In the states where the placid cultures of political violence originated, civil war did not break out. The analysis detects no regularity in the relationships between the variables because the continua of the hector-led and militant patterns overlap. However, we have to keep in mind that the civil war did not enter the states with the placid cultures of political violence, which is perfectly in the line of LaPorte and Worley.

The linear correlation between a type of a culture of political violence and the time from the date of the civil war indicator's last occurrence to the date of the first use of political violence by stakeholders of an anti-austerity movement is computed for nine cases because the civil war indicator emerged in nine from among 14 cases. The Pearson correlation coefficient equals −0.228, indicating a small negative linear correlation, and it reveals that the coefficient is significantly different from 0. The Sig. 2-tailed level is 0.555, which is considerably higher than 0.05. It is not a statistically significant correlation at the 0.05 level.

The last part of the explanatory model focuses explicitly on the revolution indicator. Just like the previous parts, it is limited to the simple fact of the occurrence of revolution. It makes us pose a question of why other forms of conflict, such as rebellion, revolt, uprising, putsch, *coup d'état*, and counterrevolution are not involved in the framework. Although they are beyond the subject matter scope of the model, their validity to account for the cultures of political violence is worth verifying in future research.

Admittedly, LaPorte and Worley avoid introducing an operationalizable definition of revolution and its essential features, but they indicate that a political type of revolution is of relevance to a culture of political violence. Political revolution is a specific type of conflict which contributes to a rapid change of the relationships between political subjects: the ruled and the ruling, springing from both the ineffectiveness of a political system and its delegitimation (Beck 2015; Davies 1962; Stone 1966). This simple definition is applied to verify whether the revolution indicator entered the European states. To put it another way, only those examples of contentious politics which meet fully all the criteria introduced in the definition are found revolutions. Accordingly, even if some events are known as revolution, e.g., the Singing Revolution (1987–1991) in Estonia (Brokaw and Brokaw 2001), but they fail to satisfy all the essential features of revolution handsomely, they are not placed into the category.

The revolution indicator found expression in the Velvet Revolution or the Gentle Revolution finished in 1989 in Slovakia (Dellinger 2016), the revolution of 1848–1849 in 1849 in Austria (Smith IV 2013), the Belgian Revolution in 1831 in the Netherlands (van Goethem 2010), the French Revolution of 1830, also known as the July Revolution, the Second French Revolution or Three Glorious Days in 1830 in France (Church 1977), the Greek War of Independence, also known as the Greek Revolution in 1829 in Greece (Church 1977), the Glorious Revolution in 1868 in Spain (Smith 1953), the Irish Revolution in 1923 in Ireland (Coleman 2013), the German Revolution or the November Revolution in 1919 in German (Lambert 1999), the Carnation Revolution in 1974 in Portugal (Cerezales 2016), the Belgian Revolution in 1831 in Belgium (van Goethem 2010), and the Revolutions of 1848, known in some countries as the Spring of Nations, the People's Spring, the Springtime of the Peoples, or the Year of Revolution finished in 1848 in Slovenia, and in 1849 in Italy (Rapport 2008). It means that the indicator occurred in 85.71 percent of the cases. Revolution did not enter two states: Estonia and Finland, where the placidly observing and indulgingly militant cultures of political violence came into sight respectively. It makes out a case that the straightforward occurrence of the revolution does not allow us to identify regularity in data between the explaining indicator and the patterns of a culture of political violence. The Pearson correlation between a type of a culture of political violence and the occurrence of the revolution indicator coefficient equals −0.279, indicating a small negative linear correlation, and it shows that the coefficient is significantly different from 0. The Sig. 2-tailed level is 0.334, which is substantially higher than 0.05. Then, it is not a statistically significant correlation at the 0.05 level.

In years, the time from the date of the revolution indicator's last occurrence to the date of the first use of political violence by stakeholders of an anti-austerity movement was: 21 in Slovakia, 163 in Austria, 181 in the Netherlands, 180 in France, 182 in Greece, 143 in Spain, 87 in Ireland, 93 in Germany, 37 in Portugal, 179 in Belgium, 164 in Slovenia, and 161 in Italy. In the states with the placid cultures of political violence, the only value was 21. The values of the states with the hector-led patterns ranged from 163 to 181. The continuum for the militant patterns had the extreme points of 37 and 182. The values of the last two types overlap, which inhibits us seeing differences between the relationships between the variables.

The research computes the correlation for 12 cases because the revolution indicator did not originate in the two other states. It scrutinizes the relationship between a type of a culture of political violence and the time from the date of the revolution indicator's last occurrence to the date of the first use of political violence by stakeholders of an anti-austerity movement. The correlation coefficient equals 0.226, indicating a small positive linear correlation, and it intimates that the coefficient is not significantly different from 0. The Sig. 2-tailed level is 0.479, which is substantially higher than 0.05. At the 0.05 level, it is not a statistically significant correlation.

All the components of LaPorte and Worley's explanatory model occurred in Austria, France, Greece, Spain, Ireland, Germany, Portugal, and Italy. The set as a whole did not enter Estonia and Slovakia whose patterns of a culture of political violence were of placid nature. It means that all the indicators emerged in

85.71 percent of the cases. Let us emphasize that in no state with the most peaceful patterns the fixed set of the indicators appeared. It entered two out of the three states with the hector-led cultures, Austria (hector-consenting) and France (hector-acknowledgment). The Netherlands (hector-consenting) lacked the civil war indicator, just like the states with the placid types.

The war, civil war, and revolution indicators were present in six from between the nine states with the militant cultures of political violence, that is, in Germany, Portugal, and Italy in the form of the obstreperously militant patterns and in Greece, Spain, and Ireland – the aggressively militant patterns. The set did not make an appearance in Finland, Belgium, and Slovenia. It appeared in all the most violent Greek, Spanish, and Irish cases representing the aggressively militant cultures of political violence. Nevertheless, apart from Greece, Spain, and Ireland, the fixed set of indicators also entered the states with less vicious patterns. It shows that the model in its current and undivided form does not allow us to see the distinct differences between the hector-led and militant cultures of political violence. Therefore, it would be advisable to consider the inclusion of additional indicators to its content and to pay more attention to the details of the existing indicators (McAdam 2003).

Despite LaPorte and Worley's assumptions, the correlation between a type of a culture of political violence and the fixed set of the war, civil war, and revolution indicators coefficient equals 0.394, indicating a moderate positive linear correlation. It testifies that the coefficient is not significantly different from 0. The Sig. 2-tailed level is 0.163, which is considerably higher than 0.05. It points out that correlation is not statistically significant at the 0.05 level.

Evidence does not allow us to reject the null hypothesis. There is no significant correlation between the war, civil war, and revolution indicators and the time of their occurrence in the history of the member states of the Eurozone and the cultures of political violence of stakeholders of anti-austerity movements in the states, at the 0.05 level. LaPorte and Worley's explanatory framework is effective to explain the diversity of cultures of political violence to a low extent.

Nevertheless, if we look at LaPorte and Worley's model, not as the fixed totality but a modifiable set of components, its empirical effectiveness is greater. According to a modified framework, if in the history of a state, the war or the war and revolution occur, it is likely that a placid pattern enters the state. The placidly-observing culture of political violence followed the war in Estonia. In Slovakia, the war and revolution preceded the placidly rationalizing pattern. The relationship between the variables is more probable to appear in the states with a placid type when just the war indicator makes an appearance in a state because some examples with not only the placid but also hector-led and militant patterns had the set of war and revolution in common. The hector-led types were fueled by this set but also by the full LaPorte and Worley's explanatory framework encompassing the war, civil war, and revolution indicators. The hector-consenting culture of political violence co-occurred with those two configurations in the history of Austria and the Netherlands. In turn, in France, the full set preceded the hector-acknowledgment pattern.

The model is invulnerable to notice the sharp differences between the sources of the hector-led and militant types. The mildest militant pattern, the indulgingly militant culture of political violence which entered Finland co-occurred in the state with the set of war and revolution which also was correlated with the hector-led types. The moderate type, the obstreperously militant pattern that entered Belgium, Germany, Portugal, Slovenia, and Italy may be explained with the appearance of the war and revolution set in Belgium and Slovenia and the full set of the indicators in Germany, Portugal, and Italy. The most vicious pattern, the aggressively militant culture might be accounted for just the complete set of war, civil war, and revolution in Greece, Spain, and Ireland. Thereby, if we observe the emergence of the comprehensive set in the history of a state, it is more likely that political subjects in its structure will represent a more relentless culture of political violence. This part of the test confirms the validity of the already discussed assumption made by LaPorte and Worley.

The explaining indicators in particular configurations are more empirically effective to explain the sources of the cultures of political violence than the fixed set of factors. The test has thrown light on the relationships between the configurations of the war, civil war, and revolution explaining indicators on the one hand and the patterns of a culture of political violence on the other. The correlation coefficient equals 0.545, indicating a high positive linear correlation between the variables, and it reveals that the coefficient is significantly different from 0. The Sig. 2-tailed level is 0.044, which is slightly lower than 0.05. It is indeed a statistically significant correlation at the 0.05 level. It provides us with a counterargument for applying LaPorte and Worley's explanatory framework in its existing form and an argument for looking at the indicators in the diverse configurations to enhance the current theories.

Noisy and Turbulent Politics of the Street, the Town Square, and the Factory

The intrastate, regional, colonial, war, civil war, and revolution indicators are beyond the interest of the next framework. According to Robert Gerwarth, a culture of political violence is the result of the noisy and turbulent politics of the street, the town square, and the factory, in which socioeconomic grievances, hostility to state authority, and new and recycled dreams of a purified community are expressed (2011, 518). The research applies this set of indicators as one explaining indicator in an empirical test for two reasons. Whereas the first is of practical nature, the second is formal. First, in political reality, the components of the approach are usually combined tightly. So, it would hardly be possible to identify and assess them separately. It would also be ineffective since they co-occur. Second, just like Ayele, in Gerwarth's model, the concomitance of the set of the explaining indicators is the necessary condition under which a culture of political violence makes an appearance. Therefore, the occurrence of all the elements involved in the explaining set is treated as the appearance of the explaining indicator.

Gerwarth's explanatory framework approaches the independent variable similarly to William Eubank and Leonard Weinberg. As they point out, if repeated expressions of political violence occur, a culture of political violence originates (Eubank and Weinberg 2000, 294). The second model is not as much elaborated as Gerwarth's model. However, after the operationalization of the explaining indicator proposed by Gerwarth, Eubank, and Weinberg, they cover the same empirical expressions. The theory-driven relationship between the indicators informs the content of the hypothesis to be tested. What derives directly from the Gerwarth theoretical approach is: if the explaining indicators enter a state, a culture of political violence might emerge in the state.

The expressions of the explaining indicator appeared in every state over the continuance of the anti-austerity movements. It means that the time from the date of the noisy and turbulent politics indicator's last occurrence to the date of the first use of political violence by stakeholders of an anti-austerity movement was equal to 0 in years in each case, regardless of a represented type of a culture of political violence.

Here, some arguments against the usefulness and empirical effectiveness of the model resurface. Presumably, a culture of political violence is always of some value, and its patterns range from the fully peaceful to extremely vicious types. Therefore, the essential features of patterns have to have different sources. Gerwarth's model is invulnerable to those differences, and thus it is useful to examine the Eurozone cases to a very low extent. Furthermore, nowadays, mass political mobilization is frequently used to achieve political goals. Thereby, it often meets fully the set of critical criteria of the explaining indicator introduced by Gerwarth. As it implies, a culture of political violence is an unceasing phenomenon. As long as the model remains unchanged, it explains almost everything because it co-occurs in a vast variety of cases with beings, phenomena, processes, and their configurations entering social reality constantly.

The employment of the conceptual framework of cultures of political violence shows that the angry anti-austerity protests took the form of noisy and turbulent politics of the street, the town square, and the factory. Participants of those events were representatives of the variety of professions. Except for Estonia and Slovakia, in the Eurozone states, the factory workers attached themselves to the movements and staged protests. Socioeconomic grievances constituted the expressed reason why people decided to use political violence in a public sphere. They were highlighted and fueled the crowd. A plethora of verbal and non-verbal expressions mirrored the demonstrable hostility to state authority when protest participants referred to representatives of state apparatuses. The messages transmitted directly to political elites were full of overt hostility as well. New and recycled dreams of a purified community presented the states free from both austerity measures and their makers. They introduced the hope for the unchained society able to lead an existence worthily. Movement participants in Austria, Belgium, Finland, France, Greece, Spain, the Netherlands, Ireland, Germany, Portugal, Slovenia, and Italy satisfied all the critical criteria of the explaining indicators handsomely. The indicators entered Austria in 2012,

Belgium in 2010, Finland in 2014, France in 2010, Greece in 2011, Spain in 2011, the Netherlands in 2012, Ireland in 2010, Germany in 2012, Portugal in 2011, Slovenia in 2012, and Italy in 2010 and took the form of anti-austerity protests. The dates are the periods of the protests that meet the critical criteria of the explaining indicators in Gerwarth's meaning.

In the remaining states, political subjects avoided holding anti-austerity protests. Although the explaining indicators occurred there, they took different forms. In Estonia, a huge anti-ACTA demonstration and numerous strikes took place in 2012 (Koorits 2012; Raun and Kund 2012). In turn, in Slovakia, the protests of various occupational class occurred in 2010 (Boyd 2010a, 2010b, 2010c).

Gerwarth's explanatory model is of very low usefulness to account for the cultures of political violence existence and differentiation. The hypothesis is not rejected, but it has a small cognitive value. Its explanatory power to delve analytically into the research field is rather scarce. In its existing form, it fails to generate any framework which would allow a researcher to observe relevant differences between the sources of various patterns of a culture of political violence. The explaining indicators and the phenomena to be explained are also connected too loosely. A culture of political violence is not a particular result of the noisy grievances, hostility to state authority, and new and recycled dreams of a purified community.

From Ruthless Military Governments to Youth's Engagement in Electoral Violence

A more detailed approach towards explaining indicators typifies the next models. Robin Theobald brings a relatively narrowly determined role under civil society (Stacey and Meyer 2005). He states that a culture of political violence originates when the highly mobilized and urbanized civil society, in the developed Latin American states with strong democratic traditions, identified with the state does not confine its militaries to the narrowly constitutional role, and ruthless and determined military governments threaten at length the civil society (Theobald 1999). Just like LaPorte and Worley, Theobald understands a culture of political violence as the use of excessive physical political violence. His approach also does not make the difference between cultures of political violence.

An extent of applicability of Theobald's framework is limited by its contextual dimension, much like LaPorte and Worley's model. Therefore, once again, it is a methodological demand to remove the reference to the territory, here to the Latin American states, to make the framework applicable to work with the European cases. It contributes to the generation of two premises. First, if a highly mobilized and urbanized civil society in the developed states with strong democratic traditions identified with the state does not confine its militaries to the narrowly constitutional role, a culture of political violence occurs. Second, if ruthless and determined military governments threaten at length the civil society, a culture of political violence emerges (Theobald 1999, 153). These explaining indicators did not enter the member states of the Eurozone under analysis

(Chandhoke 2007) when the anti-austerity movements acted. Therefore, Theobald's model is of a low empirical effectiveness to explain the diversity of the post-2008 cultures of political violence.

Thomas Waldman assumes that if tribal and religious loyalties occur, a culture of political violence emerges (2007, 70). Admittedly, the elements of the explanatory framework are undefined, but Waldman's description of a culture of political violence is semantically close to the classic definition. It is the use of extensive physical political violence. The loyalties which are to account for this phenomenon are identifiable in all the states involved because there is a resurgence of tribalism and religiosity in the contemporary world (Gao 2016). Nevertheless, in some cases, such as Estonia and Slovenia, physical political violence did not occur. Instead, they had the placid cultures of political violence. It proves that simple occurrence of tribal and religious loyalties is not useful to be the sole explaining factor. In addition, the model is not vulnerable to discern the differences between various types of the phenomenon to be explained. The potential application of the model to empirical research requires, therefore, devising a range of criteria which would allow a researcher to delve analytically into the differences between tribal as well as religious loyalties to abstract indicators from the structures of theoretical categories.

In drawing on Waldman, one might want to produce the model which would approach the intensity of religious cleavages entering the particular states rather than the sheer religious loyalties emergence (Minkenberg 2009). Then, new tribalism is also worth taking into consideration. Modern tribalism has two forms. The first, ascriptive tribalism refers to the forms of organization based on kinship, blood, and territory (Kaplan 2016). Here, it may be useful to ask about the relation between the modern tribes in a state as well as the intensity of bonds. The second, aspirational tribalism, emerges when those born outside of the tribal system desire to be accepted by actual or virtual tribal actors (Kaplan 2016). Their engagement in contentious politics in the member states of the Eurozone matters, in particular, if the citizens are put in jeopardy.

Merle Kling claims that when non-political agencies of socialization work by implanting violent role models into people, a culture of political violence originates (1963, 129–130). The phenomenon to be explained, a culture of political violence is the configuration of the use of physical political violence and the acceptance of violence as a legitimated means to take on the role of the ruling subject (Kling 1963, 121). The configuration is homomorphic, and Kling made no suggestion about its transposition potential. Then, non-political agencies of socialization are family, Church [*sic*], and less formally organized institutions (Kling 1963, 129). According to Kling, they push people to commit political violence and to accept its perpetration in the mechanisms of the change of political roles in a political structure.

The impact of the non-political agencies of socialization on denizens of the contemporary states is, however, difficult to measure. It is even harder to assert unambiguously that exactly they and only they determine a particular culture of political violence. Furthermore, in 1963, when Kling created the model, an array of influential agencies of socialization did not encompass as many objects as it should nowadays. The new powerful actors are of comparable relevance to those mentioned by Kling. For instance, it is not impossible to exaggerate the role of social or mass media in political socialization (McAdam and Kloos 2015). These drawbacks undermine the framework's empirical effectiveness to examine a contemporary political reality. Kling's model does not account for the cultures of political violence in the Eurozone because the phenomenon to be explained did not occur in the form determined by Kling in the period under scrutiny in the European states. It is also of low utility to reveal the diversity of the cultures of political violence because of the flaws of the explaining indicators.

The popularity and commonness of social media allow us to formulate one more argument against the existing explanatory frameworks of a culture of political violence. Helen Dexter and Emmanuel-Pierre Guittet reckon that the fictions of political violence defined as the novels, short stories, plays, movies, or parts thereof, where political processes and political views are reasonably close to the surface contribute to a semantically undermined culture of political violence (2014, 380). Nevertheless, the political fiction is both widely disseminated and easily accessible because the internet removes most of the barriers in the member states of the Eurozone. Anti-austerity events were not the performance of any artistic scenario. The meaning of a culture of political violence might have decreased the explanatory potential of the model, but it was necessary to adopt any definition in the light of the absence thereof in Dexter and Guittet's framework.

Atte Enyenihi Okwong contends that when the youths' engagement in electoral violence emerges in a state, an unspecified culture of political violence originates there (2012, 129). According to the data gathered by the International Foundation for Electoral Systems (IFES 2017a), electoral violence, understood as any harm or threat of harm to any person or property involved in the election process, or the process itself, during the election period (IFES 2017b), did not take place in the member states of the Eurozone in the period analyzed. Thus, the young people did not have the opportunity to engage in electoral violence and to make any contribution to a culture of political violence in the meaning accepted in the research. Once again, the absence of the semantic field of the category to be explained in the model limits its explanatory power.

Jaime M. Pensado's model consists of the internationalist spirit of the 1960s, as the explaining factor, and an undefined culture of political violence as the phenomenon to be explained (2013, 14). It is highly contextual and does not provide any theoretical assumptions applicable to account for the diversity of the cultures of political violence in the member states of the Eurozone between 2007 and 2015. Nevertheless, one may see the framework as an incentive to examine the history of European social movements, including those launched after the outbreak of the youth protest in 1968 (Horn 2007; Horn and Kenney 2004). Has the process of the 1968 protests been reflected in the post-2008 activities of the European anti-austerity movements? Has the rebellious spirit survived? Has the Spirit of '68 left its mark on the societies' cultures of political violence? (Horn 2007, 190).

What More Is to Be Done to Account for the Cultures of Political Violence

The analysis of the current explanatory frameworks proves that they only explain to a low extent why stakeholders of the post-2008 anti-austerity movements had particular patterns of a culture of political violence. Although the theories which produced the structures of the models worked in the particular time and territory contexts, they turned out to be hardly empirically effective to approach the Eurozone cultures of political violence. Being a middle-range theory is obviously not a limitation. Most of them just have a limited explanatory power to inform other models. However, some provide us with the inspiring hints of how to account for the sources of cultures of political violence and both the similarities and dissimilarities between them.

The fixed set of the intrastate, regional, and colonial indicators are not applicable to explain the diversity of the cultures of political violence because there is no significant statistical correlation between the variables at the 0.05 level. Nevertheless, Ayele's proposal has an explanatory potential. Although it is not important if all the indicators occur in a state, it matters in what configuration they emerge. In this case, the correlation coefficient equals 0.651, indicating a strong positive linear correlation, and it shows that the coefficient is significantly different from 0. The Sig. 2-tailed level is 0.012, which is substantially lower than 0.05 and proves a statistically significant correlation at the 0.05 level.

Furthermore, it may be of relevance to delve analytically into the structures of the configurations of the indicators which typify the particular patterns of a culture of political violence. The proceedings and results of the intrastate, regional, and colonial indicators manifestations are worth taking into consideration. The research has indicated that if in the history of a state the set of the intrastate and colonial indicators occur as well as the regional one does not take place, a placid pattern may originate. More violent patterns show up in the states where the intrastate indicator appears. In fact, this feature typifies the hector-led and militant types, but it is the only feature that characterizes the former. The latter may also originate when the full set of the intrastate, colonial, and regional indicators entered the state history, or just the configuration of the intrastate and regional was observed there. In one state, however, the research has identified no explaining indicator, which reduces the explanatory power of the framework. It encourages us to the further looking for the stronger and more appropriate explanation that may be informed by Ayele's inspiring and promising model.

The frequency and intensity of the events may also be meaningful (McAdam *et al.* 2008). The point is, nonetheless, that there is an urgent requirement to determine precisely a conceptual framework which would apply to approach what contributes to the paradigms of the use of political violence and how, and the differences between them.

What the research incontestably has revealed in addition is that the fixed and undivided explaining set of the war, civil war, and revolution indicators is also far from being empirically effective. Its correlation with the types of a culture of political violence is not significant statistically at the 0.05 level. The various configurations of the explaining indicators are applicable to the research on the Eurozone cases to a higher extent than LaPorte and Worley's original model to account for the placid, hector-led, and militant cultures of political violence. The Sig. 2-tailed level is there 0.044, which is considerably lower than 0.05. It sets a statistically significant correlation at the 0.05 level.

When in the history of a state, only the war indicator makes an appearance, it is likely that a placid pattern of a culture of political violence enters this state. The complete configuration of the war, civil war, and revolution indicators is the feature of the more violent patterns. When the full set appears, it is probable that a hector-led or militant type originates. Nevertheless, the combination of the war and revolution indicators is the feature of no pattern. The results may challenge the students of cultures of political violence to adopt the model in a modified and extended form and to make further changes to bolster its empirical effectiveness.

Onslow's explanatory model incentivizes a researcher to concentrate on the details of the war indicator, but Ayele's, LaPorte and Worley's indicators and contentious politics are not to be forgotten (Onslow 2011; Tarrow 2015; Tilly and Tarrow 2015). Just as in Ayele, it may be effective to explore the frequency and intensity of the events in the states' history and to determine their features potentially significant to the development of cultures of political violence (McAdam *et al.* 2008). Finally, they are not the only types of the contentious politics worth including in an explanatory framework (Tilly 1978). It may also be worthwhile to consider looking at violence in economic, cultural, and social spheres rather than focusing merely on the political phenomena as the explaining indicators of a culture of political violence (Steenkamp 2011; 2005).

Gerwarth's explanatory framework, assuming that a culture of political violence is a result of the noisy and turbulent politics of the street, the town square, and the factory, in which socioeconomic grievances, hostility to state authority, and new and recycled dreams of a purified community are expressed, is invulnerable to explain the differences between the types of a culture of political violence. Not unlike Eubank and Weinberg, it is too general to deal with the nature and roots of the complex phenomenon. The explaining indicators occurred in each state over the continuance of the post-2008 anti-austerity movements. The events being the empirical manifestations of the indicators were common and did not contribute to our understanding of the sources of the cultures of political violence. Despite the premises made by Gerwarth, it would be useful to shed light on the intensity and frequency of the indicators. It may be of vital relevance to analyzing the relative deprivations of the political subjects engaged in contentious politics to empower the model. Beyond argument is the requirement to develop the model by proposing the conceptual framework which would enable a researcher to address significant differences between the expressions of the indicators.

The other models involved the following explaining indicators: the situation when the highly mobilized and urbanized civil society, in the developed Latin American states with strong democratic traditions, identified with the state which does not confine its militaries to the narrowly constitutional role and ruthless and determined military governments threatens at length the civil society (Theobald 1999), the tribal and religious loyalties (Waldman 2007), the non-political agencies of socialization (Kling 1963), the youths' engagement in electoral violence (Okwong 2012), the fictions of political violence defined as the novels, short stories, plays, movies, or parts thereof, where political processes and political views are reasonably close to the surface (Dexter and Guittet 2014), and the internationalist spirit of the 1960s (Pensado 2013).

Nonetheless, there was no need to conduct empirical tests to state that they do not work under the theoretical and methodological assumptions made by their authors when the Eurozone cultures of political violence are to be accounted for. Their rejection has drawn on the history of the states and essential features of the context in which the anti-austerity movements acted. Some of them have an explanatory potential, such as those which point out tribal and religious loyalties, but they have to be elaborated according to state of the art. They also spur us to think about the role of elections and political campaigns in the process of shaping the cultures of political violence, but they avoid establishing directions to do so.

This part of the research has shown that much is to be done to develop the explanatory frameworks of the cultures of political violence. It is not very likely that a single indicator will account for its types. More likely is that the configurations of indicators will provide the more plausible research results concerning similarities and differences between them. Undoubtedly, delving analytically into the previous contentious politics in particular states may be useful to inform the future conceptual and explanatory frameworks.

Bibliography

Ahlbäck, Anders. 2016. *Manhood and the Making of the Military: Conscription, Military Service and Masculinity in Finland, 1917–39*. London and New York: Routledge.

Annus, Epp. 2012. "The Problem of Soviet Colonialism in the Baltics." *Journal of Baltic Studies* 43(1): 21–46.

Arosalo, Sirkka. 1998. "Social Conditions for Political Violence: Red and White Terror in the Finnish Civil War of 1918." *Journal of Peace Research* 35(2): 147–166.

Ayele, Negussay. 2011. "Legitimacy, Culture of Political Violence and Violence of Culture in Ethiopia." In *Terrorism, Identity and Legitimacy: The Four Waves Theory and Political Violence*, edited by Jean E. Rosenfeld, 212–231. Abingdon and New York: Routledge.

Balogová, Beata. 2010. "Unions Rally against Austerity Package." *The Slovak Spectator*, October 18. Accessed February 18, 2017. https://spectator.sme.sk/c/20037746/unions-rally-against-austerity-package.html.

Bäcker, Roman. 2011. *Nietradycyjna teoria polityki*. Toruń: Wydawnictwo Uniwersytetu Mikołaja Kopernika w Toruniu.

BBC. 2010a. "European Cities Hit by Anti-Austerity Protests." *BBC*, September 29. Accessed February 3, 2017. www.bbc.com/news/world-europe-11432579.

BBC. 2010b. "Italian Student Protesters Occupy Leaning Tower of Pisa." *BBC*, November 25. Accessed February 12, 2017. www.bbc.com/news/world-europe-11841199.

Beas, Diego. 2011. "How Spain's 15-M Movement is Redefining Politics." *Guardian*, October 15. Accessed February 7, 2017. www.theguardian.com/commentisfree/2011/oct/15/spain-15-m-movement-activism.

Beck, Colin J. 2015. *Radicals, Revolutionaries, and Terrorists*. Cambridge: Polity Press.

Bosi, Lorenzo, Niall Ó Dochartaigh, and Daniela Pisoiu (eds.). 2015. *Political Violence in Context: Time, Space and Milieu*. Colchester: ECPR Press.

Boyd, John. 2010a. "Breweries: Government Tax Hike Will Bury Us." *The Daily.SK*, October 13. Accessed March 4, 2017. www.thedaily.sk/brewers-say-government-hike-in-excise-tax-will-bury-them/.

Boyd, John. 2010b. "Metal Unions Spark Up Protests." *The Daily.SK*, September 23. Accessed March 4, 2017. www.thedaily.sk/metal-unions-spark-up-protests/.

Boyd, John. 2010c. "Trade Unions Storm Out of Labour Ministry Talks." *The Daily.SK*, December 16. Accessed March 4, 2017. www.thedaily.sk/trade-unions-storm-out-of-labour-ministry-talks/.

Brady, Henry E., David Collier, and Jason Seawright. 2006. "Toward a Pluralistic Vision of Methodology." *Political Analysis* 14(3): 353–368.

Brokaw, Alan J. and Marianne A. Brokaw. 2001. "Identity Marketing: The Case of the Singing Revolution." *Journal of Nonprofit & Public Sector Marketing* 8(4): 17–29.

Carter, Jeff, Michael Bernhard, and Glenn Palmer. 2012. "Social Revolution, the State, and War." *Journal of Conflict Resolution* 56(3): 439–466.

Cerezales, Diego Palacios. 2016. "Civil Resistance and Democracy in the Portuguese Revolution." *Journal of Contemporary History*. First published date: January 1, 2016.

Christodoulakis, Nicos. 2016. "Conflict Dynamics and Costs in the Greek Civil War 1946–1949." *Defence and Peace Economics* 27(5): 688–717.

Chandhoke, Neera. 2007. "Civil Society." *Development in Practice* 17(4–5): 607–614.

Church, C. H. 1977. "Forgotten Revolutions: Recent Work on the Revolutions of 1830 in Europe." *European History Quarterly* 7(1): 95–106.

Coleman, Marie. 2013. "Military Service Pensions for Veterans of the Irish Revolution, 1916–1923." *War in History* 20(2): 201–221.

Collard, Christophe. 2014. "'Bye Bye Belgium': Remediating Flemish Nationalism in Prime Time." *Rethinking History: The Journal of Theory and Practice* 18(4): 543–555.

Connolly, Kate and Angelique Chrisafis. 2012. "Anti-Austerity Movements Gaining Momentum across Europe." *Guardian*, April 27. Accessed February 7, 2017. www.theguardian.com/world/2012/apr/27/anti-austerity-movements-europe.

Cooper, Frederick. 2005. *Colonialism in Question. Theory, Knowledge, History*. Berkeley, Los Angeles, and London: University of California Press.

Daly, Gavin. 2016. "'Barbarity More Suited to Savages': British Soldiers' Views of Spanish and Portuguese Violence during the Peninsular War, 1808–1814." *War & Society* 35(4): 242–258.

Davies, James C. 1962. "Toward a Theory of Revolution." *American Sociological Review* 27(1): 5–19.

Davies, Joan. 1990. "Seeking Answers: Questioning the Fronde." *Seventeenth-Century French Studies* 12(1): 217–223.

Dellinger, Todd. 2016. "Velvet Disillusionment: Czech Performing Arts and Twenty-Five Years of Transition, 1989–2014." *The Journal of Arts Management, Law, and Society* 46 (3): 122–132.

Dexter, Helen and Emmanuel-Pierre Guittet. 2014. "Teaching (Something About) Terrorism: Ethical and Methodological Problems, Pedagogical Suggestions." *International Studies Perspectives* 15: 374–393.

Dhiarmada, Bríona Nic. 2016. *The 1916 Irish Rebellion*. Notre Dame, IN: Notre Dame University Press.

Duncan, Pamela. 2010. "Up to 500 Students Protest over Garda Behaviour." *The Irish Times*, November 11. Accessed February 7, 2017. www.irishtimes.com/news/up-to-500-students-protest-over-garda-behaviour-1.675042.

Durić, Džemal and Danijel Žibret. 2017. Respond to query 630–36/2017/4: Slovenian National Police. Register: 630–36/2017/4(262–03) [in the author's records].

Eubank, William and Leonard Weinberg. 2000. "The Italian Regions and the Prospects for Democracy." *Terrorism and Political Violence* 12(3/4): 293–307.

Finland Times. 2014. "Police Use Pepper Spray to Quell Demonstration in Helsinki: Huge Protest against Govt's Austerity Policy." *Finland Times*, April 26. Accessed February 2, 2017. www.finlandtimes.fi/national/2014/04/26/6436/Huge-protest-against-govt%E2%80%99s-austerity-policy.

Fishman, Robert M. 2011. "Democratic Practice after the Revolution: The Case of Portugal and Beyond." *Politics & Society* 39(2): 233–267.

Gao, Eleanor. 2016. "Tribal Mobilization, Fragmented Groups, and Public Goods Provision in Jordan." *Comparative Political Studies* 49(10): 1372–1403.

Gerwarth, Robert. 2011. "Control and Chaos: Paramilitary Violence and the Dissolution of the Habsburg Empire." In *Control of Violence Historical and International Perspectives on Violence in Modern Societies*, edited by Wilhelm Heitmeyer, Heinz-Gerhard Haupt, Stefan Malthaner, and Andrea Kirschner, 517–534. London: Springer.

Guralnik, Clara. 2017. Respond to query 1.1–14/368–2: Police and Border Guard Board. Register: 70008747 [in the author's records].

Hart, Russell A. 2013. "Rommel and the 20 July 1944 Bomb Plot." In *Rommel: A Reappraisal*, edited by Ian F. Beckett, 137–156. Barnsley: Pen & Sword Military.

Hartzell, Caroline A. 2009. "Settling Civil Wars." *Conflict Management and Peace Science* 26(4): 347–365.

Hill, Christopher. 2007. *The Role of Elites in the Spanish Transition to Democracy (1975–1981): Motors of Change*. Lewiston, NY: Edwin Mellen Press.

Horn, Gerd-Rainer. 2007. *The Spirit of '68: Rebellion in Western Europe and North America, 1956–1976*. New York: Oxford University Press.

Horn, Gerd-Rainer and Padraic Kenney. 2004. "Introduction: Approaches to the Transnational." In *Transnational Moments of Change in Europe: 1945, 1968, 1989*, edited by Gerd-Rainer Horn and Padraic Kenney, ix–xix. Lanham: Rowman and Littlefield.

Hull, Roger H. 2015. *The Irish Triangle: Conflict in Northern Ireland*. Princeton and Surrey: Princeton University Press.

IFES. 2017a. "Europe." *The International Foundation for Electoral Systems*, No date. Accessed March 10, 2017. www.ifes.org/europe.

IFES. 2017b. "Electoral Violence." *The International Foundation for Electoral Systems*, No date. Accessed March 10, 2017. www.ifes.org/issues/electoral-violence.

Jeffrey, Charlie. 1995. *Social Democracy in the Austrian Provinces, 1918–1934: Beyond Red Vienna*. London: Fairleigh Dickinson University Press.

Kaplan, Jeffrey. 2016. *Radical Religion and Violence: Theory and Case Studies*. London and New York: Routledge.

Kissane, Bill. 2000. "Explaining the Intractability of the Irish Civil War." *Civil Wars* 3(2): 65–88.

Kling, Merle. 1963. "Violence and Politics in Latin America." *The Sociological Review* 11(S1): 119–132.

Klösch, Christian. 2007. *Des Führers heimliche Vasallen. Die Putschisten des Juli 1934 im Kärntner Lavanttal*. Vienna: Czernin Verlag.

Koorits, Vahur. 2012. "2012 – A Year of Discontent in Estonia." *VahurKoortis* December 31. Accessed March 5, 2017. http://vahurkoorits.blogspot.com/2012/12/2012-year-of-discontent-in-estonia.html.

Lambert, Carolyn. 1999. *An Overview of the Historiography of the German Revolution 1918–19*. Newfoundland and Labrador: Memorial University of Newfoundland.

LaPorte, Norman and Matthew Worley. 2008. "Towards a Comparative History of Communism: The British and German Communist Parties." *Contemporary British History* 22(2): 227–255.

Loomba, Ania. 2005. *Colonialism/Postcolonialism. The New Critical Idiom*. 2nd edition. London and New York: Routledge.

Lukes, Igor. 2011. "The 1948 Coup d'État in Prague through the Eyes of the American Embassy." *Diplomacy & Statecraft* 22(3): 431–449.

Matthews, James. 2014. " 'The Vanguard of Sacrifice'? Political Commissars in the Republican Popular Army during the Spanish Civil War, 1936–1939." *War in History* 21(1): 82–101.

McCarthy, Ronald M., Gene Sharp, and Brad Bennett. 2013. *Nonviolent Action: A Research Guide*. London and New York: Routledge.

McAdam, Doug. 2003. "Beyond Structural Analysis: Toward a More Dynamic: Understanding of Social Movements." In *Social Movements and Networks: Relational Approaches to Collective Action*, edited by Mario Diani and Doug McAdam, 281–298. New York: Oxford University Press.

McAdam, Doug. 2014. "Revisiting the Civil Rights Movement: Toward a More Synthetic Understanding of the Origins of Contention." In *Rethinking Social Movements: Structure, Meaning, and Emotion*, edited by Jeff Goodwin and James M. Jasper, 201–232. Lanham: Rowman and Littlefield.

McAdam, Doug and Karina Kloos. 2015. *Deeply Divided: Racial Politics and Social Movements in Post-War America*. New York: Oxford University Press.

McAdam, Doug, Sidney Tarrow, and Charles Tilly. 2008. "Methods for Measuring Mechanisms of Contention." *Qualitative Sociology* 31(4): 307–331.

Mertelsmann, Olaf and Aigi Rahi-Tamm. 2009. "Soviet Mass Violence in Estonia Revisited." *Journal of Genocide Research* 11(2–3): 307–322.

Minkenberg, Michael. 2009. "Religion and Euroscepticism: Cleavages, Religious Parties and Churches in EU Member States." *West European Politics* 32(6): 1190–1211.

Munck, Gerardo L. 2016. "Assessing Set-Theoretic Comparative Methods: A Tool for Qualitative Comparativists?" *Comparative Political Studies* 49(6): 775–780.

Müsgen, Hanne. 2017. Respond to query O3–12007/1#1. Federal Police. Register: 170213 [in the author's records].

Myant, Martin. 1992. "Centre Periphery Relations in Czechoslovakia." *Journal of Interdisciplinary Economics* 4(3): 269–280.

O'Kane, Rosemary H. T. 2015. "Revolutions, Revolts and Protest Movements: Focusing on Violence and Transnational Action." *Political Studies Review* 13(3): 317–328.

Okwong, Atte Enyenihi. 2012. "IT-Based Solutions to the Electoral System in Nigeria." *West African Journal of Industrial and Academic Research* 5(1): 127–139.

Onslow, Sue. 2011. *Zimbabwe and Political Transition*. London: The London School of Economics and Political Science.

Opp, Karl-Dieter. 2009. *Theories of Political Protest and Social Movements: A Multidisciplinary Introduction, Critique, and Synthesis*. London and New York: Routledge.

Paine, Jack. 2016. "Set-Theoretic Comparative Methods: Less Distinctive Than Claimed." *Comparative Political Studies* 49(6): 703–741.

Pavone, Claudio. 2014. *A Civil War: A History of the Italian Resistance*. London: Verso Books.

Payne, Stanley G. 2011. *Civil War in Europe, 1905–1949*. Cambridge and New York: Cambridge University Press.

Pensado, Jaime M. 2013. *Rebel Mexico: Student Unrest and Authoritarian Political Culture during the Long Sixties*. Stanford, CA: Stanford University Press.

Phillips, Brian J. 2015. "Enemies with Benefits? Violent Rivalry and Terrorist Group Longevity." *Journal of Peace Research* 52(1): 62–75.

Phillips, Leigh. 2011. "Amnesty Condemns Greek Crackdown on Anti-Austerity Protests." *EUobserver*, June 30. Accessed February 4, 2017. https://euobserver.com/economic/32571.

Prebilič, Vladimir and Damijan Guštin. 2010. "Warfare Lessons Learned: The Treatment of Prisoners of War by the Republic of Slovenia during the Slovenian Independence War in 1991." *Studia Historica Slovenica* 10(1): 181–200.

Punch, Keith F. 2014. *Introduction to Social Research: Quantitative and Qualitative Approaches*. 3rd edition. London: Sage.

Rak, Joanna. 2017a. "Intrastate, Regional, and Colonial Contributions to Post-2008 Cultures of Political Violence." *Polish Political Science Yearbook* 46(1): 281–293.

Rak, Joanna. 2017b. "What Constitutes the State's Culture of Political Violence?" *Insight Turkey* 19(2): 231–237.

Rapport, Mike. 2008. *1848: Year of Revolution*. New York: Basic Books.

Raun, Alo and Oliver Kund. 2012. "ACTA meeleavaldus jäi oodatust kesisemaks." *Postimees*, February 11. Accessed March 5, 2017. www.postimees.ee/735944/acta-meeleavaldus-jaei-oodatust-kesisemaks.

Redação. 2011. "Lisboa junta-se hoje a protesto mundial anti-austeridade." *TVI 24*, October 15. Accessed February 10, 2017. www.tvi24.iol.pt/economia/protestos/lisboa-junta-se-hoje-a-protesto-mundial-anti-austeridade.

Sartre, Jean Paul. 2001. *Colonialism and Neocolonialism*. London and New York: Routledge.

Schneider, Carsten Q. 2016. "Real Differences and Overlooked Similarities: Set-Methods in Comparative Perspective." *Comparative Political Studies* 49(6): 781–792.

Scott, Tom and Robert W. Scribner. 1991. *The German Peasants' War: A History in Documents*. New York and London: Humanities Press.

Smith, Willard A. 1953. "Napoleon III and the Spanish Revolution of 1868." *The Journal of Modern History* 25(3): 211–233.

Smith IV, Miles. 2013. "From Savannah to Vienna: William Henry Stiles, the Revolutions of 1848, and Southern Conceptions of Order." *American Nineteenth Century History* 14(1): 27–51.

Stacey, Simon and Megan Meyer. 2005. "Civil Society and Violence: A Research Agenda." *Journal of Civil Society* 1(2): 181–190.

Steenkamp, Chrissie. 2005. "The Legacy of War: Conceptualizing a 'Culture of Violence' to Explain Violence after Peace Accords." *The Round Table: The Commonwealth Journal of International Affairs* 94(379): 253–267.

Steenkamp, Christina. 2011. "In the Shadows of War and Peace: Making Sense of Violence after Peace Accords." *Conflict, Security & Development* 11(3): 357–383.

Steinmetz, George. 2014. "The Sociology of Empires, Colonies, and Postcolonialism." *Annual Review of Sociology* 40: 77–103.

Stone, Lawrence. 1966. "Theories of Revolution." *World Politics* 18(2): 159–176.
Tarrow, Sidney. 2007. "Inside Insurgencies: Politics and Violence in the Age of Civil War." *Perspectives on Politics* 5(3): 587–600.
Tarrow, Sidney. 2015. *War, States, and Contention: A Comparative Historical Study*. Ithaca, NY and London: Cornell University Press.
The Globe and Mail. 2010. "Anti-Austerity Protests Hit France." *The Globe and Mail*, October 14. Accessed February 3, 2017. www.theglobeandmail.com/report-on-business/anti-austerity-protests-hit-france/article1370351/.
Theobald, Robin. 1999. "Conclusion: Prospects for Reform in a Globalised Economy." *Commonwealth & Comparative Politics* 37(3): 149–159.
Thomopoulos, Elaine. 2011. *The History of Greece*. Santa Barbara, CA: Greenwood.
Tilly, Charles. 1978. *From Mobilization to Revolution*. New York: Random House.
Tilly, Charles and Sidney Tarrow. 2015. *Contentious Politics*. 2nd edition. New York: Oxford University Press.
Tonge, Jon. 2014. "A Campaign without End?: 'Dissident' Republican Violence in Northern Ireland." *Political Insight* 5(1): 14–17.
Tota, Anna Lisa and Lia Luchetti. 2016. "An 'Unaccomplished Memory': The Strategy of Tension in Italy (1969–1993) and the Piazza Fontana Bombing in Milan (December 12, 1969)." In *Routledge International Handbook of Memory Studies*, edited by Anna Lisa Tota and Trever Hagen, 382–397. London and New York: Routledge.
Valeriano, Brandon. 2013. *Becoming Rivals: The Process of Interstate Rivalry Development*. London and New York: Routledge.
Valge, Jaak. 2011. "Foreign Involvement and Loss of Democracy, Estonia 1934." *Journal of Contemporary History* 46(4): 788–808.
van Goethem, Herman. 2010. *Belgium and the Monarchy: From National Independence to National Disintegration*. Brussels and Antwerp: Academic and Scientific Publishers and University Press Antwerp.
Vargas, Michael. 2015. "'Catalonia Is Not Spain': Projecting Catalan Identity to Tourists in and around Barcelona." *Journal of Tourism History* 7(1–2): 36–53.
Verkade, Willem. 1965. *Democratic Parties in the Low Countries and Germany: Origins and Historical Developments*. Leiden: Universitaire Pers.
Wada, Takeshi. 2016. "Rigidity and Flexibility of Repertoires of Contention." *Mobilization: An International Quarterly* 21(4): 449–468.
Waldman, Thomas. 2007. "British 'Post-Conflict' Operations in Iraq: Into the Heart of Strategic Darkness." *Civil Wars* 9(1): 61–86.
Wearden, Graeme. 2012. "Europe's Day of Anti-Austerity Strikes and Protests Turn Violent – As It Happened." *Guardian*, November 14. Accessed January 31, 2017. www.theguardian.com/business/2012/nov/14/eurozone-crisis-general-strikes-protest-day-of-action.
Wiener, Antje. 2014. *A Theory of Contestation*. London: Springer.
Willmott, H. P. 2008. *The Great Crusade: A New Complete History of the Second World War. Revised Edition*. Washington, D.C.: Potomac Books.
Zaccor, Albert M. 1994. "Guerrilla Warfare on the Baltic Coast: A Possible Model for Baltic Defense Doctrines Today?" *The Journal of Slavic Military Studies* 7(4): 682–702.

4 Looking for the Immediate Aftermaths of Cultures of Political Violence

DOI: 10.4324/9781351205757-5

Cultures of Political Violence and Making Things Happen

The previous chapter has scrutinized the possible sources of the cultures of political violence that emerged in the member states of the Eurozone in the times of austerity. In this chapter, the attention moves over to the after-effects of their emergence. Chapter 3 has tested empirically all the explanatory frameworks identified in the literature review that present a culture of political violence as the indicator to be explained. In Chapter 4, on the other hand, the explanatory frameworks showing a culture of political violence as the explaining indicator undergo tests. It concentrates entirely on the cultures' implications estimated through the current research results revealed in the substantive literature review. The goals are as follows: to examine the foregoing explanatory frameworks by working with the cases of the post-2008 incidents in which anti-austerity movements' stakeholders participated for a theory-verification purpose, to shed some light on expectations towards an explanatory framework meeting the correctness criteria, and to discuss the explanatory potential of the cultures of political violence which stemmed in the age of austerity for going towards a theory-generation purpose.

Methodology for Verification of the Theories that Consider a Culture of Political Violence as the Explaining Thing

The chapter solves the third research problem of the extent to which current explanatory frameworks account for the results of patterns of a culture of political violence had by stakeholders of the post-2008 anti-austerity movements. To deal with the problem, it verifies the third central hypothesis: current explanatory frameworks probably to a low extent account for the results of patterns of a culture of political violence had by stakeholders of the post-2008 anti-austerity movements. The current explanatory frameworks are the theoretical approaches identified in the literature review and already evaluated in the correctness criteria and general applicability to empirical studies. The analysis formulates the specific theory-driven hypotheses and tests them in the subsequent parts of the chapter. The methodology for the tests designated to assess the empirical effectiveness of the explanatory models does not differ from the methodological assumptions introduced in the chapter concerning a culture of political violence as the indicator to be explained.

The research employs the statistical analysis method. The Pearson correlation technique allows us to compute the type and strength of linear correlations between the explaining indicator and the indicators to be explained. A two-tail test establishes the statistical significance of the correlations. The scales to interpret the research results are not different from those introduced in the previous chapter. Nevertheless, the major theoretical category has a variant role here. A type of a culture of political violence is the independent variable which carries three values of its patterns located on a simple ordinal scale: placid, hector-led, and militant types. A placid type is aggressive narrowly (1), hector-led – moderately (2), and militant – sublimely (3). Let us bring it back that whereas Estonia and Slovakia had the placid cultures of political violence, Austria, the Netherlands, and France – the hector-led patterns, and Finland, Belgium, Germany, Portugal, Slovenia, Italy, Greece, Spain, and Ireland – the militant patterns. In the previous chapter, it was the point to explain their diversity. By contrast, this chapter makes an attempt to account for what may be explained by their variety. The statistical analysis provides us with remarks on the opportunities to increase the explanatory power of the theoretical approaches towards the aftermath of the cultures of political violence.

When there is no need to calculate, the explanatory models undergo the causal-process observations that allow us to handle the data-set observations or they are rejected by critical argumentation. The choice of a set of methods, techniques, and tools heavily depends on a type of data either qualitative or quantitative as well as on a quest for research process optimization. The theory-based explanatory frameworks undergo tests in their existing forms, adjusted and extended if necessary, or rejected if unmodifiable and unemployable to examine empirical phenomena. It contributes to the systematic and methodic evaluation of their explanatory effectiveness. The shifts made in their content do not encroach upon the hard core of the models.

The models under empirical tests treat a culture of political violence as the explaining indicator. They differ no more than slightly in the meanings of the category, but the research underlines and discusses the dissimilarities within the definitional assumptions for the sake of methodological clarity. The frameworks are much more diversified in terms of the beings, phenomena, and processes involved to function as the indicators to be explained. Dependent variables come from the theories identified in the literature review. Thus, the indicators or sets of indicators, recognized as the potential outcomes of a culture of political violence, whose validity is to be tested are as follows: the pattern of political culture: between the parochial and subject political culture, close to the former (Ayele 2011); violence of culture identified with the culture of masculinity and the political violence of culture (Ayele 2011); conditions in which the provocation and organization of violence are not the sole domain of professional soldiers (Kling 1963); bringing about revolution to being able to carry out the function of an election (Kling 1963); electoral violence (Omotola 2010); post-election violence, a substantial proportion of the population participating in protests and a reality that may be attributed to the snowball effect of grassroots mobilization (Forti and Maina 2012); problems to electoral democracy (Obi 2011); minimization of the chances of peaceful democratic rules establishment (Waldman 2007); death of democracy (Le Vine 2000); democratic breakdown (Le Vine 2000); breakdown of democracy (Siniawer 2008); creation of the conditions under which militaries and paramilitaries are routinely deployed against dissidents as well as basing a political regime on the army to cope with opposition, and harassing and killing critics of the regime in a formally democratic state (Theobald 1999); the political situation which undermines democracy (Njoku 2010); promoting riots (Taylor 1981); production of the context in which ruffianism is tacitly accepted as a routinely used tool of political life (Siniawer 2012); the political situation in which people are killed, maimed, disfigured, beaten, tortured, incarcerated and exiled because of political goals (Coleman 1998); enormous public distrust in the capacity of the major parties to come out of the destructive political legacy and usher in a new political alternative (Moniruzzaman 2009); undermining the secular and nationalist foundations of a moderate state (Gohel 2014); and the institutionalization of young activists of a movement into party politics (Siniawer 2008).

The research makes use of a qualitative method of written sources analysis to gather data sufficient and necessary to verify the main hypothesis. The research technique of data collection is a content analysis of secondary sources. The pieces of data derive from the Eurostat, the Freedom House reports, the Global Gender Gap Reports, and the secondary specialist literature concerning the indicators involved in the explanatory frameworks. They are especially helpful to determine exactly what values the indicators or the sets of indicators took on in the particular states. The data-set observations present the pieces of data. These databases are the original contribution of this research to the studies on the cultures of political violence. For the purpose of empowering the basis of arguments, the analysis employs theoretical sampling and adopts sources triangulation. The research tool is an instruction to review the secondary data.

The research generates comments on the possibilities to enhance the empirical effectiveness of the frameworks. It verifies the central hypothesis by weighing up the arguments and counterarguments formulated throughout the chapter in the process of verifying the specific hypotheses.

Breakdown of Democracy

The first type of the explanatory models adopting a culture of political violence as an explaining indicator is employable to examine democracies. In drawing on the history of the world, Victor T. Le Vine assumes that a culture of political violence leads a state to either a democratic breakdown (2000, 277–278) or the end of democracy (2000, 276). Eiko Maruko Siniawer supports his theory by claiming that the breakdown of democracy in Japan in 1930 was predominantly caused by a culture of political violence (2008, 73, 179). Cyril Obi argues that the phenomenon created seminal problems to electoral democracy in Nigeria

(2011, 373). Alphonsus O. Njoku sustains this model by asserting that it changed a political situation in Nigeria. The shift consisted in the evisceration of democracy (2010, 16). Le Vine, Obi, and Njoku understand the category accounting for the change in the trajectory of political regime continuance as the use of extensive physical political violence. This meaning generally agrees with the semantic field of the militant patterns adopted in the research. In turn, Siniawer defines it as the context in which the use of physical force is viewed by political actors as the viable and acceptable strategy. It is dynamic, altering, and helps political subjects tremendously perpetuate a violent brand of politics (Siniawer 2008, 2, 75, 2012, 629). This definition also corresponds closely to the militant types. It implies that the models have the meaning of the explaining category in common.

In drawing upon the theories, the specific hypothesis states that when a militant culture of political violence emerges, the breakdown of democracy might occur. The pieces of existing data from the Freedom House reports have been gathered in Table 4.1 to show the values of the following indicators: Freedom Rating (FR), Civil Liberties (CL), and Political Rights (PR) (Table 4.1). On an original scale, the values range from 1 to 7. The 1 marks the states to the highest extent democratic, whereas the 7 characterizes the states to the highest extent non-democratic. The breakdown of democracy occurs when a state obtains the 3. Then, the state starts to be partly free.

The choice of the Freedom House reports as the source of data justifies a need for statistically comparable information about the quality of democracy in 14 states and how the regimes changed over time in each case (Armstrong 2011). It provides the sufficient and necessary details about the indicator which were gathered by applying a systematic and the same methodology. Importantly, the Freedom House publishes reports for each of the states involved in the research once a year, and they are easily accessible (Szewczak 2011). As a result, it was manageable to identify what exactly the values of the indicators before, during, and after the occurrence of the explaining indicators were. The fellowship of both a cultural field and a historical period blunts the critics on the a-cultural and a-historical dimension of the measures (Giannone 2010; Koelbe and Lipuma 2008).

The data concerns all the member states of the Eurozone in 2001–2016 (Freedom House 2017). The dates of the first use of political violence by stakeholders of all the anti-austerity movements were between 2010 and 2014, including the caesurae. It means that 2001 and 2016 determine sufficiently broad temporal boundaries to verify if the appearance of militant cultures of political violence contributed to the breakdown of democracy in the countries (Table 4.1). It also gives the opportunity to investigate how exactly the values of the indicators changed in comparison to the cases with the placid and hector-led patterns. The causal-process observation allows us to delve analytically into the data-set observations and assess whether the values of the indicators altered pending or after the dates that were significant from the perspective of the cultures of political violence examination.

Table 4.1 Freedom House indicators in the member states of the Eurozone 2001–2016

d	*2001*			*2002*			*2003*			*2004*			*2005*			*2006*			*2007*			*2008*		
i	*FR*	*CL*	*PR*	*FR*	*CL*	*PR*	*FR*	*CL*	*PR*	*FR*	*CL*	*PR*	*FR*	*CL*	*PR*	*FR*	*CL*	*PR*	*FR*	*CL*	*PR*	*FR*	*CL*	*PR*
Placid cultures of political violence																								
EE	1.5	2	1	1.5	2	1	1.5	2	1	1.5	2	1	1	1	1	1	1	1	1	1	1	1	1	1
SVK	1.5	2	1	1.5	2	1	1.5	2	1	1.5	2	1	1	1	1	1	1	1	1	1	1	1	1	1
Hector-led cultures of political violence																								
AT	1	1	1	1	1	1	1	1	1	1	1	1	1	1	1	1	1	1	1	1	1	1	1	1
NL	1	1	1	1	1	1	1	1	1	1	1	1	1	1	1	1	1	1	1	1	1	1	1	1
FR	1.5	2	1	1.5	2	1	1	1	1	1	1	1	1	1	1	1	1	1	1	1	1	1	1	1
Militant cultures of political violence																								
FI	1	1	1	1	1	1	1	1	1	1	1	1	1	1	1	1	1	1	1	1	1	1	1	1
BE	1.5	2	1	1.5	2	1	1	1	1	1	1	1	1	1	1	1	1	1	1	1	1	1	1	1
DE	1.5	2	1	1.5	2	1	1	1	1	1	1	1	1	1	1	1	1	1	1	1	1	1	1	1
PT	1	1	1	1	1	1	1	1	1	1	1	1	1	1	1	1	1	1	1	1	1	1	1	1
SI	1.5	2	1	1.5	2	1	1	1	1	1	1	1	1	1	1	1	1	1	1	1	1	1	1	1
IT	1.5	2	1	1.5	2	1	1	1	1	1	1	1	1	1	1	1	1	1	1	1	1	1	1	1
GR	2	3	1	2	3	1	1.5	2	1	1.5	2	1	1.5	2	1	1.5	2	1	1.5	2	1	1.5	2	1
ES	1.5	2	1	1.5	2	1	1	1	1	1	1	1	1	1	1	1	1	1	1	1	1	1	1	1
IE	1	1	1	1	1	1	1	1	1	1	1	1	1	1	1	1	1	1	1	1	1	1	1	1

d	*2009*			*2010*			*2011*			*2012*			*2013*			*2014*			*2015*			*2016*		
i	*FR*	*CL*	*PR*	*FR*	*CL*	*PR*	*FR*	*CL*	*PR*	*FR*	*CL*	*PR*	*FR*	*CL*	*PR*	*FR*	*CL*	*PR*	*FR*	*CL*	*PR*	*FR*	*CL*	*PR*
Placid cultures of political violence																								
EE	1	1	1	1	1	1	1	1	1	1	1	1	1	1	1	1	1	1	1	1	1	1	1	1
SVK	1	1	1	1	1	1	1	1	1	1	1	1	1	1	1	1	1	1	1	1	1	1	1	1
Hector-led cultures of political violence																								
AT	1	1	1	1	1	1	1	1	1	1	1	1	1	1	1	1	1	1	1	1	1	1	1	1
NL	1	1	1	1	1	1	1	1	1	1	1	1	1	1	1	1	1	1	1	1	1	1	1	1
FR	1	1	1	1	1	1	1	1	1	1	1	1	1	1	1	1	1	1	1	1	1	1	1	1
Militant cultures of political violence																								
FI	1	1	1	1	1	1	1	1	1	1	1	1	1	1	1	1	1	1	1	1	1	1	1	1
BE	1	1	1	1	1	1	1	1	1	1	1	1	1	1	1	1	1	1	1	1	1	1	1	1
DE	1	1	1	1	1	1	1	1	1	1	1	1	1	1	1	1	1	1	1	1	1	1	1	1
PT	1	1	1	1	1	1	1	1	1	1	1	1	1	1	1	1	1	1	1	1	1	1	1	1
SI	1	1	1	1	1	1	1	1	1	1	1	1	1	1	1	1	1	1	1	1	1	1	1	1
IT	1.5	2	1	1.5	2	1	1.5	2	1	1	1	1	1.5	1	2	1	1	1	1	1	1	1	1	1
GR	1.5	2	1	1.5	2	1	1.5	2	1	2	2	2	2	2	2	2	2	2	2	2	2	2	2	2
ES	1	1	1	1	1	1	1	1	1	1	1	1	1	1	1	1	1	1	1	1	1	1	1	1
IE	1	1	1	1	1	1	1	1	1	1	1	1	1	1	1	1	1	1	1	1	1	1	1	1

Source: Author's study on the basis of the Freedom House reports.

Notes

FR – Freedom Rating (1 – to the highest extent democratic, 7 – to the highest extent non-democratic).
CL – Civil Liberties (1 – to the highest extent democratic, 7 – to the highest extent non-democratic).
PR – Political Rights (1 – to the highest extent democratic, 7 – to the highest extent non-democratic).
EE – Estonia, SK – Slovakia, AT – Austria, NL – the Netherlands, FR – France, FI – Finland, BE – Belgium, DE – Germany, PT – Portugal, SI – Slovenia, IT – Italy, GR – Greece, ES – Spain, IE – Ireland.
Grey color marks – the date of the first use of political violence by stakeholders of an anti-austerity movement.
d – date.
i – indicators.

In the states with the placid and the hector-led cultures of political violence, the values of the indicators did not change over the time pivotal to the theories. The same invariance made an appearance in most of the states with the militant patterns. Nevertheless, it was not the full invariance. Greece was the only exception because the FR increased slightly from 1.5 to 2 and the PR from 1 to 2. Those alterations cannot, however, be classified as the symptom of the breakdown of democracy because Greece did not reach 3 on any scale. Regardless of a type of a culture of political violence, the significant shifts of the FR, CL, and PR values did not enter the Eurozone. No breakdown occurred in the period under elaboration. Not to put too fine an edge on it, the indicator to be accounted for, in keeping with the theories, did not make an appearance within the research field.

The specific hypothesis is rejected because no relationship between a type of a culture of political violence and a breakdown of democracy existed. Accordingly, the theoretical approaches maintaining that the relationship exists and the cultures of political violence play a role of the explaining indicator in that relationship are of scant explanatory power to studies on the member states of the Eurozone.

The Freedom House reports enable us to verify a specific hypothesis formulated on the basis of Thomas Waldman's theory. The theory offers the second type of the explanatory frameworks, and it concerns the political regimes which are currently non-democratic but in tandem on the way to becoming democracies. To put in another way, it focuses on the states that make use of their regime transposition potential to transpose themselves into democracies. Just like Siniawer, Le Vine, and Obi, Waldman's explaining indicator is the use of extensive physical political violence. The meaning of a culture of political violence is equated with the semantic field of the militant pattern. In drawing on the qualitative case study of Iraq, Waldman considers a culture of political violence to be an explaining indicator of the minimization of the chances of the establishment of peaceful democratic rules (2007, 70). A culture imposes limitations on the use of the transposition potential. But does the model explain the changes in political regimes in different states? Or is it restricted merely to Iraq? The hypothesis phrased in pursuance of Waldman's theory is that when a militant culture of political violence originates, the peaceful establishment of democratic rules might fail to take place.

Nevertheless, no member state of the Eurozone was a non-democratic political regime before, over, and after the occurrence of any pattern of a culture of political violence in 2001–2016. It means that the hypothesis is rejected due to the absence of the relationships between the explaining indicator and the indicator to be explained in Waldman's meanings.

The third type of the explanatory models approaches the formally democratic political systems which do not satisfy the primary criteria of democracy and as such are of non-democratic quality. As Robin Theobald claims, the creation of the conditions under which Latin American militaries and paramilitaries are routinely deployed against dissidents, basing a political regime on the army to cope with opposition, and harassing and killing critics of the regime of Carlos Menem in formally democratic Argentina were the tangible results of a culture of political violence (1999, 153). Although Theobald avoids defining a culture of political violence, he adopts its classic meaning, that is, the use of extensive physical political violence in a political structure to achieve political objectives. Just as in the already discussed models, the explaining indicator is the militant pattern, according to the research conceptual framework. The specific hypothesis formulated on the grounds of Theobald's theory is: if a militant culture of political violence makes an appearance, the following phenomena might occur: the deployment of militaries and paramilitaries to fight with the political opponents, the stabilization of a political regime by using the army, and the abuse and murders of the critics of the political system.

In the period under scrutiny, however, militaries and paramilitaries were not routinely employed against dissidents in the member states of the Eurozone. The ruling subjects did not deploy the army to establish political relations with the opposition and to stabilize political systems. Subordinate political subjects performed the function of the ruled in the relation of public power. The critics of the regimes were neither scourged nor murdered. It means that the crucial components of Theobald's explanatory model did not originate over and after the occurrence of not only the placid and hector-led types but also the militant patterns. The hypothesis is, therefore, rejected. The empirical effectiveness of Theobald's model to examine cultures of political violence in the Eurozone of the times of austerity is low because the phenomena to be explained by a culture of political violence did not enter the European states.

Although the explanatory frameworks by Siniawer, Le Vine, Njoku, Obi, Waldman, and Theobald were useful to account for the results of the cultures of political violence in the specified territorial and temporal contexts, they have not withstood the empirical tests. The explaining category proved to be scarcely employable to examine the member states of the Eurozone because the occurrence of its forms was not followed by the theory-driven phenomena and processes to be explained. The models often functioned in the literature as the labels created just to describe in a highly general manner all the possible sources of the transposition of political regimes. Sometimes no methodological assumption supported their application. The research reveals what the results of the cultures of political violence in Europe were not, but it avoids showing any promising explanations.

Culture of Masculinity

According to Negussay Ayele, a culture of political violence contributes to the violence of culture identified with the culture of masculinity and the political violence of culture (2011, 226). As already discussed, a concept of a culture of political violence in Ayele's perspective is of low applicability to empirical study because of its semantic ambiguity and contextuality. Its essential feature is the overindulgence of physical political violence over a prolonged period in a political structure. The militant pattern proposed in the conceptual framework of the research has the proximate understanding to Ayele's culture of political violence. Thus, the research applies that meaning of the explaining indicator. In turn, it recognizes the culture of masculinity by a size of gender equality. Obviously, it is not a one-value variable, and its expressions differ in terms of an extent of equality. The smaller the size is, the higher the extent of a culture of masculinity emerges. In drawing upon Ayele's theory, the specific hypotheses are formulated.

***H_0*:** There might be no correlation between a culture of masculinity in a state and a pattern of a culture of political violence of stakeholders of an anti-austerity movement in the state.

***H_A*:** When a militant culture of political violence of stakeholders of an anti-austerity movement makes an appearance, a culture of masculinity might originate in the state where the movement acts. The more violent the culture of political violence is, the more intense the culture of masculinity is.

A gender gap indicator describes a culture of masculinity. The sufficient and necessary data to determine its values comes from the 10 Global Gender Gap Reports released in 2001–2016 (Hausmann *et al.* 2006, 2007, 2008, 2009, 2010, 2011, 2012, 2013, 201, 201, 2016). The analysis selects this source of existing data because it provides comprehensive and comparable information on gender inequality in the member states of the Eurozone in the period significant for the research. It was an important criterion for selection due to the missing pieces of data in the most popular databases. For instance, the Eurostat lacks details concerning a gender pay gap in Ireland and Greece (Eurostat 2017).

The World Economic Forum quantifies in the Global Gender Gap Reports the magnitude of gender disparities and traces their progress over time with a specific concentration on the relative gaps between women and men across four key areas: health, education, economy, and politics (Hausmann *et al.* 2016). The subindexes structure the key areas and contribute to the primary index. The first, the Economic Participation and Opportunity subindex covers five variables: female labor force participation over male value; wage equality between women and men for similar work (survey data, normalized on a 0-to-1 scale); female estimated earned income over male value; female legislators, senior officials and managers over male value; and female professional and technical workers over male value. The second, the Educational Attainment subindex encompasses four variables: female literacy rate over male value; female net primary enrolment rate over male value; female net secondary enrolment rate over male value; and female gross tertiary enrolment ratio over male value. The third, the Health and Survival subindex embraces two variables: sex ratio at birth (converted to female-over-male ratio) and female healthy life expectancy over male value. The last, the Political Empowerment subindex consists of three variables: females with seats in parliament over male value; females at ministerial level over male; and number of years with a female head of state (last 50 years) over male value (Hausmann *et al.* 2016).

The analysis interprets gender gap index (ggi) on the scale proposed by the World Economic Forum. The extreme points are 1 and 0. The 1 is the highest possible score that means equality or better for women, except for lifespan, 106 percent or better for women. The 0 is the worst possible score and indicates no equality. The scale is:

$ggi = 1.00$ – full equality
$1.00 > ggi \geq 0.90$ – almost full equality
$0.90 > ggi \geq 0.85$ – a very high extent of equality
$0.85 > ggi \geq 0.80$ – a high extent of equality
$0.80 > ggi \geq 0.75$ – a moderately high extent of equality
$0.75 > ggi \geq 0.70$ – a moderate extent of equality
$0.70 > ggi \geq 0.65$ – a moderately low extent of equality
$0.65 > ggi \geq 0.60$ – a low extent of equality
$0.60 > ggi \geq 0.55$ – a very low extent of equality
$0.55 > ggi \geq 0.50$ – almost no equality
$0.50 > ggi \geq 0$ – no equality

According to the World Economic Forum, a situation is alarming when the indicator takes on a value lower than 0.70. It indicates the occurrence of a culture of masculinity. The value of 0.70 and higher signify a culture of non-masculinity. The range $0.70 > ggi \geq 0$ is indeed relatively broad and thus it may be explored to determine the distinct patterns of a culture of masculinity, according to a next newly built and original scale. A moderately low extent of equality typifies a soft culture of masculinity; a low extent of equality – a mild type; a very low extent of equality – a harsh type; almost no equality – a fierce type; and no equality – an aggressive type. The analysis adopts this scale to interpret data and verify the specific hypothesis.

The data derived from the reports allows us to verify the hypothesis step by step (Table 4.2). The analysis shows that in the states with the placid patterns, a culture of political violence did not contribute to the appearance of a culture of masculinity. In Estonia, the gender gap indicator was 0.6977 in 2012, when stakeholders of an anti-austerity movement used political violence for the first time. The indicator had an upward tendency because in 2013 it was 0.6997, 2014 – 0.7017, 2015 – 0.749, and 2016 – 0.747. The indicator started to fall earlier, in 2006 (0.6944) and increased in 2007 (0.7008), then declined in 2011 (0.6983), and went up in 2012 (0.6977). It means that before, during, and after the occurrence of the explaining indicator, in Ayele's meaning, a culture of masculinity existed and had the soft form. In other words, the placid culture of political violence did not contribute to any change in the Estonian culture of masculinity.

Similarly, in Slovakia, in 2010, the gender gap indicator was 0.6778. Until this date, the indicator was escalating from 0.6757 in 2006 to 0.6845 in 2009. After 2010, there was a constant growth from 0.6778 in 2010 to 0.6857 in 2013, then, the loss was in 2014 (0.6806). The indicator was 0.6797 in 2011, 0.6824 in 2012, 0.6857 in 2013, 0.6806 in 2014, 0.675 in 2015, and 0.679 in 2016. Before 2010, the indicator to be explained had a higher value, but the appearance of the explaining indicator did not contribute to its reduction. Directly after 2010, the rise of the gender gap indicator made an appearance. During the whole analyzed period, a soft culture of masculinity lingered. Therefore, the placid culture of political violence did not make a shift of the Slovak culture of masculinity. The relationships between the indicators in Estonia and Slovakia confirm that the placid cultures of political violence do not influence a culture of masculinity.

Table 4.2 Gender gap indicator in the member states of the Eurozone 2006–2016

State \ *The gender gap indicator*	*2006*	*2007*	*2008*	*2009*	*2010*	*2011*	*2012*	*2013*	*2014*	*2015*	*2016*
Placid cultures of political violence											
Estonia	0.6944	0.7008	0.7076	0.7094	0.7018	0.6983	0.6977	0.6997	0.7017	0.749	0.747
Slovakia	0.6757	0.6797	0.6824	0.6845	0.6778	0.6797	0.6824	0.6857	0.6806	0.675	0.679
Hector-led cultures of political violence											
Austria	0.6986	0.7060	0.7153	0.7031	0.7091	0.7165	0.7391	0.7437	0.7266	0.733	0.716
The Netherlands	0.7250	0.7383	0.7399	0.7490	0.7444	0.7470	0.7659	0.7608	0.7730	0.776	0.756
France	0.6520	0.6824	0.7341	0.7331	0.7025	0.7018	0.6984	0.7089	0.7588	0.761	0.755
Militant cultures of political violence											
Finland	0.7958	0.8044	0.8195	0.8252	0.8260	0.8383	0.8451	0.8421	0.8453	0.850	0.845
Belgium	0.7078	0.7198	0.7163	0.7165	0.7509	0.7531	0.7652	0.7684	0.7809	0.753	0.745
Germany	0.7524	0.7618	0.7394	0.7449	0.7530	0.7590	0.7629	0.7583	0.7780	0.779	0.766
Portugal	0.6922	0.6959	0.7051	0.7013	0.7171	0.7144	0.7071	0.7056	0.7243	0.731	0.737
Slovenia	0.6745	0.6842	0.6937	0.6982	0.7047	0.7041	0.7132	0.7155	0.7443	0.784	0.786
Italy	0.6456	0.6498	0.6788	0.6798	0.6765	0.6796	0.6729	0.6885	0.6973	0.726	0.719
Greece	0.6540	0.6648	0.6727	0.6662	0.6908	0.6916	0.6716	0.6782	0.6784	0.685	0.680
Spain	0.7319	0.7444	0.7281	0.7345	0.7554	0.7580	0.7266	0.7266	0.7325	0.742	0.738
Ireland	0.7335	0.7457	0.7518	0.7597	0.7773	0.7830	0.7839	0.7823	0.7850	0.807	0.797

Source: Author's study on the basis of the Global Gender Gap Reports (2006–2016).

Notes

1 – the highest possible score that means equality or better for women, except for lifespan, 106% or better for women.

0 – the lowest possible score.

Grey color marks – the date of the first use of political violence by stakeholders of an anti-austerity movement.

When the hector-led pattern emerged in Austria, the Netherlands, and France, a culture of masculinity was not present in those states. In Austria, a phenomenon to be explained did not occur since 2006 (0.6986) when a soft type existed. In the Netherlands, it did not appear in 2006–2016. In France, a soft pattern made an appearance in 2006 (0.6520), 2007 (0.6824), and 2012 (0.6984). Nevertheless, it was not observed before, over, and after 2010, the year of the first use of political violence by stakeholders of the French anti-austerity movement. Moreover, after 2012, a culture of masculinity was not identified. The hector-led cultures of political violence are, therefore, the least useful explaining indicators here because the indicator to be accounted for followed their occurrence in no case.

Ayele's model concentrates its attention directly on the relationship between a militant pattern of a culture of political violence and a culture of masculinity. In 2006–2016, the latter was not present in five of the nine states with the militant cultures of political violence: Finland, Belgium, Germany, Spain, and Ireland, which was 55.56 percent of cases from between the militant cases. It provides an argument against a high value of Ayele's framework explanatory potential.

In Portugal, a soft culture of masculinity last asserted itself in 2007 (0.6959) in the period involved. 2011 was the year of the first deployment of political violence by stakeholders of the Portuguese anti-austerity movement. Hence, the militant pattern did not influence a culture of masculinity there, which generates one more argument against the explanatory model. Similarly, in Slovenia, a culture of masculinity failed to be distributed after 2009 (0.6982). After the occurrence of the soft pattern to the end of the period under scrutiny, a culture of masculinity was not instanced, including 2012, when the explaining indicator made an appearance. It shows another limitation of Ayele's model to explain the results of the European cultures of political violence.

In the determined period, in Italy, a soft culture of masculinity existed from 2006 (0.6456) to 2014 (0.6973). The situation altered, however, in 2015, when the indicator increased to 0.726. Nevertheless, the militant type occurred in 2010, when the score was 0.6765. A year before it was 0.6798, and a year after – 0.6796. The culture of political violence did not make a contribution to a soft pattern due to its continuance over time. Moreover, after 2010, the indicator slightly increased. It means that Ayele's explanatory framework is not empirically effective enough to examine the Italian case.

A soft culture of masculinity existed in Greece in the whole period 2006–2016. In 2011, the year of the first use of political violence by stakeholders of the Greek anti-austerity movement, the indicator was 0.6916. A year before – 0.6908, a year after – 0.6716, and two years after – 0.6782. It reveals that after the emergence of the militant pattern, the value of the indicator slightly increased. Nonetheless, a soft pattern did not transform into a mild type. Additionally, even more importantly, the change did not take the form of transposition from a culture of non-masculinity to a culture of masculinity. Then, Ayele's model does not work here as well.

As a result of the empirical study, the null hypothesis has not been rejected at the 0.05 level and, thereby, the alternative one cannot be accepted. The Pearson correlation between a gender gap indicator and a type of a culture of political violence coefficient equals 0.386, indicating a medium positive correlation, and it states that the coefficient is not significantly different from 0. The Sig. 2-tailed level is 0.173, which is considerably higher than 0.05. Therefore, a statistically significant correlation does not exist between the variables at the 0.05 level. It means that, outside Ayele's research field, or at least in the member states of the Eurozone, the militant culture of political violence does not contribute to a culture of masculinity. A researcher should not overestimate the influence of anti-austerity mobilization on gender equality (Cullen and Murphy 2017; Durbin *et al.* 2017).

Ayele's model is hardly useful to explore the austerity-driven political reality of the member states of the Eurozone. The explaining indicator, the militant type of a culture of political violence does not account for a culture of masculinity. Its explanatory power is too weak to apply it to account for the results of stakeholders of the post-2008 anti-austerity movements' cultures of political violence effectively.

Political Culture: Between the Parochial and Subject Patterns

Ayele offers another explanatory model that accounts for a qualitatively different phenomenon than the above theory. Nonetheless, in the second theoretical approach, the meaning of the explaining indicator is the same. Ethiopian culture of political violence is the source of political culture (Ayele 2011, 219) in Gabriel A. Almond, Sidney Verba, and Lucian W. Pye's view (1972). Just like Almond, Verba, and Pye, Ayele defines political culture as the set of the specifically political orientations that are the attitudes towards the political system and its parts as well as the attitudes towards the role of the self in the political regime (Almond and Verba 1972, 12). In Ayele's explanatory model, the pattern of political culture: between the parochial and subject political culture, close to the former is the result of a culture of political violence (2011, 219). The reconstruction of the semantic field of the categories is crucial to determine the distinctive features of the indicators to be accounted for.

In Almond and Verba's traditional meaning (1972, 16–17), the parochial pattern typifies the absence of specialized political roles and expectations of change initiated by the political system. The parochial type counts on nothing from the regime. A relatively pure type is likely to emerge in simpler traditional systems with minimal political specialization. In more differentiated systems, parochialism is likely to be effective and normative rather than cognitive. If the feelings towards the political regime originate, they are uncertain or negative. The members of society do not internalize norms to regulate the relations with the system.

Almond and Verba (1972, 17–18) assume that the subject political culture is marked with a high frequency of orientations towards the differentiated political system and towards the output facets of the system, but orientations towards specifically input objects and the self as an active political subject do not exist at all. Although the subject is aware of specialized governmental authority, their orientation is of an affective nature. They perhaps take pride in it, dislike it, and evaluate it as either legitimate or not. The passive relationship is towards the regime on a general level, and towards the output, administrative, or downward flow side of the system. A political competence is limited severely. The pure subject orientation is likely to make an appearance in the society in which there is no differentiated input structure. In political structures with democratic institutions, it is affective and normative rather than cognitive.

Let us underscore that according to Ayele's framework, after the occurrence of a militant culture of political violence, a participant pattern of political culture does not appear. Within the meaning of Almond and Verba (1972, 18), a participant pattern exists when the members of society strive for being explicitly oriented towards the political system as a whole and to both the political and administrative structures and processes. The input and output facets of the regime are in the spotlight. Individual members of the participant polity favorably or unfavorably orient towards the diverse classes of political objects. They aim directly to play an activist role of the self in the polity, even if their feelings and evaluations range widely from acceptance to rejection.

Unsurprisingly, the empirical studies on the cultures of political violence have shown that the cultures do not emerge in their pure form, but they are the complex combinations of the parochial, subject, and participant patterns (Blokker 2008). In fact, this is of an asymptotic nature of the ideal types which create Almond and Verba's model. Ayele discerns this feature and uses Almond and Verba's theory to formulate the indicator to be explained in his model by adopting the symptomatic linkage of the parochial and subject patterns, in which the former dominates. Ayele's model informs the anticipation that a militant culture of political violence produced by stakeholders of anti-austerity movements might have contributed to the appearance of Ayele's hybrid type of political culture. It is followed by the specific hypothesis: if a militant culture of political violence emerges, a hybrid type of political culture produced with the ascendant parochial and subject patterns might occur.

This hypothesis cannot, however, be accepted because the elements of the participant type did not disappear in the member states of the Eurozone over the presence of the militant cultures of political violence. Furthermore, there was no difference between the occurrence of the placid, hector-led, or militant types and the participant pattern appearance. Indeed, the model explains little mainly because of its excessively simplified approach towards political culture (Lane 1992).

Though Ayele's model explained Ethiopian political culture in its strictly determined temporal boundaries, it proved empirically ineffective to examine the Eurozone cases. Nevertheless, we are not the proponents of forsaking the attempts to build political culture into the studies on a culture of political violence. Instead, we are in support of making use of more nuanced frameworks than Almond and Verba's theory. In their current form, the superficial ideal types do not allow a researcher to point out sharply the differences between the contemporary political cultures in the Eurozone (Bhambra 2016). Thus, we would stand for approaching the category from the perspective of a more comprehensive conceptual framework employable to empirical research (Welch 2013). Note should be taken, however, that the application of the frameworks which would be able to capture subtle differences between political cultures demands to deploy a survey methodology. In the case of this study focused on the past events, the ex-post facto evaluation is hardly enforceable (Paine 2016). The test of Ayele's framework reveals the weakness of not only the explaining indicators but also the structures of relationships between them. We would argue that the direction of the causal relation orientation should not be taken for granted. Hence, a tool for analyzing a causal complexity is also to be devised.

From Electoral Violence to Revolution

In case studies of African states, Shola Omotola assumes that a culture of political violence in the classic meaning contributes to electoral violence (2010, 70–71). Nevertheless, as stated in the previous chapter, according to the data gathered by the International Foundation for Electoral Systems (IFES 2017a), electoral violence, defined as any harm or threat of harm to any person or property involved in the election process, or the process itself, during the election period (IFES 2017b), did not take place in the member states of the Eurozone after the occurrence of the anti-austerity movements. The absence of the indicator to be explained in the European states indicates that Omotola's model avoids shedding light on the results of cultures of political violence in non-African context.

Merle Kling's explanatory framework finds the use for studying states in Latin America. As it assumes, a culture of political violence triggers off the potential of revolution. Thus, the revolution achieves the ability to carry out the function of an election (Kling 1963, 131). Irrespective of an adopted definition of the explaining indicator, Kling's model does not account for the indicators to be accounted for because they did not appear in the member states of the Eurozone after the emergence of the anti-austerity movements. In the post-2008 Europe, there has been no revolution and, therefore, it could not have done double duty as an election.

As a result of the research on Latin America, Kling offers one more explanatory model. The researcher claims that a culture of political violence produces conditions in which the provocation and organization of violence are not the sole domain of professional soldiers (Kling 1963, 126). Kling defines a culture of political violence as the political behavior which is manifestly violent and the acceptance of violence as a legitimate means for the pursuit of power (1963, 121). The explaining phenomenon and the phenomena to be explained share a semantic field partly, as in Stan Taylor's model that indicates that a culture of political violence contributes to the promotion of riots (1981, 170). When stakeholders of anti-austerity movements participated in angry anti-austerity protests in the Eurozone, the provocation and organization of violence were not the exclusive area of professional soldiers. The same situation was in the states where the protests against austerity measures did not occur. There, an anti-ACTA demonstration, strikes (Koorits 2012; Raun and Kund 2012), and protests of various occupational classes took place (Boyd 2010a, 2010b, 2010c). Simultaneously, the ordinary people who assumed roles brought under professional soldiers behaved in a blatantly violent way. The fundamental characteristic of the explaining category employed to delve analytically into the research field provides an additional argument against Kling's model. In the member states of the Eurozone, during and after the operation of the anti-austerity movements, the acceptance of violence as a legitimate measure to change the relation of political power did not emerge. Kling's explanatory framework is, therefore, of the low applicability to address the consequences of cultures of political violence in the European context.

M. Moniruzzaman's model points out that a semantically undetermined culture of political violence spawns enormous public distrust in the capacity of the major parties to come out of the destructive political legacy and usher in a new political alternative (2009, 96). However, as has already been described, anti-austerity movement participants expressed no confidence in party politics, and more broadly political elites. They blamed institutions and politicians for destructive consequences of austerity measures. Other research on political mistrust after the 2008 financial crisis confirm the absence of confidence (Muro and Vidal 2017). The mistrust fueled arguments for the use of political violence in a public sphere. Thereby, the framework is of low applicability to account for the results of cultures of political violence in the Eurozone.

Those arguments also support the criticism of Daniel Forti and Grace Maina's explanatory framework. As the researchers assume, the post-election violence, substantial proportion of the population participating in public protests, and a reality that may be attributed to the snowball effect of grassroots mobilization are the after-effects of an undefined culture of political violence (2012, 74). As just stated, the post-election violence did not emerge in the member states of the Eurozone after the activities of the anti-austerity movements (IFES 2017a, 2017b). The broad-based participation of the population in mass protests took place pending anti-austerity events. The mobilization was present also before the first use of political violence by stakeholders of the movements. The anti-austerity activities often took the form of the mobilization of street protests and grassroots campaigns. Forti and Maina's model contributes to the explanation of the European political reality to an infinitesimal extent.

Eiko Maruko Siniawer shows that, in Japan, a culture of political violence produces the context in which ruffianism is tacitly accepted as a routinely used tool of political life (2012, 629). Siniawer defines a culture of political violence as the context in which the use of physical force is viewed by political actors as a viable and acceptable strategy (2012, 629). Hence, in Siniawer's model, the explaining indicator has the classic meaning which is a militant pattern, according to the conceptual framework adopted in the research. Nonetheless, the phenomenon to be accounted for did not make an appearance in the member states of the Eurozone over and after the occurrence of the anti-austerity movements. Siniawer's theoretical design is, therefore, not applicable to handle the problem of the aftermath of the cultures of political violence in Europe.

Another Siniawer's model is also a result of studies of Japan. According to the framework, a culture of political violence makes a contribution to the institutionalization of *sōshi*, young activists of the Freedom and People's Right Movement into party politics (2008, 73, 179). Those idiosyncratic phenomena were not present in Europe obviously. The names are anchored in the historical context, but if we generalize their key components, we identify the theoretical categories. Notably, the anti-austerity movements were heterogeneous rather than created merely by the youth. Then, a militant culture of political violence may be viewed as the phenomenon leading to the institutional setting of a social movement into a party politics. The occurrence of the explaining indicator (2011) was followed by the rise of Podemos in Spain (2014) (Rodríguez-Teruel *et al.* 2017; Stoehrel 2017) and the Coalition of the Radical Left known as the SYRIZA in Greece (2012) (Nikolakakis 2017; Spourdalakis 2014). It is thought that it also empowered the Five Star Movement (2009) in Italy founded a year before the occurrence of the Italian anti-austerity movement (2010) (Bordignon and Ceccarini 2014; Natale 2014; Passarelli and Tuorto 2017). Nonetheless, a militant culture of political violence did not lead to the transposition of the social movements into party politics in the remaining Eurozone states (Mosca 2014b).

Not all of the explanatory indicators mixed into Stephen Coleman's explanatory framework occurred in the Eurozone. Coleman's model presents an undefined culture of political violence as a source of the political situation in which people are killed, maimed, disfigured, beaten, tortured, incarcerated, and exiled because of political goals (Coleman 1998). The occurrence of the set to be explained was not confirmed in the Eurozone states. Therefore, although Coleman's model depicted the political situation in Northern Ireland in the historical period, it failed to find a use for dealing with the consequences of political cultures in different territorial and time contexts.

According to Sajjan M. Gohel, a semantically unestablished culture of political violence undermines the secular and nationalist foundations of moderate Bangladesh (2014, 88–89). Let us skip a contextual reference to the state and focus on the undermining the secular and nationalist foundations. This indicator to be explained did not occur in most of the cases: Estonia, Slovakia, Austria, the Netherlands, France, Belgium, Portugal, Slovenia, Italy, Spain, and Ireland (Torfs 2010). Although Germany does not have a state church, the relationships between the state and the religious communities are established as a partnership (Torfs 2010). In Finland, the Evangelical Lutheran Church of Finland and the Finnish Orthodox Church have the right to collect church tax from their members in conjunction with governmental income tax (Ketola *et al.* 2014). Furthermore, businesses also pay taxes for the church. Finally, the Greek Constitution recognizes Eastern Orthodoxy as the prevailing faith of the country (Diamantopoulou 2012; Mavrogordatos 2003). The militant cultures of political violence did not make a contribution to the relationships between the states and the church (Molokotos-Liederman 2016). The absence of the explaining indicator reveals a low extent of applicability of Gohel's model to explore the aftermath of the Eurozone cultures of political violence.

Culture of Political Violence as a Whipping Boy

The research tests the models that avoided introducing operationalizable definitions of a culture of political violence after the adoption of the authorial conceptual framework. Those offering the full explanatory frameworks have undergone a test in their existing forms. Then, if the meanings proposed in the theories were consistent with the proposed in the research, the analysis accepted the latter to provide the semantic consistency in the analysis. Thereby, the validity of the test is not blunted by the use of the new conceptual framework to describe the cultures of political violence. All the methodological choices were indeed discussed and justified in the research process.

Regrettably, however, no explanatory model has turned out to be empirically effective enough to introduce the resonance of the explaining indicator. In most cases, the beings, phenomena, and processes to be accounted for in line with the frameworks did not make an appearance in the member states of the Eurozone. It precluded dealing with the relationships between the cultures of political violence and their results determined by the existing theories. They proved utterly useless to explain the violent behavior paradigms of stakeholders of the anti-austerity movements in the context designated territorially and temporally.

The theories somewhat accused a culture of political violence of contributing to beings, phenomena, and processes assessed by the authors of the theories negatively. The category was deployed to play a role of a label of the undesired events. It often did double duty as an umbrella term, but it was not clear what was concealed under the umbrella of the label. Nevertheless, it has to its name being the agent undermining democracy or forbidding the establishment of democratic regimes (Le Vine 2000; Njoku 2010; Obi 2011; Siniawer 2008; Theobald 1999; Waldman 2007), leading to the occurrence of the hybrid of the parochial and subject political culture (Ayele 2011), creating the violence of culture identified with the culture of masculinity and the political violence of culture (Ayele 2011), producing the conditions in which the provocation and organization of violence are not the sole domain of professional soldiers (Kling 1963), bringing about revolution to being able to perform the function of an election (Kling 1963), triggering electoral and post-election violence (Forti and Maina 2012; Omotola 2010), sparking the context in which ruffianism is tacitly accepted as a routinely used tool of political life (Siniawer 2012) and in which people are killed, maimed, disfigured, beaten, tortured, incarcerated, and exiled because of political objectives (Coleman 1998), inciting enormous public distrust in the capacity of the major parties to come out of the destructive political legacy and usher in a new political alternative (Moniruzzaman 2009), eroding the secular and nationalist foundations of a moderate state (Gohel 2014), and starting the institutionalization of the corruptive social movements into party politics (Siniawer 2008).

Nevertheless, the research has found no evidence that the models work when applied to account for the consequences of stakeholders of the anti-austerity movements' cultures of political violence. The explanatory frameworks might have been empirically effective to examine other empirical political contexts, but in most cases, they were not the results of research conducted by using strong methodological assumptions. They were more than often developed by drawing on the commonsense discussion on political violence. However, the theoretical approaches are worth underpinning because they may become the theories of medium range.

Last but not least, we do not accept the value-laden treating a culture of political violence like a whipping boy. Instead, we stand for working on a new explanatory framework of the aftermath of its patterns without making premises that they have to be negative. It is also interesting whether there is a mechanism that differentiates the sources of the indicators to be explained that are expressed through the dissimilarities from among cultures of political violence. Indeed, it would be useful to trace and compare the history of the member states of the Eurozone after the activity of the anti-austerity movements to find out how a political reality changed in the states with diverse cultures of political violence.

Bibliography

Almond, Gabriel A. and Sidney Verba. 1972. *The Civic Culture: Political Attitudes and Democracy in Five Nations*. Princeton, NJ: Princeton University Press.

Armstrong, David A. 2011. "Stability and Change in the Freedom House Political Rights and Civil Liberties Measures." *Journal of Peace Research* 48(5): 653–662.

Ayele, Negussay. 2011. "Legitimacy, Culture of Political Violence and Violence of Culture in Ethiopia." In *Terrorism, Identity and Legitimacy: The Four Waves Theory and Political Violence*, edited by Jean E. Rosenfeld, 212–231. Abingdon and New York: Routledge.

Bhambra, Gurminder K. 2016. "Comparative Historical Sociology and the State: Problems of Method." *Cultural Sociology* 10(3): 335–351.

Blokker, Paul. 2008. "Multiple Democracies: Political Cultures and Democratic Variety in Post-Enlargement Europe." *Contemporary Politics* 14(2): 161–178.

Bordignon, Fabio and Luigi Ceccarini. 2014. "Protest and Project, Leader and Party: Normalisation of the Five Star Movement." *Contemporary Italian Politics* 6(1): 54–72.

Boyd, John. 2010a. "Breweries: Government Tax Hike Will Bury Us." *The Daily.SK*, October 13. Accessed March 4, 2017. www.thedaily.sk/brewers-say-government-hike-in-excise-tax-will-bury-them/.

Boyd, John. 2010b. "Metal Unions Spark up Protests." *The Daily.SK*, September 23. Accessed March 4, 2017. www.thedaily.sk/metal-unions-spark-up-protests/.

Boyd, John. 2010c. "Trade Unions Storm Out of Labour Ministry Talks." *The Daily.SK*, December 16. Accessed March 4, 2017. www.thedaily.sk/trade-unions-storm-out-of-labour-ministry-talks/.

Coleman, Stephen. 1998. "BBC Radio Ulster's Talkback Phone-In: Public Feedback in a Divided Public Space." *Javnost – The Public* 5(2): 7–19.

Cullen, Pauline and Mary P. Murphy. 2017. "Gendered Mobilizations against Austerity in Ireland." *Gender, Work & Organization* 24(1): 83–97.

Diamantopoulou, Elisabeth A. 2012. "Religious Freedom in the Light of the Relationship between the Orthodox Church and the Nation in Contemporary Greece." *International Journal for the Study of the Christian Church* 12(2): 164–175.

Durbin, Sue, Margaret Page, and Sylvia Walby. 2017. "Gender Equality and 'Austerity': Vulnerabilities, Resistance and Change Gender." *Work & Organization* 24(1): 1–6.

Eurostat. 2017. Gender Pay Gap. Accessed March 7, 2017. http://ec.europa.eu/eurostat/web/equality/statistics-illustrated.

Forti, Daniel and Grace Maina. 2012. "The Danger of Marginalisation: An Analysis of Kenyan Youth and Their Integration into Political, Socio-Economic Life." In *Opportunity or Threat: The Engagement of Youth in African Societies*, edited by Grace Maina, 55–86. Umhlanga Rocks and Durban: African Centre for the Constructive Resolution of Disputes.

Freedom House. 2017. The Freedom House Reports 2001–2016. Accessed March 17, 2017. https://freedomhouse.org/.

Giannone, Diego. 2010. "Political and Ideological Aspects in the Measurement of Democracy: The Freedom House Case." *Democratization* 17(1): 68–97.

Gohel, Sajjan M. 2014. "Bangladesh: An Emerging Centre for Terrorism in Asia." *Perspectives on Terrorism* 8(3): 84–91.

Hausmann, Ricardo, Laura D. Tyson, and Saadia Zahidi. 2006. The Global Gender Gap Report 2006. Accessed March 7, 2017. www3.weforum.org/docs/WEF_GenderGap_Report_2006.pdf.

Hausmann, Ricardo, Laura D. Tyson, and Saadia Zahidi. 2007. The Global Gender Gap Report 2007. Accessed March 8, 2017. www3.weforum.org/docs/WEF_GenderGap_Report_2007.pdf.

Hausmann, Ricardo, Laura D. Tyson, and Saadia Zahidi. 2008. The Global Gender Gap Report 2008. Accessed March 9, 2017. www3.weforum.org/docs/WEF_GenderGap_Report_2008.pdf.

Hausmann, Ricardo, Laura D. Tyson, and Saadia Zahidi. 2009. The Global Gender Gap Report 2009. Accessed March 10, 2017. www3.weforum.org/docs/WEF_GenderGap_Report_2009.pdf.

Hausmann, Ricardo, Laura D. Tyson, and Saadia Zahidi. 2010. The Global Gender Gap Report 2010. Accessed March 11, 2017. www3.weforum.org/docs/WEF_GenderGap_Report_2010.pdf.

Hausmann, Ricardo, Laura D. Tyson, and Saadia Zahidi. 2011. The Global Gender Gap Report 2011. Accessed March 11, 2017. www3.weforum.org/docs/WEF_GenderGap_Report_2011.pdf.

Hausmann, Ricardo, Laura D. Tyson, and Saadia Zahidi. 2012. The Global Gender Gap Report 2012. Accessed March 11, 2017. www3.weforum.org/docs/WEF_GenderGap_Report_2012.pdf.

Hausmann, Ricardo, Laura D. Tyson, and Saadia Zahidi. 2013. The Global Gender Gap Report 2013. Accessed March 11, 2017. www3.weforum.org/docs/WEF_GenderGap_Report_2013.pdf.

Hausmann, Ricardo, Laura D. Tyson, Yasmina Bekhouche, and Saadia Zahidi. 2014. The Global Gender Gap Report 2014. Accessed March 12, 2017. www3.weforum.org/docs/GGGR14/GGGR_CompleteReport_2014.pdf.

Hausmann, Ricardo, Laura D. Tyson, Yasmina Bekhouche, and Saadia Zahidi. 2015. The Global Gender Gap Report 2015. Accessed March 12, 2017. www3.weforum.org/docs/GGGR2015/cover.pdf.

Hausmann, Ricardo, Laura D. Tyson, Yasmina Bekhouche, and Saadia Zahidi. 2016. The Global Gender Gap Report 2016. Accessed March 12, 2017. www3.weforum.org/docs/GGGR16/WEF_Global_Gender_Gap_Report_2016.pdf.

IFES. 2017a. "Europe." *The International Foundation for Electoral Systems*, No date. Accessed March 10, 2017. www.ifes.org/europe.

IFES. 2017b. "Electoral Violence." *The International Foundation for Electoral Systems*, No date. Accessed March 10, 2017. www.ifes.org/issues/electoral-violence.

Ketola, Kimmo, Tuomas Martikainen, and Hanna Salomäki. 2014. "New Communities of Worship: Continuities and Mutations among Religious Organizations in Finland." *Social Compass* 61(2): 153–171.

Kling, Merle. 1963. "Violence and Politics in Latin America." *The Sociological Review* 11(S1): 119–132.

Koelble, Thomas A. and Edward Lipuma. 2008. "Democratizing Democracy: A Postcolonial Critique of Conventional Approaches to the 'Measurement of Democracy.' " *Democratization* 15(1): 1–28.

Koorits, Vahur. 2012. "2012 – A Year of Discontent in Estonia." *VahurKoortis* December 31. Accessed March 5, 2017. http://vahurkoorits.blogspot.com/2012/12/2012-year-of-discontent-in-estonia.html.

Lane, Ruth. 1992. "Political Culture: Residual Category or General Theory?" *Comparative Political Studies* 25(3): 362–387.

Le Vine, Victor T. 2000. "Violence and the Paradox of Democratic Renewal: A Preliminary Assessment." *Terrorism and Political Violence* 12(3/4): 261–292.

Mavrogordatos, George. 2003. "Orthodoxy and Nationalism in the Greek Case." *West European Politics* 26(1): 117–136.

Molokotos-Liederman, Lina. 2016. "The Impact of the Crisis on the Orthodox Church of Greece: A Moment of Challenge and Opportunity?" *Religion, State and Society* 44(1): 32–50.

Moniruzzaman, M. 2009. "Party Politics and Political Violence in Bangladesh: Issues, Manifestation and Consequences." *South Asian Survey March* 16(1): 81–99.

Mosca, Lorenzo. 2014a. "Methodological Practices in Social Movement Online Research." In *Methodological Practices in Social Movement Research*, edited by Donatella della Porta, 397–417. New York: Oxford University Press.

Mosca, Lorenzo. 2014b. "Austerity and the Crisis of Traditional Representation: The Five Star Movement: Exception or Vanguard in Europe?" *The International Spectator: Italian Journal of International Affairs* 49(1): 36–52.

Muro, Diego and Guillem Vidal. 2017. "Political Mistrust in Southern Europe since the Great Recession." *Mediterranean Politics* 22(2): 197–217.

Natale, Paolo. 2014. "The Birth, Early History and Explosive Growth of the Five Star Movement." *Contemporary Italian Politics* 6(1): 16–36.

Nikolakakis, Nikolaos. 2017. "Syriza's Stance Vis-à-vis the European Union Following the Financial Crisis: The Persistence of Left Europeanism and the Role of the European Left Party." *European Politics and Society*. Published online: June 17, 2016: 1–20.

Njoku, Alphonsus O. 2010. "Political Violence and Its Implications to Democratic Consolidation in Niger." *Knowledge Review* 21(4): 16–22.

Obi, Cyril. 2011. "Taking Back our Democracy? The Trials and Travails of Nigerian Elections since 1999." *Democratization* 18(2): 366–387.

Omotola, Shola. 2010. "Explaining Electoral Violence in Africa's 'New' Democracies." *African Journal on Conflict Resolution* 10(3): 51–73.

Paine, Jack. 2016. "Set-Theoretic Comparative Methods: Less Distinctive Than Claimed." *Comparative Political Studies* 49(6): 703–741.

Passarelli, Gianluca and Dario Tuorto. 2017. "The Five Star Movement: Purely a Matter of Protest? The Rise of a New Party between Political Discontent and Reasoned Voting." *Party Politics*. First published date: April 14, 2016.

Pye, Lucian W. and Sidney Verba (eds.). 1972. *Political Culture and Political Development*. Princeton, NJ: Princeton University Press.

Raun, Alo and Oliver Kund. 2012. "ACTA meeleavaldus jäi oodatust kesisemaks." *Postimees*, February 11. Accessed March 5, 2017. www.postimees.ee/735944/acta-meeleavaldus-jaei-oodatust-kesisemaks.

Rodríguez-Teruel, Juan, Astrid Barrio, and Oscar Barberà. 2017. "Fast and Furious: Podemos' Quest for Power in Multi-level Spain." *South European Society and Politics*. Published online: November 8, 2016: 1–25.

Siniawer, Eiko Maruko. 2008. *Ruffians, Yakuza, Nationalists: The Violent Politics of Modern Japan, 1860–1960*. Ithaca, NY and London: Cornell University Press.

Siniawer, Eiko Maruko. 2012. "Befitting Bedfellows: Yakuza and the State in Modern Japan." *Journal of Social History* 45(3): 623–641.

Spourdalakis, Michalis. 2014. "The Miraculous Rise of the 'Phenomenon SYRIZA'." *International Critical Thought* 4(3): 354–366.

Stoehrel, Rodrigo Ferrada. 2017. "The Regime's Worst Nightmare: The Mobilization of Citizen Democracy. A Study of Podemos' (Aesthetic) Populism and the Production of Affect in Political Discourse." *Cultural Studies*. Published online: December 26, 2016: 1–37.

Szewczak, Wiktor. 2011. "Jak zmierzyć demokrację? Skale pomiaru demokracji politycznej stosowane w politologii porównawczej." *Przegląd Politologiczny* 1: 122–137.

Taylor, Stan. 1981. "Riots: Some Explanations." *Journal of Ethnic and Migration Studies* 9(2): 167–172.

Theobald, Robin. 1999. "Conclusion: Prospects for Reform in a Globalised Economy." *Commonwealth & Comparative Politics* 37(3): 149–159.

Torfs, Rik. 2010. "Religious Organizations and the Rule of Law in Comparative Perspective: The Religion–State Relationship in Europe." *The Review of Faith & International Affairs* 8(2): 15–20.

Waldman, Thomas. 2007. "British 'Post-Conflict' Operations in Iraq: Into the Heart of Strategic Darkness." *Civil Wars* 9(1): 61–86.

Welch, Stephen. 2013. *The Theory of Political Culture*. New York: Oxford University Press.

Conclusions and Discussion on the Limitations of the Research

DOI: 10.4324/9781351205757-6

The comprehensive literature review has shown that a culture of political violence is a forceful but understudied issue. Although most of the works under scrutiny have been neither widely cited nor commonly known, their elaboration has allowed us to see the broad range of promising scientific approaches towards the use of the term in empirical studies. The analysis of its definitions, classification schemes, and explanatory frameworks considering it to be either the explaining indicator or the indicator to be explained has uncovered the methodological challenges for the researchers who might want to employ them effectively to their empirical studies. Indeed, this research has made use of its exploratory and explanatory potential by developing a theoretical framework of a culture of political violence and putting it into work on the research field of stakeholders of the post-2008 anti-austerity movements in the member states of the Eurozone.

The hard core structuring and organizing the theoretical framework is the category of a culture of political violence defined as a paradigm of using political violence in a political structure, which is determined by the temporal, subject, and subject matter indicators. This paradigm indicates who takes advantage of the use of political violence, what their mutual legitimation to the use is, how they justify and account for the deployment, what forms of violence they employ, and how intense physical political violence is. The definition has been a foundation of an original conceptual framework applicable to describe and analyze cultures of political violence. The model, however, may and should be refined according to state of the art and empirical demands of particular research fields to enhance its empirical effectiveness.

The application of the conceptual framework of a culture of political violence to the empirical study enabled us to verify the first main hypothesis. When the post-2008 anti-austerity movements acted, their cultures of political violence were undifferentiated in the political subjects that employed violence to achieve political goals over the duration of the movements. They were, nevertheless, diversified with respect to the values of its remaining four essential features: mutual legitimation to use political violence, modes of the legitimation of the perpetration, the intensity of the use of physical political violence, and forms of political violence.

Furthermore, the structure of the conceptual framework allowed us to approach the problem of a classification scheme in a qualitatively different manner than social movements have been addressed thus far. The simultaneous and joint application of the five critical criteria paved the way for the typology which consists of seven patterns of a culture of political violence: placidly observing, placidly rationalizing, hector-consenting, hector-acknowledgement, indulgingly militant, obstreperously militant, and aggressively militant. The qualitative comparative analysis enabled us to identify similarities and differences between them and contributed to our knowledge of the variety of the cultures of political violence among stakeholders of the anti-austerity movements in the member states of the Eurozone.

The analysis has shown that whereas the hector-led and militant types prevailed on the European political scene, the peaceful patterns were in the minority. It indicates the constantly developing civil society willingly deploys physical force to perform its political goals. Worth pursuing are, therefore, studies on the mechanisms and dynamics of radicalization and deradicalization of not only terrorist groups but also a priori non-violent interest groups.

This part of the study might be criticized for not providing a detailed description of some events under scrutiny, which the method of observation would have allowed to generate. If the research had not been conducted from the ex-post 2008–2015 anti-austerity mass political mobilization perspective, it would have offered a detail-rich presentation of the activities of the anti-austerity movements in which their stakeholders engaged. Then, the presentation of the cultures of political violence would have been more vivid. The goal of the chapter was not, however, to describe public actions of political subjects in the times of austerity. Much more important was to glean the pieces of data relevant, necessary, and sufficient to verify the hypothesis. Therefore, mass media conceptual qualitative content analysis has been carried out.

The content analysis of the existing written sources allowed us to access the information concerning the inevitably bygone past. They were nonreactive and did not influence the researcher. Nevertheless, we should keep in mind a potentially selective continuance of the sources. The authors of sources might not have captured some pieces of information relevant to the cultures of political violence. They also might have decided to publish some news due to such reasons as political correctness, mass media profile, or particular interest, and ignore other facts, which contributes to the effect of media attention. We cannot sweep aside misinterpretation of events and their actors by a journalist. Furthermore, the sources are incomplete due to the archival longevity of particular titles. Their content may be partial, inaccurate, and inadvertently or deliberately distortional (Basu 2017; Raynor 2016). The researcher's unintended misinterpretation, interpretation, or omission of some details might have undermined the research results as well. Data are inherently composite if we take a look at the content of all the sources needed to verify the hypothesis as a whole.

The substantive information, the pieces of data from public, commercial, and social media often differed widely in the number, for instance, of political subjects involved in anti-austerity events, detained, arrested, and injured, the types of objects deployed as weapons, the narratives developed by political subjects, the tenor of their activities, and the intensity of physical political violence. Not to contribute to the conclusion contorting and thus undermining research results, the study excogitates analytical tools by excluding from the subject matter field the potential distortion factors which were not necessary to examine cultures of political violence.

The researcher devised data by applying the conceptual framework to approach the cultures of political violence methodically, systematically, and intersubjectively. Additionally, she took measures to verify if data are reliable because there was no practical alternative to the sources. First, she confronted all the details relevant to determine the patterns of a culture of political violence from the media with other media information from at least five different sources published in native for the states and foreign languages. Thus, the researcher rejected the unsubstantiated claims of journalists. Second, she sent official letters to the police stations located in the states involved in the research to request for documentation of police and riot police actions and statistics from December 1, 2007 to December 31, 2015.

In contrast to the first highly effective precaution measure, the second was only moderately effective. On the one hand, the data from police stations allowed us to verify the solidity of the data concerning Estonia, Germany, Slovenia, and Spain due to the information facilitated by the Police and Border Guard Board (Guralnik 2017), the Federal Police (Müsgen 2017), the Slovenian National Police (Durić and Žibret 2017), and the Spanish National Police (Horsman 2017) respectively. Thus, data considerably contributed to the hypothesis verification and accelerated the discovery process. On the other hand, a number of the police stations that decided to provide the pieces of data was relatively low. The Polícia de Segurança from Portugal refused to send the requested data for undetermined legal reasons (Freitas 2017). In similar tone was the response of the Federal Police from Austria that claimed they did not have the competence to make data available (Jedelsky 2017). The Politie from the Netherlands denied access to the police information by quoting having other priorities in their work (Politie 2017). Irish An Garda Síochána referred the researcher to the Garda Research Unit which, in turn, after asking the researcher for completion of an application form for access to data, stated that the unit must prioritize operational requests for data and did not provide the access (Copeland 2017a, 2017b; Kavanagh 2017). The Hellenic Police from Greece declined to answer the request because of its "unclear substance" (General Policing Division 2017). Finally, the other police entities from Belgium, Finland, France, Slovakia, and Italy took a rain check.

Additionally, guided by the research problem and emerging directions in the analysis, the researcher collected a set by set of data. According to the principle of theoretical sampling, the theoretical developments that occurred in an analysis of previously gathered data led the following stages of data collection. The cycle of alternation between data collection and analysis did not stop at two repetitions but continued until theoretical saturation was gained: in other words, until new pieces of data were not introducing the exemplifications of new theoretical elements but instead were confirming what the research already discovered.

The media discourse was crucial to establish what stakeholders of the anti-austerity movements acted in the given set of states and to make sense of the structures of relationships between them. The analysis of data enabled us also to formulate arguments concerning mutual legitimation of political subjects to commit political violence. Information was accessible about the details of how political subjects reacted to the misuse and perpetration of mental, and active and passive physical violence and to what extent they were prone to accept each other's violent behavior. It was used to place the cases on the continuum established by the maximum extent and the total lack of mutual legitimation. Furthermore, data provided us with information on how political subjects explained and justified their violent action, which was vital to explore modes of the legitimation of the use of political violence. The intensity of physical political violence was tough to measure because of limited data. The information was, however, adequate to observe if the threat and active physical force were in use, if political subjects crossed the qualitative line between active and passive physical violence within a political structure, and, if so, which stakeholders of the anti-austerity movements did so. It enabled us to place the cases on the continuum determined by constant and maximally intense use of political violence and its abandonment. Although the fragmentariness of data inhibited the comprehensive assessment of how political subjects deployed mental political violence, it proved to be sufficient to estimate the general types of configurations of forms of political violence. The evaluation of if and how political subjects made use of mental, passive and active physical violence served to locate the cases on the continuum determined by soft and hard power approaches.

Police data was of equal relevance to the media discourse in achieving plausibility of the process of theoretical sampling through theoretical saturation. It showed how police stations legitimated their use of political violence springing from political roles and its actual usage over anti-austerity events. The discursive creation indicated how a particular type of representatives of state apparatuses accounted for and justified their aggressive behavior. It also neatly revealed how and to what extent they delegitimated the perpetration of political violence by movement participants. The police perspective allowed us to complete data from the media discourse to evaluate mutual legitimation of political subjects to act violently. Thereby, it contributed to locating the cases on the continuum determined by the maximum extent and the total lack of mutual legitimation. Furthermore, it was useful to identify and elaborate the modes of the legitimation of the use of political violence. The properties of authorization and rationalization were stated by policemen, and as such, they provided details relevant to apply effectively Theo van Leeuwen's typology of legitimation (2007, 92) to the analysis of the cultures of political violence.

The existing data were, however, insufficient to adopt a more specific tool to identify and compare modes of the legitimation of the use of political violence.

Van Leeuwen's typology of legitimation (2007, 92), which consists of authorization, moralization, rationalization, and mythopoesis, allowed us to analyze how political subjects justified and accounted for resorting to violent means while they were creating relationships within political structures. It turned out, however, to be moderately vulnerable to observe any critical differences between political discourses. Although it appeared useful to determine three general clusters of the modes, two of them contained no more than one case. Whereas in Slovakia, the configuration of authorization and rationalization occurred, in Estonia, the set of authorization, rationalization, and mythopoesis was in use. The variety of the cultures of political violence in Austria, Belgium, Finland, France, Greece, Spain, the Netherlands, Ireland, Germany, Portugal, Slovenia, and Italy shared authorization, rationalization, and moralization but the character of the three-element set for particular types remained unapproached. Future studies should put emphasis on how to deal with the similarities and dissimilarities of the placid, hector-led, and militant patterns in the discursive creation of justification and explanation of the deployment of political violence. The restricted choice of methods applicable to generate useful data and the existing evidence makes this challenge demanding.

One may argue against the comprehensiveness of the research by claiming that it has not dealt with mental political violence in depth, or it has understudied the types of relationships between representatives of state apparatuses and movement participants (della Porta and Reiter 1998; Tarrow 2012). The counter-argument is that protest policing has not been the exact research field, even if it potentially might have enriched the view of the cultures of political violence. Moreover, the intensity of mental political violence might have been examined like physical political violence. However, it would be hardly possible to generate necessary and sufficient data to identify and compare the extents of intensity from the ex-post facto perspective. For instance, it is hindered to determine an extent of the vulgarity of verbal and non-verbal communication used during anti-austerity protests and other collective actions initiated by movements' stake-holders because of the elusive nature of their physical media such as banners or comments on web pages. No database contains information on the key features of the category exemplifications which emerged in social media. The chance of studying this aspect of a culture of political violence should not be abandoned in planning future studies if data are accessible. Overall, the validity of the research results may and ought to be discussed critically as long as it leads us to the development of the field.

Criticism may also flow directly from the thesis of the research that a culture of political violence is a forceful theoretical category to explore and explain violent behavior in austerity-driven Europe. The thesis circumscribed the scope of the tested theories to those literally coping with a culture of political violence. On the one side, the assumption has established what explanatory frameworks are to be verified, which spawned a more intersubjective selection of theories than any other criterion. On the other side, it inevitably left several potentially forceful theories behind. It would be particularly interesting to see in future research how the theoretical approaches concerning a culture of violence, not only and exactly political violence, compete while explaining why some anti-austerity movements turned to violence and others did not (Rak 2017b). The research perspective of cultures of violence deals with a question of why societies are more or less violent, and it may challenge a researcher to adopt a broader understanding of violence that may carry a political meaning but do not have to be political by its very nature.

Furthermore, although an attempt to include political culture in the studies on a culture of political violence occurred in the specialist literature, the causal relation suggested by its author has not been empirically confirmed by this study. Social science methods do not offer a reliable means to assess the direction of influence in the relationships between those two categories. It may be of importance in the field to look at political culture as a theoretical category and use it to examine the differences and similarities within political structures created by stakeholders of anti-austerity movements and, then, to explain sources and consequences of different patterns of political cultures. A relationship between the categories and the empirical expressions of a culture of political violence and political culture is still puzzling.

It may also be analytically challenging to determine the categories of narrower and broader semantic fields than a culture of political violence, and verify their empirical effectiveness by following the methodological assumptions proposed in his research changed in the core category organizing a research process.

The second main hypothesis relates to what accounts for a culture of political violence. The research tested the explanatory frameworks identified in the literature review by using statistical analysis, causal-process observation, and critical argumentation. The current theories of cultures of political violence have informed the research process. On the one hand, the study has shown that the existing explanatory frameworks to a low extent explain why stakeholders of the post-2008 anti-austerity movements had the particular patterns of a culture of political violence. On the other, it has established a new avenue into accounting for the sources of their diversity.

The particular configurations of the explaining indicators have turned out to have greater explanatory power than individual indicators or their full fixed sets. Interestingly, the combo of the intrastate, regional, and colonial indicators is not applicable to explain the diversity of the cultures of political violence because there is no significant statistical correlation between the variables. Nonetheless, the Negussay Ayele proposal has an explanatory potential. Although it is not a major issue if the three indicators originate in a state in the fixed set, it matters in what configuration its components emerge. In this case, the correlation coefficient equals 0.651, indicating a strong positive linear correlation and letting us see that the coefficient is significantly different from 0. The Sig. 2-tailed level is 0.012, which is substantially lower than 0.05 and proves a statistically significant correlation. The research has indicated that if in the history of a state both the intrastate and colonial indicators occur as well as the regional one does not take place, it is probable that placid cultures of political violence originate in the state. More violent patterns show up in the states where the intrastate indicator appears. This feature typifies hector-led and militant types, but it is the only feature that characterizes the former. The latter may also originate in the states where the full set of the intrastate, colonial, and regional indicators or just the configuration of the intrastate and regional made an appearance in the state history. In one state, however, no indicator occurred, which undermines the model.

It seems to be promising to delve analytically into the structures of the configurations of the indicators which typify particular cultures of political violence. The proceedings and results of the already recognized intrastate, regional, and colonial indicators are worth taking into consideration. The frequency and intensity of the events may also be meaningful (McAdam *et al.* 2008). For the purpose of empowering the empirical effectiveness of the model, it would be advisable to determine precisely a conceptual framework applicable to approach what contributes to the paradigms of the use of political violence, and how, and the differences between them.

Let us draw one more conclusion on other explanatory frameworks. As the research has pointed out, the war, civil war, and revolution indicators as the fixed and undivided explaining set are far from being effective because its correlation with the types of a culture of political violence is not statistically significant. More importantly, however, the various configurations of the explaining indicators are to a greater extent applicable to explain placid, hector-led, and militant cultures of political violence than Norman LaPorte and Matthew Worley's original model. The Sig. 2-tailed level is there 0.044, which is considerably lower than 0.05, and it sets a statistically significant correlation. The analysis has revealed that when in the history of a state only the war indicator makes an appearance, it is likely that a placid pattern of a culture of political violence enters this state. Perfectly in the line of LaPorte and Worley, the complete configuration of the war, civil war, and revolution indicators is a feature of more violent patterns. When it appears, it is probable that a hector-led or militant type originates. Nevertheless, the set of war and revolution indicators is a property of no pattern. The results may encourage a researcher to adopt the model in a modified and extended form and to make further changes to reinforce its explanatory potential.

Here, it is worth discerning that Sue Onslow's explanatory model challenges a researcher to concentrate on the details of the war indicator but, note should be taken, other indicators are not to be left aside. Just as in Ayele, it may be effective to explore the frequency and intensity of the events in the states' history and to determine their features potentially significant to the development of the cultures of political violence (McAdam *et al.* 2008).

Robert Gerwarth's explanatory model, assuming that a culture of political violence is a result of the noisy and turbulent politics of the street, the town square, and the factory, in which socioeconomic grievances, hostility to state authority, and new and recycled dreams of a purified community are expressed, is invulnerable to explain the differences between the cultures of political violence. Not unlike William Eubank and Leonard Weinberg's, Gerwarth's model is too general to deal with the nature and roots of the complex phenomenon. The explanatory indicators occurred in each state pending the measurement of the cultures of political violence. It was purposeless to verify just the straightforward occurrence of the indicators because their empirical manifestations were common in Europe. In spite of Gerwarth's assumptions, it would be useful to shed light on their intensity and frequency. It may be of vital importance to analyzing the relative deprivations of political subjects engaged in contentious politics to empower the model. Beyond argument is the requirement to develop the model by proposing the conceptual framework which would enable a researcher to address significant differences between expressions of the indicator.

The other models involved the following explaining indicators: highly mobilized and urbanized civil society, in the developed Latin American states with strong democratic traditions, identified with the state which does not confine its militaries to the narrowly constitutional role and ruthless and determined military governments threatens at length the civil society, tribal and religious loyalties, non-political agencies of socialization, the youths' engagement in electoral violence, the fictions of political violence defined as novels, short stories, plays, movies, or parts thereof, where political processes and political views are reasonably close to the surface, and the internationalist spirit of the 1960s. Nonetheless, there was no need to conduct statistical analysis to state that they do not work under their original theoretical and methodological assumptions to account for the Eurozone cultures of political violence. Their rejection was justified mainly by drawing upon the history of the states and essential features of the context in which the anti-austerity movements acted. Although some of them have an explanatory potential, such as those which point out tribal and religious loyalties, they have to be elaborated according to state of the art to develop their empirical effectiveness. They also inspire a researcher to think about the role of elections and political campaigns in the process of shaping cultures of political violence, but they avoid establishing directions to do so.

This part of the research has pointed out that much is to be done to elaborate explanatory frameworks of a culture of political violence. It is not very likely that a single indicator will account for its types. More likely is that the configurations of indicators will provide more plausible research results. Undoubtedly, it may be useful to inform future conceptual and explanatory frameworks by delving analytically into the previous contentious politics in the particular states.

The third hypothesis focuses on the empirical effectiveness of the current explanatory frameworks that treat a culture of political violence as the explaining indicator. Unfortunately, no explanatory model has turned out to be useful to introduce the resonance of the explaining indicator. In fact, in most cases, the beings, phenomena, and processes to be accounted for in line with the frameworks did not make an appearance in the member states of the Eurozone. It precluded dealing with the relationships between patterns of a culture of political violence and their results determined by the existing theories. The current explanatory models are empirically ineffective to explain violent behavior paradigms of stakeholders of the anti-austerity movements in the Eurozone.

The study has uncovered that the authors of the frameworks fixed the blame on a culture of political violence for contributing to the beings, phenomena, and processes recognized by the researchers as having an adverse influence on society. The term served as a label of the undesired events. It often served as an umbrella term, but what the umbrella of the label concealed was unclear. Nevertheless, a culture of political violence is often blamed as the agent of undermining democracy or forbidding the establishment of democratic regimes, leading to the occurrence of the hybrid of the parochial and subject political cultures, creating the violence of culture identified with the culture of masculinity and the political violence of culture, producing the conditions in which the provocation and organization of violence are not the sole domain of professional soldiers, bringing about revolution to being able to perform the function of an election, triggering off electoral and post-election violence, sparking the context in which ruffianism is tacitly accepted as a routinely used tool of political life and in which people are killed, maimed, disfigured, beaten, tortured, incarcerated, and exiled because of political objectives, inciting enormous public distrust in the capacity of the major parties to come out of the destructive political legacy and usher in a new political alternative, eroding the secular and nationalist foundations of a moderate state, and starting the institutionalization of the corruptive social movements into party politics. As the discussion on the explanatory framework has underscored, the scientific approaches towards a culture of political violence are often biased because of treating the category as a whipping boy. It is a result of the value-laden determination of relations between the explaining indicator and the indicators to be explained.

The research contributes to social sciences by proposing and testing a non-traditional research design built around a methodologically structured literature review. It formulates the sets of problems and correctness criteria which are of universal applicability to evaluate theories in terms of their methodological effectiveness. The extensive literature review of works on cultures of political violence is the first attempt to put scientific ways of thinking about that phenomenon in order. It informed the creation of a semantic universe of a culture of political violence and its types. As a result, the study offers an operationalizable definition of the category and generates its new conceptual framework. Their application to qualitative comparative analysis methodologically shaped a comparison distinguished by the use of the category. The analysis of the cultures of political violence of stakeholders of the anti-austerity movements in the member states of the Eurozone contributes to comparative politics by showing the crucial patterns of similarities and differences between the cases.

The literature review allowed us to determine methodically and intersubjectively two sets of explanatory models with the potential to develop our knowledge of the cultures of political violence. The research has tested the empirical effectiveness of the models which treat the category either as an explaining indicator or an indicator to be explained by employing a unique blend of statistical analysis, causal-process observations, and critical facts-driven discussion. Some theories have been found to be ineffective to account for the Eurozone cultures of political violence which were beyond their original research fields. Others have turned out to have explanatory power, and they marked out ways for delving analytically into the sources of the cultures of political violence. They also have revealed potentially exact directions for future studies in the field. As the research results indicate, the most important are the issues of the intensity of contention and the frequency, features, and dynamics of intrastate, regional, colonial, factors in the history of states.

The volume presents original databases for 14 states formulated especially for the research, but they may be successfully employed in other studies on anti-austerity movements. They contain the dates of the occurrence of the anti-austerity movements, patterns of the cultures of political violence, characteristics of stakeholders of the anti-austerity movements – who they are, forms of political violence, modes of the legitimation of the perpetration, mutual legitimation to the use, and the intensity of physical political violence – and explanatory indicators – intrastate, regional, colonial, experiences of war, civil war, revolution, noisy and turbulent politics, breakdown of democracy, and culture of masculinity.

The research contributes as well to our knowledge of the context-determined cultures of political violence, which is of relevance for the state plans of crisis management in protest policing, the role of state police as stakeholders of social movements, the impact of the police on increasing and decreasing violent behavior, the means employed by representatives of the state apparatus within the relationships with movement participants. The analysis provides decision-making authorities with information about the patterns of violent behavior whose specificity has to be taken into consideration to prevent the transposition of the less violent cultures of political violence into the more aggressive types. As the research points out, negotiations of the standards through discursive and actual legitimation of representatives of state apparatuses and movement participants to perform their political roles and not deploy peaceful means mirrored the processes of fueling and quenching political violence. It reveals the meaning of responsibility for earning the standards of demeanor and co-operation in times of social mobilization.

The non-traditional research design may cause a backlash in conservatively oriented circles of social scientists, but constructive criticism is very welcome to pave new avenues for future research in the field. In fact, the work does not challenge the empirical effectiveness of traditional research designs. Rather, it encourages us to rethink our insight into how a given analysis should and should not be structured and conducted. It offers one of many formulas to come to grips with why some anti-austerity movements turned to force when others did not, and how it influenced political structures. Despite not being free of a drain on the research results, the study proposes a new way for investigating the cultures of political violence. As long as the category is about how political subjects see themselves and each other in their political roles within political structures, how they perceive, justify, and explain the deployment of political violence, and how they make use of it, we cannot take its structure for granted. Instead, we have to elaborate individually for every research field its conceptual framework structured with theoretical categories, a classification scheme to discern differences between its expressions, and explanatory frameworks to account for its sources and results. We should generate up-to-date empirical evidence that leads the design of any theoretical framework to discover the very nature of the changeable cultures of political violence.

Bibliography

Basu, Laura. 2017. "Living within Our Means: The UK News Construction of the Austerity Frame over Time." *Journalism*. First published date: June 22, 2017.

Copeland, Caroline. 2017a. Respond to query 2/17/2017: Garda Research Unit. Register: 17/02/2017 [in the author's records].

Copeland, Caroline. 2017b. Respond to query 3/3/2017: Garda Research Unit. Register: 3/03/2017 [in the author's records].

della Porta, Donatella and Herbert Reiter. 1998. "The Policing of Protest in Western Democracies." In *Policing Protest: The Control of Mass Demonstrations in Western Democracies*, edited by Donatella della Porta and Herbert Reiter, 1–34. Minneapolis and London: University of Minnesota Press.

Durić, Džemal and Danijel Žibret. 2017. Respond to query 630–36/2017/4: Slovenian National Police. Register: 630–36/2017/4(262–03) [in the author's records].

Freitas, Jorge. 2017. Respond to query no 271/JF: Polícia de Segurança Pública. Register: 3F05–2017 [in the author's records].

General Policing Division. 2017. Respond to query 2/13/2017: Hellenic Police Headquarters. Register: 13/02/2017 [in the author's records].

Guralnik, Clara. 2017. Respond to query 1.1–14/368–2: Police and Border Guard Board. Register: 70008747 [in the author's records].

Horsman, Marjolein. 2017. Respond to query 2017.00000005: Railpol on behalf of the Spanish National Police. Register: 2017.00000005 [in the author's records].

Jedelsky, Peter. 2017. Respond to query 35049/17: Federal Police. Register: 0003506 [in the author's records].

Kavanagh, Gerry. 2017. Respond to query 2017–02–13: An Garda Síochána. Register: 2017–02–13 [in the author's records].

McAdam, Doug, Sidney Tarrow, and Charles Tilly. 2008. "Methods for Measuring Mechanisms of Contention." *Qualitative Sociology* 31(4): 307–331.

Müsgen, Hanne. 2017. Respond to query O3–12007/1#1. Federal Police. Register: 170213 [in the author's records].

Politie. 2017. Respond to query 170207–00391234534: Politie. Register: 170207–00391234534 [in the author's records].

Rak, Joanna. 2017a. "Intrastate, Regional, and Colonial Contributions to Post-2008 Cultures of Political Violence." *Polish Political Science Yearbook* 46(1): 281–293.

Rak, Joanna. 2017b. "What Constitutes the State's Culture of Political Violence?" *Insight Turkey* 19(2): 231–237.

Raynor, Ruth. 2016. "Dramatising Austerity: Holding a Story Together (and Why It Falls Apart…)." *Cultural Geographies* 24(2): 193–212.

Tarrow, Sidney. 2012. *Strangers at the Gates: Movements and States in Contentious Politics*. Cambridge and New York: Cambridge University Press.

van Leeuwen, Theo. 2007. "Legitimation in Discourse and Communication." *Discourse & Communication* 1(1): 91–112.

Index

Page numbers in **bold** denote tables, those in *italics* denote figures.